What reviewers say of Marjorie Simmins

Memoir: Conversations and Craft

Memoir is one of the ascendant literary forms of our time. Now, fortunately, Marjorie Simmins has provided a road map for all of us, from first-timers right through to seasoned memoirists. Her own tricks of the trade are in there. But Simmins also talks to some of the most accomplished writers working today to plumb the depths of their knowledge. A great addition to any writer's bookshelf.

— John DeMont, journalist and author of
The Long Way Home: A Personal History of Nova Scotia

Marjorie Simmins has written a comprehensive primer on memoir that showcases her long experience as a writer, researcher, and teacher of the genre. But Memoir: Conversations and Craft is also a deep reflection on the ways in which memoir – done well – resonates powerfully and universally, and tells important truths. Her insightful interviews with some of Canada's leading practitioners of memoir make this required reading for both writers and readers.

— Pauline Dakin, journalist and author of
Run, Hide, Repeat: A Memoir of a Fugitive Childhood

Coastal Lives: a memoir

A brilliant, intimate heart-warming memoir, cleverly organized with its back-and-forward chronology, and a charmingly written tribute to a loving relationship that began on Canada's West Coast and flourished on the East Coast.

— William Deverell, author of the *Arthur Beauchamp series*

Simmins is a terrific writer with a terrific tale to tell. It's the urgency and passion of her prose that makes her memoir such gripping reading. At the heart of the story is the unfolding of an extraordinary love affair between her on the Pacific Coast and, 4,000 miles east on the Atlantic, fellow writer Silver Donald Cameron.

— Harry Bruce, author and journalist

Through Simmins' collage of essays, the core story draws the author towards the risk of honesty, a leap of faith and an ultimate trust in the promise of love waiting on the other side of the continent. Coastal Lives is a professional and honest telling of something rare in many memoirs, a happy ending.

— Frank Macdonald, *Atlantic Books Today*

Year of the Horse: A Journey of Healing and Adventure

This is the tale of a remarkable woman who falls hard from horses but never ceases to fall for horses. The result is an illuminating and heartfelt chronicle of the horse-human bond.

— Lawrence Scalan, author of *Wild About Horses*.

Memoir
Conversations and Craft

by

Marjorie Simmins

Includes conversations with

Lawrence Hill, Plum Johnson, Linden MacIntyre,
Edmund Metatawabin, Donna Morrissey,
Claire Mowat, and Diane Schoemperlen

POTTERSFIELD PRESS
Lawrencetown Beach, Nova Scotia, Canada

Copyright © Marjorie Simmins, 2020

All rights reserved. No part of this publication may be reproduced or used or stored in any form or by any means – graphic, electronic or mechanical, including photocopying – or by any information storage or retrieval system without the prior written permission of the publisher. Any requests for photocopying, recording, taping or information storage and retrieval systems shall be directed in writing to the publisher or to Access Copyright, The Canadian Copyright Licensing Agency (www.AccessCopyright.ca). This also applies to classroom use.

Library and Archives Canada Cataloguing in Publication

Title: Memoir : conversations and craft / Marjorie Simmins.

Names: Simmins, Marjorie, author.

Identifiers: Canadiana (print) 20200171747 | Canadiana (ebook) 20200171771 | ISBN 9781988286990

(softcover) | ISBN 9781989725009 (HTML)

Subjects: LCSH: Autobiography—Authorship.

Classification: LCC CT25 .S546 2020 | DDC 808.06/692—dc23

Front cover design by: Denise Saulnier

Cover design by Gail LeBlanc

Pottersfield Press gratefully acknowledges the financial support of the Government of Canada for our publishing activities. We also acknowledge the support of the Canada Council for the Arts and the Province of Nova Scotia which has assisted us to develop and promote our creative industries for the benefit of all Nova Scotians.

Pottersfield Press
248 Leslie Road
East Lawrencetown, Nova Scotia, Canada, B2Z 1T4
Website: www.PottersfieldPress.com
To order, phone 1-800-NIMBUS9 (1-800-646-2879) www.nimbus.ns.ca

Printed in Canada

Pottersfield Press is committed to preserving the environment and the appropriate harvesting of trees and has printed this book on Forest Stewardship Council® certified paper.

*For Don, who brings light, love, and peace
to every day we are together.*

"I believe that the memoir is the novel of the 21st century; it's an amazing form that we haven't even begun to tap … we're just getting started figuring out what the rules are."

– Susan Cheever

Contents

Preface	11
Introduction	13

Section I: Understanding Memoir

Chapter One: What is a memoir? ... 18
Conversation with Linden MacIntyre ... 31
Craft ... 54

Chapter Two: Who writes memoirs? ... 57
Conversation with Edmund Metatawabin ... 59
Craft ... 74

Chapter Three: When do we write a memoir? ... 79
Conversation with Donna Morrissey ... 82
Craft ... 94

Chapter Four: Why do we write memoirs? ... 98
Conversation with Claire Mowat ... 100
Craft ... 114

Chapter Five: How do we write memoirs? ... 118
Conversation with Lawrence Hill ... 125
Craft ... 136

Chapter Six: Life Before and After Memoir ... 140
Conversation with Diane Schoemperlen ... 142
Craft ... 164

Chapter Seven: Character and Setting in Literature and Memoir ... 168
Conversation with Plum Johnson ... 173
Craft ... 189

Section II: Creating Your Memoir

Chapter Eight: Style and Content — 194

Chapter Nine: The Outline Dilemma: Plotting versus "Pantsing" — 199

Chapter Ten: Before You Start Writing; Finding Your Story — 202

Chapter Eleven: Collecting up your Writing, and "The Truth" — 209

Section III: The Audacity of Memoir

Chapter Twelve: Maps of the Heart and Mind — 216

Chapter Thirteen: The Minefields of Memoir — 219

Appendix

Seven Tips for Writing a Memoir — 222

Writing Prompts and Lists — 225

Ghosts of Our Past — 230

The Voices of Our Ancestors — 231

Acknowledgements — 232

Bibliography — 234

About the Author — 250

Books by Marjorie Simmins — 251

Preface

What's not to love about memoir – life stories from every land, culture, and people, which inspire us all to live better, more meaningful, or perhaps simply more adventurous lives? Memoir's most essential and lovable quality is its democratic openness. Doors we could never ordinarily walk through are flung open to us – into the lives of Olympians, or queens, victims of war and other tragedies, teenage rock stars, former streetwalkers or geishas – and also the doors to extraordinary, ordinary lives. We step in tentatively at first and then we lose ourselves to those foreign worlds. *Take me there*, we say, take me there in your backpack, Rolls Royce, kayak, or perhaps keep me at your side while we walk the ancient pilgrimage Camino de Santiago. *Tell me a story.*

We may even think, Tell me *how* to tell a story; I want to write a memoir of my own.

This book offers comprehensive help for those who want to write their own memoir: how to start, keep on, and – crucially – finish a memoir; inspiration and some practical how-to; and even those seemingly elusive Memoir Muses to guide your efforts.

In classic Greek mythology, there are nine Muses. All ancient writers appealed to them when they sat down to write. No less a scribe than Homer asks the Muses both in *The Iliad* and *The Odyssey* to help him tell the story well. Today, the Muses remain symbols of encouragement and artistic creation.

But for this musing on memoir, my heart was set on talking to a particular group of Literary Muses, whose work I often refer to or read when I teach workshops on memoir. With many thanks, then, to the following writers: Lawrence Hill, Plum Johnson, Linden MacIntyre, Edmund Metatawabin, Donna Morrissey, Claire Mowat, and Diane Schoemperlen.

May *Memoir: Conversations and Craft* give you the drive and knowledge to write your own memoir, and may these Memoir Muses show you the more accessible paths to beauty and universal truths within that life tale. Your story counts. There's always room for more magic in this world.

Introduction

My lifelong love of story began with a mother who read to her four children every night, and took them to the library every week, armed with a fat wicker laundry basket to cart home books. My mother, Barbara Simmins (*née* Atkinson), an English and philosophy major who taught high school, also taught her children how to write letters – an activity that has stayed with us and brought us deep satisfaction. After letters came hard-bound journals, introduced to me and my siblings by our father, Richard Simmins, a freelance journalist at the time.

From readings, letters, and journals, my older siblings and I progressed onto assorted liberal arts degrees, writing and teaching careers, and books of our own. For all my family, there is always time in our lives for *story* – "an account of imaginary or real people and events told for entertainment," says the *Oxford English Dictionary* – in our letters to friends and each other; in our personal and professional writings; in the vast variety of young or mature students' life stories that we read and assess; and always, in the greedy intake of the world's writings. Whether we are reading a novel or a memoir or a poem, each of us reads with the same open heart and curious mind our mother had when she read to us.

In our love of story, my family and I are specks of sand in the Sahara Desert. There are literally billions of "results" or listings for "story" on the Internet. Storytelling, says Jeremy Hsu in "The Secrets of Storytelling: Why we Love a Good Yarn" in *Scientific American*, "is a human universal, and common themes appear in tales throughout history and all over the world." Says the late novelist and memoirist Pat Conroy: "The most powerful words in English are 'tell me a story,' words that are intimately related to the complexity of history, the origins of the language, the continuity of the species, the taproot of our humanity, our singularity, and art itself."

Scientists now believe story helped to save our lives, changed our very beings: "It is in our nature to need stories," declares Jag Bhallaa in *Scientific American*. "They are our earliest sciences, a kind of people-physics. Their logic is how we naturally think. They configure our biology and how we feel, in ways long essential for our survival."

Story has shaped my life. Since 1991, I have been a freelance writer, editor, and writing teacher. I have written for Canadian and American newspapers, magazines, and anthologies. For six years I covered the commercial and sport fisheries on the west coast of Canada and published many essays or short, personal stories in provincial and national magazines and newspapers. At this time, I also taught memoir writing to seniors. Now based in Nova Scotia, I continue to work as a freelance writer and editor, and teach memoir writing to writers of all ages and experience levels, from east to west. (And yes, I hope to include the Arctic coast in coming years.)

I started reading memoirs and biographies as a teenager, gulping down the lives of the rich and famous, in particular Hollywood actors. I also distinctly remember preferring memoir, naively trusting that the "I" and not "she" or "he" guaranteed a more truthful or "real" account. Decades after these first reading experiences, I wrote in my blog on memoir writing: "For me, a memoir can be entry to worlds I know nothing about – and I almost always find that experience exciting." Some things don't change: I still love the worlds of theatre, film, and memoir.

Worldwide, memoir is prolific, evolving, and defiantly varied in its forms. I have come to think of memoir as a "renegade," a genre that is rebellious and non-conforming. While generally accepted by the reading public to be truthful, circumscribed, narrative accounts of a person's life, memoirs in fact have a long history of defying conventional expectations of narrative. They can be fictionalized or fraudulent (Daniel Defoe, in both *Moll Flanders* and *Journal of the Plague Year*, 1722; *Love and Consequences*, 2009, by "Margaret B. Jones"; *The Angel at the Fence*, 2008, by Herman Rosenblat); they can be exceedingly long (former American President Bill Clinton's memoir, *My Life*, 2004, is 957 pages); and the narrative structure can vary to include a range of forms and formats: recipes, letters, e-mails, journal entries, photographs, artwork of all sorts, poems, and more.

Memoirs such as these are similar to what is called *bricolage,* or *hybrid.* The term "hybrid" is attributed to writer and memoirist Natalia Rachel Singer, the author of *Scraping by in the Big Eighties.* Singer views hybrid memoirs as works "in which a writer presents a life through a lens that reflects both inward and outward."

Whether hybrid or conventionally rendered, memoirs record our histories, our movements through life. "Memoir," writes author Abigail Thomas, "is the story of how we got here from there." Fittingly, my memoir essay about my sister Karin, written in 1993, was titled "Trips From There to Here."

In 2009, after being a professional writer for nearly twenty years, I was surprised to find I had not yet published a book of any kind. It was something I'd expected to do earlier on – and, for a variety of reasons, had not. I was beginning to wonder if I could, as I was starting to term it, "write long," in any genre.

In the end, I chose memoir – or memoir chose me – because it was the genre that made the most sense for a writer of my background to write. All those letters, all those journals, all the essays I'd published over the years – they all used variations of the same "voice" – my direct-to-the-reader voice – which enabled me to be candid and personal, as though talking to a good friend, and yet, conversely, somehow gave me enough artistic distance to craft a story.

In 2009, I enrolled in a master's program at Mount Saint Vincent University, wanting to study and understand memoir in a more systematic way. I also hoped to use my thesis as the basis for a traditionally published memoir.

I knew the stories I loved best from my years of teaching memoir writing to a seniors' group in Vancouver – the stories that took me away to another time, place, and outlook, and satisfied me both in form and emotional content. So with those reading memories and many others in mind, I sat down to "write long" about my first fifteen years in the Maritimes. So much had happened in that decade and a half. I (the once-upon-a-journal-keeper) wanted to see what it all looked like, down on paper. I (the storyteller) also wanted to see how it compared and contrasted with other emotionally significant parts of my earlier life.

I finished my M.A. in 2011. In 2014, I published my first book, *Coastal Lives: A Memoir* (Pottersfield Press). In 2016, I wrote a second book, a blend of memoir and non-fiction, *Year of the Horse: A Journey of Healing and Adventure* (also with Pottersfield Press).

Now, after two traditionally published memoirs, I am circling around once again, to re-examine other matters I am curious about, mine the stacks of material I've amassed during decades of memoir writing workshops, and to write a book on crafting a memoir. It's called *Memoir: Conversations and Craft* because I believe we benefit from in-depth conversations about the genre, and we are further enabled by learning about craft. Therefore, approximately half of the book focuses on the how-to and why-to of memoir, and half focuses on conversations with top Canadian writers who, despite their professional experience, had their own struggles with producing memoirs, but ultimately triumphed. I've learned a lot from these writers' experiences and I am delighted to share them.

Let's celebrate the dream of memoir and its realization ... starting now.

Section I
Understanding Memoir

Chapter One
What is a memoir?

Let's start with the basics.

The terms memoir and autobiography are often confused. In fact, a memoir is a chapter of a person's life, not the entire life. An autobiography covers a whole life.

While a memoir covers some of the pivotal, even transformative events in our lives, it is not intended to be a résumé. Do not include all your life achievements unless you are writing a book about your working life. Even then, if the tale is nothing more than a brag-fest, no one will want to read it.

In terms of book sales – it can be the bestselling and lowest-selling genre going. Because, let's be honest, if you're not famous, most people don't really care about you. What they do care about is being entertained and given singular reading experiences. Your memoir, then, needs to sell the "story" of your life as deftly as a novel can, while still bringing in the benefits (life lessons/information on interesting subjects) for the reader as a non-fiction book does.

Striking this balance is a challenge. And in the end, this means that all authors can learn from studying a memoir description, or blurb, done well. Your would-be reader should be drooling to get started on your memoir.

The majority of memoirs are self-published and these authors, of course, don't need to worry about sales, as they only print what they need. And having a family history to pass down is a priceless accomplishment.

The best memoirs are "effortlessly" engaging. (Translated, this means many hours at your computer.) Engaging refers both to content and style, which, in turn, means rapid page-turning by the reader. And it's not unattainable, even for the emerging writer. Enjoy yourself, and chances are readers will enjoy themselves, too. Even if your story has sad or tragic elements, there is satisfaction in expressing the story well, so that others will be affected by it, or will learn from it.

Related to this — humour is crucial. People do love to have a laugh. Self-deprecating humour always goes over well. And if you are dealing with difficult subjects, careful use of humour is a *must*.

The story of your life should focus on your own adventures and challenges. Of course you will have other people in your memoir, but you can't speak directly for them, unless you truly know how they felt on an issue, or if you are remembering dialogue as closely as you can.

The first premise of a memoir is that it is truthful — that stories are "taken from life." One thing this means is doing your absolute best to remember things as they occurred. That said, if someone disagrees with you, that's their problem, not yours. It's your story to record as you see fit. Sometimes, bizarrely, you may even have to tell a lie, to get to the truth. Omission, commission, paltering or misleading (saying something that is not true, with the intention to deceive), individual truths, collective truths, selective truths — we'll talk much more on this complicated subject later in the book.

Memoirs are often evocative of time and place. One of the joys of reading a good memoir is feeling as though you've travelled to a particular world that may no longer exist, or that you know you will never see. As a writer, your job is to bring that personal remembrance to vivid life. You do this by providing detail. What was the music like? The clothing of the time? The attitudes of the day? The food? How did people speak? What did their cars and homes look like? What did they work at?

Finally, use dialogue. You might not remember exactly what your mother used to say to you as a child … but if you think carefully, you'll come darn close. If you feel more comfortable using italics to indicate it's an approximate quote, go ahead.

Memoirs should also contain universal themes. We suffer neither joy nor bereavement in total isolation. With the exception of the housebound or hermits, we are interacting with people each and every day. This includes our families and friends, acquaintances or strangers, and on some days, all of these groups. How did others help or hinder your progress in life? How did you learn from others?

Like a novel, a memoir needs a narrative arc. Essentially, you need a beginning, middle, and end, with escalating tension and a satisfying resolution. How does the old saw go? "Act One: Put your character up a tree. Act Two: Throw stones at her. Act Three: Bring her down." No drama – no bruises, cuts, and scars, and extreme worry about our central figure – no story. And finally, you will need a climax (or epiphany) near the end of the story.

The climax is the most exciting moment in your story. This is the moment when the reader's commitment pays off. You've kept your reader all the way along and they have been really worried for you, wondering how you will resolve your troubles. Don't let them down! Every life has drama, and (most) of our difficulties are resolved, one way or another. Pay special attention to your pacing.

If you are writing a collection of essays, there will be arcs in each and every one of the stories, and overarching themes, as well. Imagine the text equivalent of a photograph album, "Summer of '99," or what have you. But the writer needs to be careful here, and lead the reader on a connective, open-minded journey. Too much navel-gazing or settings-only writings and you'll lose your reader.

Of course you must use excellent grammar and diction, which includes using the active voice (i.e., Jill threw the ball, not, The ball was thrown by Jill); precise verbs, which reduce the need for adverbs; carefully chosen adjectives, few in number; and sentences of different lengths. Mix it up! And when needed, use short sentences to add tension and drama.

It is so important to have polished and error-free text; no reader wants to think you just slapped your memoir together and didn't check it over when you finished. For most of us, this means the story has been rewritten and edited many times, and proof-read countless times. Do consider engaging a professional editor to help you with this, whether or not you seek traditional publishing. Provincial or national (state or national) writers' organizations can direct you to a professional editor, or ask any professional writer you know for recommendations.

Your memoir will require determination, honesty, bravery, *time*, imagination, and fact-checking. If you find yourself stalled, then go back and find the story's elemental truth and purpose, and start again. Now, let's go deeper.

Definitions of memoir

The *Oxford English Dictionary* defines memoir as "a historical account or biography written from personal knowledge," and defines memoirs (plural) as "an account written by a public figure of their life and experiences, and an essay on a learned subject." The word's origin is late fifteenth century (denoting a memorandum or record): from French *mémoire* (masculine), a special use of *mémoire* (feminine) "memory."

It should also be noted that *mémoire* (French) does not mean the same as the English "memoir," the former meaning a mini personal essay – not the longer account that English speakers would expect. As well and interestingly, the word "memory" comes from the same root as the word "mourn," which, says author Abigail Thomas, "should tell you something."

In the *Oxford English Dictionary*'s definition, the example used, "she published a short memoir of her husband," can be interpreted several ways: did the author write the memoir *with* her husband (a combined effort), *for* her husband (ghost-written) or *about* her husband (biography)? Memoirs can be written with someone ("as told to"), or for someone (Farley Mowat's *Bay of Spirits*, 2009, which details his meeting and marriage to his second wife, Claire), or about someone (Sally Armstrong's *The Nine Lives of Charlotte Taylor*, 2008, a fictional memoir written about one of her early Canadian ancestors).

Memoir/Memoirs: The Genre and Its Cousins, Autobiography and Essay

Historically, says memoir specialist Ben Yagoda, the memoir did focus on others, not the self, by contrast with the autobiography. He offers the somewhat recent example of A.E. Hotchner's 1966 *Papa Hemingway: A Personal Memoir*. In this, Hotchner plays a bit part, and Hemingway is the headliner. This distinction between autobiography and memoir "held sway as late as 1984," writes Yagoda, "when another scholar, Richard Coe, observed that while in an autobiography 'it is the writer himself who is the centre of interest,' in a memoir, 'the writer is, as a *character*, essentially negative, or at least neutral.'"

Although the terms are often used interchangeably now, most contemporary writers on memoir distinguish the memoir form from autobiography. Autobiography is typically taken to mean a more historical account of a life, relying more on research, dates, and facts, rather than just memories.

Yagoda writes: "The one clear difference [between autobiography and memoir] is that while 'autobiography' or 'memoirs' usually cover the full span of that life, 'memoir' has been used by books that cover the entirety *or* some portion of it." As for the memoir's twenty-first-century presentation, Yagoda observes, "Attention is resolutely focused on the self, and a certain leeway or looseness with the facts is expected." This does not encompass, he adds, "gross liberties or outright fabrications perpetrated by James Frey [*A Million Little Pieces*] and many other recent fraudulent memoirists ..."

George Fetherling, editor of *The Vintage Book of Canadian Memoirs*, places memoir under the catch-all field of "life-writing." He elaborates:

> Life-writing is the general term whose specifics include autobiography (about one's public self), memoir (frequently about others but with oneself as a thread), diary (day-by-day record), and journal (a discontinuous and often more private or intense product of the same impulse to record). Many argue compellingly that life-writing today is popular because it's connected to the traditional realistic novel in which a recognizable world is created in a recognizable manner through the telling of a story. Fictional characters are flesh-and-blood figures whom their creators care about passionately, but they're essentially inventions.
>
> Memoirists or other life-writers create from actual experience but allow themselves the fiction writer's freedom of rearranging and telescoping in order to make what happened worthy of being called a tale.

You might wish to take special note of those two informative terms, *rearranging* (to rearrange story/life highlights for best dramatic sense) and *telescoping* (making something slide into itself, so that it becomes smaller) as sooner or later, you'll find yourself using these writing techniques in your memoir. In the first instance, rearranging serves the story arc, and quite possibly, and in relation to other parts, the beauty of the story. In the second, you may just need to pare down the content leading in and out of an event to increase the drama quotient. We don't need to know every detail.

The Esssay

Also in the category of memoir is the essay. The history of the essay is long, honourable, and fascinating. French writer Michel Eyquem de Montaigne (1533-1592) is sometimes called the "father of the [literary] essay." His collection, *Essais,* established a new literary form. In this, according to the *Encyclopedia Britannica*, "… he wrote one of the most captivating and intimate self-portraits ever given, on a par with Augustine's and Rousseau's."

The essay has had many incarnations, from New York's "New Journalism" (also the title of a collection of essays, edited by Tom Wolfe and E.W. Johnson, in 1973), practised by the likes of Joan Didion, Truman Capote, and Norman Mailer in the United States, and by journalists Harry Bruce, Peter Gzowski, Christina McCall, and Barbara Moon in Canada, to its current and popular guise as the short, personal story, published in anthologies, newspapers, and magazines. The essay, as a form of scholarly argument, is also taught in high schools and universities.

Essays are also a way of living a life. Writer, essayist, and self-described "cripple" (she has multiple sclerosis) Nancy Mairs finds the impetus to write and ponder all around her: "Out of the new arrivals in our lives – the odd word stumbled upon in a difficult text, the handsome black stranger who bursts in one night through the cat door, the telephone call out of a friend's silence of years, the sudden greeting from the girl-child – we constantly make of ourselves our selves."

Cultural anthropologist and author Mary Catherine Bateson has written extensively about the life story and the varied forms it can take, essays among them. She, too, sees the impetus for story all around the writer and, additionally, sees story as something humans need:

> Wherever a story comes from, whether it is a familiar myth or a private memory, the retelling exemplifies the making of a connection from one pattern to another: a potential translation in which narrative becomes parable and the once upon a time comes to stand for some renascent truth.

> This approach applies to all the incidents of everyday life: the phrase in the newspaper, the endearing or infuriating game of a toddler, the misunderstanding at the office. Our species thinks in metaphors and learns through stories (www.storyteller.net/articles/160).

Yet another distinguished writer, Virginia Woolf, prolifically used the essay to live a considered life. While known primarily for her fiction, Woolf in fact authored over five hundred works of non-fiction, and spent most of her working life as a book reviewer and essayist. Of her essays in *The Essays of Virginia Woolf*, non-fiction pieces dating from 1904, when she was twenty-three, to 1912, the year she married Leonard Woolf, the *Library Journal* says: "These are polished works of literary journalism – shrewd, deft, inquisitive, graceful and often sparkling" (*www.libraryjournal.com/*).

It is the term "literary journalism" that is of interest here – a reminder of the pinnacle the essay can reach, and has done, with Woolf and many others. Beloved children's author E.B. White was also known for his elegant essays, which he often published in *The New Yorker*, *Harper's*, and *The Atlantic*. Christopher Lehman-Haupt, a book reviewer with *The New York Times*, says he was given the lucky "break" of reviewing of White's 1977 collection of essays and writes of their timelessness:

> … E.B. White will always be coming back into style. That's because, as he himself observes of Thoreau, he writes sentences that resist the destructiveness of time. Besides, he's an essayist's essayist. With his relaxed serendipitous technique of seeming to stumble on his subject by way of the back door, he lends you confidence that you don't really have to know much about a thing to write about it intelligently; you need only possess the skill to write, along with a lot of sanity. Thus, if you've got the hang of it, you can arrive at the subject of disarmament by way of Mary Martin's furniture, or at the prospects of American democracy by the route of a dachshund named Fred.

Light years away from the wry wit of E.B. White's essays is the more common and rigid understanding of the essay form, as taught in high schools and universities. Writer and memoirist Natalie Goldberg acknowledges this negative perception, and adds her own opinion:

Unfortunately, the word "essay" usually gets a bad rap in our society. Hand your essays in by Friday. You must write a five-hundred-word essay on the American flag. As adults we hear the e-word and flee, but in truth essays are a delectable form and have the potential to be a baby memoir – fresh, alert, compact, rather perfect. They are short invitations to come along with the writer as she excavates a memory or rolls around in a nuanced thought. As the picture unfolds, the reader can be there in an organic way.

Other definitions of memoir, particularly of the "good" or well-written memoir, come from literary critic and writer William Zinsser:

> A good memoir requires two elements – one of art, the other of craft. The first element is integrity of intention. … The other element is carpentry. Good memoirs are a careful act of construction. … Memoir writers must manufacture a text, imposing order on a jumble of half remembered events. With that feat of manipulation, they arrive at a truth that is theirs alone …

Memoir: A Contemporary Genre

"This is the age of memoir," pronounced Zinsser in 1998. He continued: "Never have personal narratives gushed so profusely from the American soil as in the closing decade of the twentieth century. Everyone has a story to tell, and everyone is telling it."

Similarly, Yagoda writes: "As ubiquitous as memoirs seem in the United States, they are – if there are degrees of ubiquity – even more so in Britain, accounting for seven of the top ten bestselling nonfiction hardcovers in both 2007 and 2008." In 2019, bestselling non-fiction memoirs in the U.K. for the week of October 21 included *Me*, by Elton John; *Tall Tales and Wee Stories*, by Billy Connolly; and *Twas the Nightshift Before Christmas*, by Adam Kay. Earlier in 2019, *The Language of Kindness: A Nurse's Story*, by Christie Watson, sold over 100,000 copies in only a few weeks. Celebrity memoirs are always popular, along with stories from the other end of the spectrum, those of the Everywoman/man.

Sven Birkerts claims that the appetite both for the writing and reading of memoir is growing in contemporary life. It is a form of what he calls "creative self-inquiry." He writes:

> *This really happened* is the baseline contention of the memoir, and the fascination of the work – apart from the interest we have in what is told – is in tracking the artistic transformation of the actual via the alchemy of psychological insight, pattern recognition, and lyrical evocation into a contained saga …"

Canadian writers are equally enthusiastic about memoir, publishing their own memoirs and in memoir collections. Published in 2011, *Slice Me Some Truth: An Anthology of Canadian Creative Non-Fiction* was edited by award-winning writers Luanne Armstrong and Zoë Landale. In addition to memoir, the anthology covers the areas of personal essay, literary travel, nature writing, and lyric essay as well as researched literary journalism and cultural criticism. Some memoir anthologies tend to focus on particular subjects, such as *Fathers: A Literary Anthology*, published by Patremoir Press in 2011 and edited by André Gerard.

Also in October, 2011, two Canadian music superstars, Jann Arden (*Falling Backwards*) and Michael Bublé (*Onstage Offstage*), had memoirs on *The Globe and Mail's* Bestsellers list, as did hockey commentator Ron MacLean, with his memoir, *Cornered*. Jann Arden penned a second bestselling memoir in 2017, titled *Feeding My Mother: Comfort and Laughter in the Kitchen as a Daughter Lives with her Mom's Memory Loss*.

In 2018, a former American First Lady (*Becoming*, by Michelle Obama), a British composer (*Unmasked*, by Andrew Lloyd Webber), and a raw and brilliant new indigenous voice from the Seabird Island Reservation in British Columbia (*Heart Berries*, by Terese Marie Mailhot) all produced hugely successful memoirs. In 2019, more diversity flowed from Canadian non-fiction pens: *The Unexpected Cop: Indian Ernie on a Life of Leadership*, by Ernie Louttit; *To the River: Losing my Brother*, by Don Gillmor; and *Chop Suey Nation: The Surprising History and Vibrant Present of Small-Town Chinese Restaurants from Victoria, BC, to Fogo Island, NL*, by Ann Hui. Memoir's range is only matched by its steady production.

Oh, and that memoir by Michelle Obama? It sold 1.4 million copies in its first week. In two weeks, the book became the bestselling book in the U.S. in 2018. And by March 26, 2019, *Becoming* had sold 10 million copies. Now there's a record that won't be topped for a long time …

Sub-Genres

In the proliferation of this genre, its sub-genres appear to be infinite. During the two years I kept a blog on my memoir readings, I noted that sub-genres can include:

- spiritual or religious
- wartimes and Holocaust
- "misery" or "shockers"
- revenge
- subject-focused, related to: family, place, event, hobby, food, life-philosophy, or animals
- fraudulent (the world has such a long, fine history of "fake" memoirs)
- fictional
- children's
- writers/literary
- groups of people (sports or rock stars; Hollywood figures; politicians; relatives of successful memoirists; average Joes/Josephines), and
- forms (serial, hybrid or mixed genre, magazine- or newspaper-length memoirs)

And again, this is only a handful of sub-genres, in an ever-growing list – and they often mix and overlap.

Memoir as Renegade: The Hybrid Memoir

Memoir is a renegade genre. If memoir were a fish, it would dart past your hand when you reached out to touch it. It's not meant to be caught, only to swim against currents of accepted form.

I further believe that the memoir reaches its renegade apex in its hybrid form, and that the hybrid exists within all sub-genres of memoir. By hybrids, again, I mean memoirs that will not suffer any constraints of any sort: not in form, length, content, or presentation. (Joni Mitchell's newly released *Morning Glory on the Vine: Early Songs and Drawings*, first published for friends only in 1971, contains handwritten lyrics and drawings. It was re-released, this time to the public, in 2019.)

To qualify as hybrid, the memoir must add that "something different" – not just prose, but photographs, sketches, maps, e-mails, letters, or previously published work; recipes, boat or house plans; poetry, unusual fonts, illustrations, or presentations; unusual subject matter or themes, etc. – this list, like the list of sub-genres, is long, defiantly creative, and open-ended.

Hybrids fear no reader or critic, nor any subject. They will horrify with tales of bestiality (*Secret Life*, by Michael Ryan), titillate with confessions of promiscuity (*Love Junkie, A Memoir*, by Rachel Resnick), and taunt with conditional titles such as *If I Did It* (O.J. Simpson).

Examples of Hybrids

Not Quite What I was Planning, from *Smith Magazine*, is a memoir collection of six-word memoirs. The editors of *Smith Magazine* explain how the idea for the book came about: "Legend has it that Ernest Hemingway was once challenged to write a story in six words. Papa came back swinging with, 'For sale: baby shoes, never worn.' Some say he called it his best work. Others dismiss the anecdote as a literary folktale. Either way, the six-word story was born, and it's been popping around the writing world for years."

The 100-Mile-Diet: A Year of Local Eating takes the form of a two-handed play of a single year of living. The two "players," writers and freelance journalists Alisa Smith and J.B. MacKinnon, write in the fashion of a journal, dating the entries by month as they go along, and taking turns "speaking," from chapter to chapter.

Another memoir that uses two-handed play is *Jack & Rochelle: A Holocaust Story of Love and Resistance*. Jack and Rochelle Sutin told their story of love and survival as part of a band of Jewish resistance fighters in the forests of Poland during World War Two to their journalist son, Lawrence Sutin, who then ably edited the two tales. I believe this memoir's deep emotional resonance was heightened by the two different perspectives.

Denise Chong's *The Concubine's Children* could be called an investigative hybrid – with fictionalized features. Chong, a writer and political advisor, explores her family history through research, discussions with family in Canada and China, and a visit to China to meet family members and see where the family originated. She then writes a fictionalized account of the families' lives in both China and Canada. (Another British Columbia writer, journalist Rick Ousten, wrote a similar investigative memoir, *Finding Family*. His did not include fictionalized narrative – though the excellent pacing and development led it to read as a novel would. A fine memoir, then, but not a hybrid.)

From another Chinese-Canadian memoirist comes the *Wong Family Feast, Our Recipes and Stories*, by Joanna Claire Wong. A Vancouver writer, filmmaker, and communications strategist, Wong wrote and self-published a classic mixed-medium hybrid, which includes poems, photographs, family stories and history, and recipes. To do this, Wong travelled to China to study Mandarin and Chinese culture and foods. Together with her parents, who had come to visit her, Wong made a "pilgrimage" to the Wong ancestral village in South China. The seeds for writing a family history were planted during this time. The fact that Wong chose to do this within the hybrid form makes the memoir-family history unique to this family and its times in history, both in China and the west coast of Canada. The memoir is touchingly of this family and none other.

This is perhaps what the hybrid does best: provides uniqueness in a prolific genre where a writer must work hard to go beyond commonalities for any degree of freshness and originality.

Mentioned earlier is *The Nine Lives of Charlotte Taylor*, Sally Armstrong's memoir of her long-ago settler-ancestor. Once again a woman writer is consumed by curiosity and compassion about a figure in her family history – and once again the hybrid memoir provides a framework for exploration. Armstrong, a journalist, author, filmmaker, teacher, and former editor of *Homemakers* magazine, then applies her formidable researching and writing skills to a detailed imagining of her ancestor's life in New Brunswick. The memoir blurs genres – historical fiction, memoir, biography – which, thanks to a forgiving renegade aspect to the genre and an experienced writer's hand, makes for an absorbing read.

On one hand, the reading public has the sometimes fraudulent, often embellished, always unpredictable, and occasionally brilliant, unforgettable memoir (*Walden*, by Henry David Thoreau; *Angela's Ashes*, by Frank McCourt). On the other, the memoir's sub-genre, the hybrid, fights conformity and propriety even harder – to the point, perhaps, of estranging its reader (*Running with Scissors*, by Augusten Burroughs). But when sitting down to write in a renegade genre, how can the writer predict what might transpire? Conventional incarnations exist, certainly, but any scan of the bestselling lists shows they are in the minority.

Regardless of the ultimate form the memoir might take, conventional or hybrid, basic premises still guide its progress onto paper. As Sven Birkerts notes, the injunction from Socrates to "Know Thyself" underpins memoir writing. Writing a memoir is necessarily a phenomenological enterprise (the philosophical study of the structures of experience and consciousness). In order to write a memoir, I had to draw upon my own experiences and examine them in detail. I did this for greater self-understanding and to make the larger connections to other lives in other memoirs.

Some memoirists focus on a single, large event in their lives, which is experienced personally, but takes place in the larger world, where many others are affected by it, too. One such writer is journalist and author Linden MacIntyre, in his memoir, *Causeway*.

Conversation with Linden MacIntyre, author of
Causeway: A Passage from Innocence

Linden MacIntyre was born in Newfoundland and grew up in Cape Breton. He is a graduate of St. Francis Xavier University in Antigonish, Nova Scotia, and worked for many years as a journalist, first in print, then broadcasting. MacIntyre spent twenty-four years as the co-host of *the fifth estate* and won ten Gemini awards for his work there.

His bestselling first novel, *The Long Stretch*, was nominated for a Canadian Booksellers Association (CBA) Libris Award and his boyhood memoir, *Causeway: A Passage from Innocence*, won both the Edna Staebler Award for Creative Nonfiction and the Evelyn Richardson Prize. His second novel, *The Bishop's Man*, a #1 national bestseller, won the Scotiabank Giller Prize, the Dartmouth Book Award, and the CBA Libris Fiction Book of the Year Award, among other honours. The third book in the loose-knit trilogy, *Why Men Lie*, was also a #1 national bestseller as well as a *Globe and Mail* "Can't Miss" Book for 2012. His most recent novels are *Punishment*, in 2014, and *The Only Café*, 2017. His most recent book, a non-fiction project, part memoir and part history, *The Wake: The Deadly Legacy of a Newfoundland Tsunami*, was published in August 2019, becoming an immediate bestseller.

SIMMINS: Could you tell me how you came to write a memoir?

MACINTYRE: I was visited a couple of times by an agent on behalf of a publisher to write a memoir and I never wanted to. I refused. Because I felt what they wanted was my journey through journalism and all the places I've been and all the people I've met and stories I've done and I wasn't interested in that. In journalism everything you do is public anyways, so what's the point to sit down and craft it into a narrative? I think [that would be] a work of vanity more than anything else.

It hit me once that memoir can also be about and should also be about other people and places. The memoir that's egocentric probably should not be written. So I started thinking about the causeway from mainland Nova Scotia to Cape Breton and what it meant to a kid, probably a lot of kids, especially a kid whose father could never get a job around here. All you heard at the time from politicians was all life was going to change, a whole new era.

I can remember there was a very talented sketcher, his name was Stuart Kennedy. I remember for one of the concerts – the little school I went to would be used for community concerts – Kennedy drew this huge picture of Port Hastings in the future. It was skyscrapers and airplanes. It was massive; it looked like the skyline of Manhattan. And this was the kind of thinking that was cultivated by all the politicians and all the dreamers when they talked about the Canso Causeway. You know, the commitment had been made, it was going to be built, it was actually being built and so of course it was a huge project for a couple of years. My father came home from working in the mines in St. Lawrence, Newfoundland.

And it was the first time that he had relatively steady work in this area from the time he was a child. He left as a kid; I mean he was sixteen when he left. So there he was, he was home, and he had all kinds of dreams. He knew the project would end, but he thought that it would launch him into some sort of trucking business, or some kind of sawmill business. With all the new economic activity generated by this link, he would definitely be able to make a business for himself.

Because he was never going to be able to get employed. As I point out in the book, he'd never gone to school. Every place he went looking for work they'd say, well, let's see your grades and stuff. He'd say, well, I never went to school. Oh, my God, so the automatic assumption would be illiterate, stupid, and he was totally literate and articulate and smart. But he didn't have the certification. So he thought, Okay, I'll leapfrog over that and I'll have a business of my own. I'll be my own boss in this bold new world of post-causeway Strait of Canso.

And of course it was huge disappointment. It was a bit of a boom for a while but he never could quite get part of it. Ten years later he finally got a grip on something that was related to the new economy – and he dropped dead. So I thought there was an interesting existential story there about dreams – a kid's dream connected to an adult dream, and promises of people with a stake in optimism, whether it's a political stake or a commercial stake in public widespread optimism. Good for politics, good for business, so they try to generate this optimism and people get caught up in it. Little kids get caught up in it, adults get caught up in it, people say there's going to be great opportunities for material growth and inevitably it never pans out.

SIMMINS: This is a fascinating process you've described. One of the questions I wanted to explore was the subjects that choose us, as writers. You return to a gem idea from your childhood, a gem that you hold to the light to look at the colour and faceting. Your writer's heart knew, even though everyone was pressing you to write about your career, and the people you met along the way, your writer's heart knew that there had to be a story in that long-ago gem.

MACINTYRE: Well, yes, and it had to be larger than me. It doesn't matter who you are – if the story is ultimately about you and your narrow perceptions – and all our perceptions when we're inside ourselves are fairly narrow – then who wants to read it? A good memoir is about the time you're living in. It's about the place you're living in. It's about the people you know either intermittently or over a lifetime. I thought, Okay, I can do this as long as they understand this is not going to be the story of the journalist travelling around doing stories. This is going to be an insight into life in a small place, a story about failure and the struggle of people who are born with huge deficits, either socially, or in my father's case physically, too. He was sickly as a kid and so he had to overcome all these deficits and struggle through hard, lean times. I call my parents 'the hungry generation' because they didn't really have much starting out and everything kind of fell away from them during the '30s and the struggle to make a living, and then war, and all the rest of it.

So it was a hungry period of time until the '50s and then they began to lift up. I thought, Okay, I'll write an insight into where they come from, where my father came from, that eighteenth-century world – it wasn't even nineteenth-century – that so many of his generation came out of. And suddenly they're thrown into this optimistic prosperity-driven 1950s period and the causeway was a symbol of all that.

SIMMINS: You also said at some point that one of the reasons you hesitated about writing a memoir was being perceived yourself as having 'big feeling,' or an overabundance of pride and ego. I'd never heard that expression until I came to Cape Breton.

MACINTYRE: Big feeling [in Cape Breton] is a terrible scar to carry; it's the scarlet letter.

SIMMINS: That's right! So that certainly would have been in your considerations before starting a memoir.

MACINTYRE: Yeah, you don't act like that. I studied at St. Francis Xavier University, and one professor there was an old country Scotsman who was a Celtic historian and he said, 'I know around here you do not draw attention to yourself in a good way or a bad way, unless you run for office.' And it's changing now but in my formation period you did not really, you did not want to do that. And I just thought that was like modesty and virtue.

But the older professor was explaining that once upon a time, to draw attention to oneself was to draw the attention of the evil spirits. So, for me to say, for example, 'Marjorie Simmins, that's a great book you just published,' you would be offended by that because it would draw the attention of evil spirits and the book would flop. I mean, if you walk up to somebody and said, 'That's a lovely new car you've got,' you'd be putting bad luck on the car. There was a tendency not to draw attention to oneself. The people who did draw attention to themselves were 'big feeling' – because they thought they were more than they really were.

SIMMINS: It is interesting that the professor viewed this behaviour on a spiritual level of sorts, or supernatural. But really, when you think about it, any sort of bringing yourself to the forefront, such as penning a memoir, is making yourself vulnerable.

MACINTYRE: Well, there's that, too.

SIMMINS: You are literally going to the front of the stage and there you are, for the audience to see.

MACINTYRE: Yes, exactly, and if you're in a culture where quite frankly people are prepared to shoot the person who gets out front ...

SIMMINS: Canadians do that, and newspapers do that.

MACINTYRE: Yeah, they do that.

SIMMINS: So you get a double whammy.

MACINTYRE: You think twice before you expose yourself or you expose your back. Because out front is to expose your back, too.

SIMMINS: The third thing you said at one point was that as a journalist, with one non-fiction book, *Who Killed Ty Conn,* already published, you still hesitated. As a journalist you knew how to prove things. But memoir, that was different. It was a bunch of reflections and memories.

MACINTYRE: Yeah, that's the essence of memoir.

SIMMINS: But you were distrustful of that feature.

MACINTYRE: Yes, of the whole genre, and I had to come to terms with that. That memoir is a creative process that sort of sits halfway [between fiction and non-fiction]. [Also], I'm not sure that factual non-fiction is all that factual either.

SIMMINS: Genres are hard to pin down.

MACINTYRE: They are. Then you have memoir, which is based on memory to a large extent. And then you have fiction. I've always found one of the reasons I prefer fiction is because you put more truth in fiction.

SIMMINS: Yes, but as soon as you write fiction someone says, 'Oh, that happened in his life, did you know that?'

MACINTYRE: Oh, God yeah, they do. Ashley MacIsaac [a multi-award-winning Canadian fiddler, singer, and songwriter from Cape Breton Island, Nova Scotia] was telling me that his mother and father each bought a copy of my novel *The Bishop's Man* and they'd sit in the living room with their respective copies arguing who was who. They did this because they were living in Creignish where the novel was set. But memoir, in this particular case, was backed up by research. I had a whole lot of historical research back in the '70s when Father John Angus Rankin in Glendale was publishing a history of the parish and he asked me if I would research the MacIntyres from the Mountain.

So I did all that and I ended up tied to a whole lot of people who when I was writing this were no longer around. There was a little community-based newspaper called *The Victoria Inverness Bulletin*, which was very big in the area during the '50s. I think it was printed in Truro. It was essentially an assembly of what we used to call at *The Chronicle Herald* 'bush notes,' handwritten notes from people all over – Port Hawkesbury, Petit-de-Grat, Judique, Creignish – wherever there was someone who was somebody who was interested in what was going on, and they were writing gossip down and the gossip was all getting in the paper. I went through – in the archives in Halifax – year after year of this little *Bulletin* and it would be, 'Dan R. MacIntyre is visiting his family home from such and such a place'; 'So-and-so got a new car'; 'So-and-so is gone to Boston to visit relatives.' It was full of that kind of stuff, and the real nitty-gritty, such as 'Sylvia Reynolds had a lovely birthday party, and the following people attended, including me, you know.' And so it was school stuff, community stuff, right down to the grassroots. I don't know who was ever writing it, but it was essentially as factual as you will ever get.

SIMMINS: Sure. It's no different really than a journal, but about the community.

MACINTYRE: Yes, it was a community journal. Every little place had that. Port Hastings was one of them. Other communities did, too. I spent ages sitting up in the archives just going through these reels and reels. It was fascinating. There was one funny one – I was flipping through 1955, which I think was the year the causeway opened, and the *Bulletin*, they used to publish on the front page huge wedding pictures. These were just ordinary pictures, not like Princess Diana. More like 'Mary and John MacDonald got married and this is the wedding party.'

So I was seeing all the people I knew who got married in the '50s and then I'm scrolling through and I see one big picture. It was the usual collection of people, three or four rows of them. I noticed that they were all female except one person so I stopped and I went back and I looked. Yes, it was all girls and one guy and it was the 1955 graduating class of the Provincial Normal College in Truro and that one guy was Alistair MacLeod.

He'd come from such a poor background. He went to the Normal College [the Teachers' College] for a year, got a teaching license, and he taught in places like Port Hood Island and a few little places like that until he saved up enough money to go to St. FX and get a degree. Then he taught some more and then he saved up and got more degrees and ended up as a university professor. But it was just so great to see him in that photo. There he was, Alistair MacLeod [the master short story writer and author of the bestselling novel *No Great Mischief*], sitting there, big grin on his face, totally unselfconscious about the fact he was the only male in this mob of women.

SIMMINS: Well, he got what he wanted, didn't he? He got that piece of paper.

MACINTYRE: He had the piece of paper. So anyway, it was great fun researching that. But then, you can't make it into a recitation, as you know. You fold it all into the consciousness of your central voice. In my case, that was this ten-, eleven-year-old kid who I remember quite well. So I fed all this stuff to that voice.

All of it was informed by memory. I have a good memory from that period because it was a very vivid period and I was the kid who went around selling the newspapers. I also read the newspaper. Our house was full of newspapers; I don't know why. I remember there was a Winnipeg weekly paper, a *Toronto Star Weekly*, a Halifax paper coming and going, and the Sydney paper also. I was selling the Sydney paper, which was a fairly real daily newspaper at the time. And so I was always following the crises of the world and the crises of the country and all the stories of the time. And then you had this massive construction project going on in Port Hastings …

SIMMINS: I would guess that the average Cape Breton kid at the time would not have been as aware of the wider world the way you were, by reading so many newspapers.

MACINTYRE: Yeah, I was.

SIMMINS: I mean you were thinking about, let's say, Winnipeg – and who the heck in Cape Breton in the '50s was thinking about Winnipeg?

MACINTYRE: Exactly. And Winnipeg was thinking about the world, too, because I can remember the first time – this would have been much later – I really read about Stephen Truscott. [Truscott was sentenced to death in 1959 for the rape and murder of classmate Lynne Harper; CBC's *the fifth estate*, and MacIntyre, later covered the story of his wrongful conviction and ten-year incarceration, under a life sentence. He was parolled in 1969, which meant living outside prison walls, but under the stringent conditions of his sentence. *The fifth estate* was a key part of an effort to have the sentence overturned in 2007. Between 1969 and until the documentary, Truscott lived under a different name and under the cloud of being a convicted murderer. Then, in 2000, on *the fifth estate*, he showed his face and spoke as Stephen Truscott for the first time since his release from prison.]

It was in the *Free Press Weekly* from Winnipeg, I'm pretty sure it was there. So that would have been in 1960, but back in the '50s, the kid that ran around on the bicycle dropped the paper at houses that wanted it and then what I had left over I took to the construction camps and there was a tugboat, too. You could just wander through construction sites in those days into the bunkhouses and into the cookhouse and into the staff-house and then down onto the tugboat and to the dredge and all the facilities down where they were actually doing the work.

SIMMINS: All the fun places you'd never be allowed to go now.

MACINTYRE: Oh, you wouldn't be allowed near it now. I just went there and they loved to see me come. The old cook on the tugboat would feed me. They'd feed me stuff at the cookhouse on the construction camp and then they'd feed me on the dredge and they'd feed me on the tugboat. I had like three suppers by the time I got home – and had to eat another one there.

SIMMINS: A boy's or girl's dream, wandering around free.

MACINTYRE: And dumping the papers off, which was kind of secondary to the whole thing, which was just shooting the breeze with all these strangers. I had a fascination with strangers. There's an anecdote in there, the memoir about the old Hungarian caretaker at the camp who shot himself practically under my nose. But I was fascinated by these people because, again, they were bringing this vast world into this place I called home.

So I gather all that stuff and I put it into a kind of personal hopper and I told the publisher, 'Look, this is not going to be what you would expect from somebody who you think you know – a reporter who works at the CBC, who's been around for decades, covering all kinds of stories, big and small. It isn't going to be that kind of a memoir.' I was working with a guy named Jim Gifford at Harper Collins who said, 'Look, you make it what you want to make it.' And I was so anxious to keep myself out of it that I wanted to put it in the third person.

SIMMINS: Did you actually try that?

MACINTYRE: I actually tried a chapter and I showed it to him and he said, 'No, no …

SIMMMINS: … it's not working.'

MACINTYRE: It's gotta be first person. So okay, I got past that and I wrote in the first person.

SIMMINS: I came to memoir after many, many, many decades of journal writing so there was going to be no other pronoun than 'I,' and off I went and that was it. Whereas you would be on television saying, '*The fifth estate* has discovered,' or even 'we,' I suppose, to indicate collective effort. Anything but the 'I' word.

MACINTYRE: I was anxious to distance the self, the predictable self from this product. I wanted people to approach it as if they'd never heard of me. I wanted them to read it as though it were only about the dreams of a father, and dreams of the kid, and the disappointments that are going to have to be overcome by people who are born on the wrong side of the tracks.

SIMMINS: And you succeeded, because it is so much a Cape Breton story and a young boy's story and a moment in time in this particular part of the world. It's not Linden MacIntyre the journalist.

MACINTYRE: No, not him. It was interesting ... we wanted the book to have wide appeal. I don't know how many copies it sold, but it seemed as though everybody who read it wrote to me. I had letters from a South Asian woman who said that she identified with the kid and the kid's thinking. A friend of mine who is a journalist, a very brave woman from the former Yugoslavia – she lived in Sarajevo – and she just adored the book. She read it twice, I think. The whole sense of what home means really resonated for her.

SIMMINS: It did for me, too, with my two coastal homes, and deep loves for them. Coastal people are a particular people, so passionate about place. For me, I literally thought I wasn't going to be able to breathe away from the West Coast.

MACINTYRE: My wife Carol [journalist Carol Off] grew up in Winnipeg, Ottawa, and London, Ontario. That first summer she was down here in Cape Breton, I was working on the boat. We were in Little Judique Harbour. Carol asks the stranger, 'Are you from here?' He replies, 'No.' She's thinking that, like her, he's 'from away.' She asks, 'So where are you from?' He replies, 'Little Judique.'

SIMMINS: One mile away ... but he's not from Judique Harbour, you get that straight. As a seasoned Maritimer now, I can understand the subtleties of this story. Let's review. You came to the memoir and you said, 'I'm going to do it my way,' and as any good journalist would, you found psychological comfort in surrounding yourself with some facts and figures. You say, 'Ah, okay, so I can talk capably about this if I have my historical framework.' And then you accepted the fact that you couldn't hold the personal aspect at bay, that you were going to have to not just dive, but dive deep, which you did. And then I presume you started to roll with the writing.

MACINTYRE: You have to. I think in anything you write, you have to find that universal or nobody's going to read it. Who cares about how I grew up unless they can relate to it? So that's where I wanted to get to, before I could really embrace the project. I have to write this from a point of view that's shared by a lot of people and not only in this culture, but people that come from any kind of marginalized place or culture, or anyone who has to sort of face struggle that requires them to improve themselves beyond, without a whole lot of help.

SIMMINS: But it's interesting, isn't it, and even counterintuitive, that to get to your comfort zone you basically had to decide to go deep and to open yourself up and to present yourself in even a less-than-flattering light at times.

MACINTYRE: Absolutely.

SIMMINS: That's where you found your comfort zone. That's fascinating, for me being able to tell that to people when I'm teaching memoir and say, 'Listen, you're going to find comfort when you get to …

MACINTYRE: … an uncomfortable place.'

SIMMINS: Right, an uncomfortable place. Then you'll know you've hit some gold. Again, it's not the simple fact of, let's say, loss, it's the complexities and universals surrounding that loss. I find it really interesting that that's where you hit your stride – when you were slightly uncomfortable and certainly feeling exposed.

MACINTYRE: Mm'hmm.

SIMMINS: How long did it take to write the book?

MACINTYRE: Well, I wrote the book fairly quickly; I thought it was going to take a long time, but [in 2005], the CBC locked us all out, so I ended up with a three- or four-month stretch that I didn't expect I was going to have. So it took probably five months, not counting the amount of time I spent in the archives. I probably spent a year researching and thinking, and then the writing I thought would take a lot longer. But once I got in the voice and the rhythm of it, it just sort of rolled along. I would post the end of a chapter and suddenly the next chapter would be sitting there waiting for me.

SIMMINS: How nice. And you hadn't written journals as a younger person, had you?

MACINTYRE: Well, no, I didn't really keep a journal, although I was a very solitary kid in many ways because there weren't many other kids of my generation so I spent a lot of time inside of myself, talking to myself. So once I really returned to that state, I suddenly found the voice was still there, still echoing around. And so I just let it run.

SIMMINS: How did you access the voice? Were you just literally sitting down and doing this and it came to you?

MACINTYRE: Well, it was strange. I didn't know how I was going to start this book and I decided the sort of the momentous point of the book will be where my father dies. So I woke up in the middle of the night and I thought about the last time I had seen him alive and I was just thinking, Okay, maybe I should start the book with the last time I saw him alive. And then I realized that the last time I saw him alive I could barely see I was so hungover because it had been a weekend of complete bingeing with my friends. I had come down to visit my parents but ended up getting off with a bunch of friends and had very little time with them. My father and I spent an hour or two in the old tavern down here – Billy Jo's first tavern, which is down on the other street. And then of course, we were sitting there, connecting a little bit and then an old friend comes along, and the two of them started to talk Gaelic to each other. And you know, I knew what they were talking about but I wasn't going to, I couldn't get involved. I wasn't fluent enough to participate and I didn't want to participate. A friend of mine comes over and says, 'Where you going this afternoon?' and I said, 'I'll catch up with you.'

So the next thing was getting driven to the airport on Sunday and I could hardly speak. My last memory of my living father was looking out an airplane window and in the days everybody could come right into the departure lounge and stand, he was standing in the window of the departure lounge. I'm sitting in the airplane; it was a government airplane and I'm looking out. I'm seeing this guy stand there with his hands in his pockets and I'm feeling guilty, I'm feeling guilty, never realizing that I'd never see him alive again.

SIMMINS: So you weren't even worried that you might not see him again.

MACINTYRE: No, it never crossed my mind. So I wrote the first chapter and I just sort of sat there and I'm going to do that straight, so the chapter was entitled Getting Loaded. The old man and I got loaded Friday night and then we go to the tavern Saturday morning. He had some business in town and just had a beer and we were getting on maybe, I don't know, going visiting maybe, but he got off on this conversation with one of his friends, I got off in conversation with my friends, so the whole thing was getting loaded and getting that close to a connection and at that point I had reached that point where I was uncomfortable, but I'm going to keep on going.

And then, then I pick up in the next chapter as the ten-year-old voice and the causeway and the rest of it and then I come back to the next time I saw my father it was when he was dead. And that's sort of, I think, either the penultimate or the last chapter of the book. But it was all true. There's a scene in the book where my father's dead and I got to get home from Ottawa and I had no money and this envelope had come in the mail and I had a look at it and it was a plastic card with Chargex written on it, unsolicited notice from the bank, and the wife said, 'That's a credit card.' I said, 'Yeah,' but I was thinking I had to go to the bank and borrow some. 'No, no,' she says, 'that's what that thing is for. Try it out.'

So I went to the airport and yeah, no problem. Next thing I'm standing talking to the Premier of Nova Scotia, G.I. Smith, who was coming from some federal-provincial thing and he recognized me and says, 'Where are you going?' and I said, 'I'm going home.' And it was an odd time of the year, it was March and he says, 'Oh, family visit?' I said, 'No,' I said, 'there's been a death.' 'Who died?' he says. 'My father,' I said, and you know, suddenly there was no more Premier of Nova Scotia, he was just a friend, relative, whatever. He was very warm. It was like one of those strange things that, looking back on it, I said I'm going to write that in, too.

All that stuff just flowed out. Once I woke up in the middle of the night. It was like early morning and I said to myself first chapter's going to be about the last time I saw him, and it was going to be about us getting shit-faced, and how much time you waste. So that was the first chapter and then it just took off from there. All the research, the scribblers full of stuff from the archives, again I wasn't going through it. It was just there and okay, I need to know a date and I'd go back through, or I'm stuck, so I'll just go through these notebooks and get something, something will connect. But I knew what I wanted to do, I knew what I wanted to achieve and I knew where I wanted to end and that to me, to know *where you want to end is key to the journey*. I know a lot of writers sort of meander, but I don't. I have to know how the story is going to wrap and the same with the memoir.

SIMMINS: Did you actually do an outline then?

MACINTYRE: No, no, it was in my head.

SIMMINS: That's a lot of story to keep in your mind.

MACINTYRE: It wasn't all that difficult because the structure of the book was going to be the couple of years it took to build the causeway with outcroppings, and then fast forward to 1969 when my father died. So no, there was no outline. It was very organic, like rolling out, all driven by the voice of this kid alternating with the voice of this callow twenty-something-year-old supposed adult.

SIMMINS: What did your family think when it came out?

MACINTYRE: Well, that's a good point. I was a little nervous about some of it. One of the people who I talked to a lot was my cousin from out in MacIntyre's Mountain, Archie. And Archie was terminally ill with cancer, but it didn't affect his outlook, it didn't affect his morale much. He was living in St. Catharine's, so I would make frequent visits in to St. Catharine's and like I'm not researching a book, I'm just talking to Archie and we'd journey back into our memories and make, check things off, refer things back and forth.

And then I told him one day during one of the visits, I said, 'You know, I'm writing a book about the causeway, about my growing up there, and there's an awful lot about the mountain and our people and all that stuff and when I finish the manuscript, I want to give it to you to read.' In the back of my mind I knew he wouldn't be alive to see that so I wanted him to see it anyway. 'So,' I said, 'it would be a great favour to me if you'd read this manuscript and you know what, just tell me flat out what you think – if it's offensive, if it's wrong, anything.' Well, I gave it to him on a Saturday and left it with him and the following Saturday morning he phoned up, and said, 'I read it.' And I said, 'Okay, what'd you think?' He said, 'It's accurate. There's some rough stuff in there, but it's all true.' Then he said, 'As a matter of fact, if you wanted to get some really rough stuff, I could add to it.'

So the next hurdle was my mother. My father's long gone, I didn't care about my siblings because that would just be competing memories, but if somebody in the earlier generation, like a parent first of all, well, there's a reflection on domestic relations, the domestic situation.

So I said I'm going to bite the bullet on this one. I was down for a visit in the fall of late 2005. I had the manuscript with me. It was just printed off, wasn't in a galley or anything like that. I left it in the room that I was occupying and when I got back to Toronto I called up my mother and I said, 'I left something in that room and you can read it or you can not read it, suit yourself.'

I never heard anything else and Christmas Day I phoned to say Merry Christmas. In the middle of the phone call she says, 'Oh, by the way,' she says, 'I found that manuscript and read it.' And I said, 'Ahh, and you're still talking to me …" And she said, 'That's a beautiful book.' I said, 'Well, I must have missed something' but she said no, she says, 'It was all true and it's all well presented.' And that's about all she ever said about it.

SIMMINS: What more would you want?

MACINTYRE: Yeah, she was a huge fan of the book.

SIMMINS: 'That's a beautiful book.' Nice.

MACINTYRE: Yeah, and then of course the rest of it was the book comes out around here [in Cape Breton]. The only static I got was from a former schoolteacher from Judique who said, 'Why didn't you put your years of going to school in Judique?' I said, 'Well, because that's not what the book is about.'

SIMMINS: Isn't that sweet, though?

MACINTYRE: I've been in the public eye with TV; you can't get much more public so, and I'm accustomed to people coming up and saying, 'Really liked that piece you did, great show,' because that's the way Canadians are, that's the way people are. Nobody comes out and says, 'Holy shit, how you could possibly have come up with that piece of garbage?' So the book, you know, people come up and say, 'Loved that book,' saying gave it away, given it to people all over the place, you know, and I say, 'That's great.' I also know that there's probably numbers like the law of physics, equal and opposite reactions. But everybody that comes up to me on a subway car and says, 'I love that piece you did,' there's somebody else saying, 'I hate that piece he did.' And I'm sure there are a lot of people who think the book is wrong, it's drivel, it's the rest of it but, you know what, the book is the book. The book is a *living* – it's one of my kids, you know.

SIMMINS: You were about to say it's like a living creature?

MACINTYRE: It *is* a living creature. The book is a living creature and it's the property of whoever reads it. That's the same with the novels, you know. People will tell me about stuff in the novel that I never realized was there; they find stuff in there. Okay, good.

SIMMINS: Of course that's the time to take credit, as though every aspect was planned for their enjoyment.

MACINTYRE: A book is a very strange thing. It's your kid. You take your kid and put him school that first day and the kid is gone, the kid starts to become something that is, has a lot to do with other relationships. So you know I don't judge my kids, I don't judge my book, I don't judge anybody's reaction to the book or to my kids. I mean, the book is just something that people will absorb into themselves and respond to the effect of that.

SIMMINS: I love the idea that it's a living creature, though it's not, of course. Invariably somebody will say about my memoir, *Coastal Lives*, 'Oh, my goodness you write about some very difficult things.' And I say, 'Yes, I had to.' And they say, 'Oh, well, didn't you, you know, worry about this or worry about that?' I say, 'It's a piece of art, it's not me. I can't slice it open and have blood come out of it, right? It's produced as art.'

MACINTYRE: I know, and I have run into a lot of this with fiction where characters in fiction say and do the most godawful things, the language that comes out of their mouths, and people will say, 'Oh, my God, did you have to use all that?' No, it's not me. I create a character and the character just ends up talking that way because did you ever hear a police officer or a corrections officer or, you know, a drunk person or an angry person talk? And for me to start censoring them is silly …

SIMMINS: That would be the word, yes, or even toning it down.

MACINTYRE: Now I will, you know, run a filter sometimes. In fiction, I do what I call the Audrey edit.

SIMMINS: Audrey?

MACINTYRE: There's a woman named Audrey, so Audrey becomes my, a particular reader. I like Audrey, I respect Audrey, I don't want to offend Audrey, and Audrey has broadened my world; she's not a prude but even so, I want to say, okay, so I do a word search, fuck. I will revisit every fuck in the book or every piece of vulgarity in the book and I'll run it through the Audrey test and she may very well question it, but I don't back away just because she's going to ask. I back away if I don't think I have an answer.

SIMMINS: Right, right.

MACINTYRE: If she says, 'Does he really have to say that?' and I say yes, 'He did, for the following reason,' and Audrey being a smart woman will say, 'Okay, I get it.' Now my mother, she goes through most of it with a felt tip pen and there's no hope there, you know. It's like, whatever, it's your book, you can use it for toilet paper, if you want to. But, you know, to go back to the book as a living creature, is that the living creature isn't composed of living, breathing people. It's a big, big universal I.

SIMMINS: It really is.

MACINTYRE: I always say to people you can't write a successful book, you can only write a good book if you really work hard. And the factors that turn a book into a successful book are way beyond your control. It's like playing golf. [People] don't even know all the factors that go into a good golf shot and it's the same with a book. You don't even know the factors that contribute to a successful book. I will read successful books and say I don't understand why this is a successful book.

SIMMINS: I do it all the time. Sometimes I'll double check with Don [my husband and writer, Silver Donald Cameron] and say, 'What did you think of this?' and he'll go, 'I was underwhelmed,' because we often agree when it comes to literature. But now, one thing I'm interested in – how this has gone for you, the writerly process. You basically found a comfort level, produced the book in what I would call pretty timely fashion, including a year of research. Did you find any surprises along the way?

MACINTYRE: That's a good question. I've never thought of that before. I was surprised by my own emotional reaction to a couple of things that persuaded me when the book was finished, that regardless of what else the book and the project might achieve, to have written it was therapeutic. The suicide of the old fellow in the camp, I hadn't realized how deeply that had buried itself, way down deep. I actually went back to a couple of people who were working in the camps at the time just to say, 'Did that really happen?' Did I really come down to the camp on a Saturday afternoon and sort of walk, almost step over, this guy who was dead and not realize, spoke to him, went into the bunkhouse and distributed the newspapers and came back and stopped and spoke to him again, climbed on my bicycle and drove away. It is possible, did that …? 'Oh, of course that happened,' they said. 'You were seen, we know when he shot himself and you came along and you walked over him and something in you just blanked that out.'

And then, when I began to deal with it, it was very difficult. And the other part, my father's death, was difficult. I knew that my father's sudden death was a total surprise and had affected me, but it was also that there was a whole lot of stuff going on in my life at the time, so I had to defer all kinds of aspects of that. And of course when I started to write about it the deferral was over. It was all okay.

I remember vividly every moment, starting with the afternoon I think was, the day escapes me, but it was like a Wednesday afternoon, I think, when we were pounding away at this weekly newspaper I worked for and the door was closed and there was a knock on the door. Nobody ever knocked on the door and I went and I opened the door and it was this friend of mine.

He was a priest, a local guy from Judique who was teaching in Ottawa. I'd never seen him with his priest suit on, but he was all dressed up in his priest suit. What are you doing downtown, I thought. He'd been meeting the Bishop or whatever. He says, 'Come on out for a second,' and I said, 'No, no I'm busy, come in.' 'No, no,' and he grabbed the door I was in, and he grabbed me, and he said, 'You gotta come out in the hall' and he told me about my father's death.

And you know, I said what people often say foolishly – that was, 'You're kidding.' It was absurd. And he said, 'You have to come with me,' and then I realized, well, yeah, I have to go with him. I'm in the middle of a job with typewriter paper rolled in and I'm writing something for the weekend paper and I went and I tell the guy, 'I'm working on a story but I gotta go.' And he said, 'What do you mean, you gotta go?' and I said, 'My father, it seems my father dropped dead. I have to leave.' And he says 'Well, sit down for a second. We have to talk about what you're working on.' I said, 'No, I'm leaving.' He said, 'Can you spare just five minutes?' and I said, 'No, I can't, Mike, I'm out of here.' And this was a guy who – well, we'd often talked about the fact his father had been a big shot in the early days of the CCF [Co-operative Commonwealth Federation] Party, one of the brains with Woodsworth and all those people, and we had talked about how this guy's famous father had just dropped way before his time. And I was thinking afterwards what a cold reaction that was. So all this shit came back, you know.

SIMMINS: The deferral was over. You said a minute ago the deferral was over. I got a little chill when you said that, you know, because we do this, we say, 'Well, I'll think about that later when I'm a little stronger or steadier and not so busy or not so this or that or whatever it is.' Then the deferral was over. And you preceded that by saying that there was a cathartic effect by the end of the memoir. I'm really fascinated to hear that. When I teach memoir I often say, 'Please don't expect that. It's all very nice, we all would want a catharsis after tough times, but don't look to memoir to necessarily give that to you.' And yet, that gift was given to you.

MACINTYRE: Yeah, yeah, and it was compliments of the fact, I think, of the last chapter, called Cadillac. It all sort of came back as I was dealing with that last chapter. I never really knew my father. He was away in the mines all the time and it was only when I got older and I needed work and I went off and I said, 'Can you get me on?' wherever it was. He'd get me on and we'd spend time together and we got to know each other in the mining camps. And then afterwards I would bump into him here and there as I travelled around in journalism.

I remember one night we sat in a bar in Gander, Newfoundland, long, late into the night and I remember him saying, 'So how much money did they pay you for that work you do?' And I said I think they pay – I think at the time I was making $5,000 a year. 'Oh, you're getting there,' he says. 'When you make it to $6,000 a year, you can stop worrying about stuff.' $6,000. He said, 'I've pretty well given up. I'm going to be working in the mines until I'm done,' but, he says, 'I've bought some bonds, I bought some Canada Savings Bonds. They're going to come due in I think 1970 or something like that.' He says, 'You know what I'm going to do with that money from those bonds?' He says, 'I'm buying a Cadillac, that's what I'm going to do with the money from those bonds – I'm going to buy a Cadillac. I'm going to have one fancy car in my life.' So that was … it. He had reduced the dream down to that. And at the time I'm in my twenties with all of life ahead of me.

SIMMINS: Hey, but somebody's dream is somebody's dream; it wasn't a reduction for him. That was his shiny dream.

MACINTYRE: Yeah, and I was in my early twenties and he was in his forties and I say, 'Well, he's old.' So I was thinking afterwards, you know, and when I was writing the final pages, they took him to the cemetery in a Cadillac hearse and so I just made the scene in my mind. You know, the family in the car behind the hearse and the hearse is a Cadillac and this all comes back; you know, the futility of it all. And it was cathartic, the whole thing became an unspooling of the various bits and pieces that had been in the deferral, had been jammed into a cupboard with no organization or no logic, just jammed in there. Because like I said, you know I was having a lot of trouble at home in my own personal home, I was having trouble. I didn't like this job very much, I wasn't very good at it, I didn't think I was, anyway, and my wife at the time was from here and hated it in Ottawa and was having trouble with that, and promptly after my father died she had a nervous breakdown.

I don't want to get into any of that, but I was raising a bunch of small children and it was just chaos. So I didn't have time to deal with this sudden death. No, that's done, I can't do anything about that, it's out of here and in the closet it goes. And fast-forward many years and then I have to revisit that closet for purposes of that and it all comes crashing out.

SIMMINS: But what is the particular cathartic element here? Where does the catharsis come in? Is it just like the fact that those poor memories are allowed to reach air?

MACINTYRE: I'm not quite sure. For me to finally sit down and deal with the incredible story of disappointment in this one guy's life and how he never really showed it, and it sort of came together, I don't know, with the Cadillac symbol … It was just a realization that when somebody dies in those circumstances, you do have to really take the time to process it at the time, because all these things start coming back. I remember, vividly, the priest comes to the door of the office, I go out with him, I get my coat, I go out, I have this encounter with my colleague, and I remember it's raining, it's miserable and I remember as we were waiting to cross Wellington Street that his father had dropped dead exactly the same, former hard rock miner, the priest's father came home from the mines, died in his own home just early in the morning, just about a year before. And we went across the street, at the other side of the street, and I said, 'How am I supposed to feel now?' Because I don't feel anything, I feel, like, paralyzed.

SIMMINS: Shock.

MACINTYRE: And he said, 'Where did you park the car?' and I said, 'I don't know.' He says, 'Just give me the keys and I'll find it.' And he loaded me in the car and took me home. And it was one of those old-fashioned things, you know, the body in the house, no funeral parlour and people come in waves and waves of people twenty-four hours a day, for three days and then back on an airplane, go to Ottawa and back to work. It was unreal. So it was nothing, there was no particular discovery, there was no particular insight, it was just to have to work through all those particulars, all the details, all the moments and the memories. To realize that everything had been preserved intact somewhere inside of me and now I'm reviewing it, I'm going through – I gotta go through it – I have to actually make sense of it, I actually have to draw conclusions from it.

SIMMINS: It's a bit of a miracle, isn't it? Because it's in this filing cabinet, way in the back there, it's all kept in.

MACINTYRE: Yeah, and I opened it up. I finished writing that last page of the book in Judique. And I stood up and I didn't want to tell anybody I had finished. I didn't want to let on because I didn't know I'd finished it. I said I've written the end of the last page and there's nothing else, nowhere else to go with it. And I stood up from the laptop and I walked in and I sat down on a couch in the next room and I realized that I was weeping. Now whether it was because I couldn't [go on], I had to leave this now, forever.

SIMMINS: And this sounds like such an extraordinary experience on all levels for you. I mean, to weep when you finish a manuscript – I don't think is common. You didn't do it with your novels.

MACINTYRE: No, I just pour a drink. You finish a novel, you pour a drink and say, 'Thank Christ.' But with this one I just wanted to be all alone. I wanted – I didn't want to talk about it. Like I say, it was finished but it wasn't complete. And it never will be. And I think that's the way memoirs are doomed to be. A memoir is always going to be a work in progress because the only completed memoir, you can't write, because you're dead. But that experience – writing the memoir – made a big difference with my novels.

SIMMINS: Did it?

MACINTYRE: I had written a novel called *The Long Stretch* and it took me ten years to get it in the shape that it could be published. I had tried to write two more and one of them was an underfed [creation], and one of them was stuck. And, you know, I wasn't interested in it. I finally did the memoir and since I've published the memoir I've published four novels. So something got cleaned out, something got cleared away.

SIMMINS: You would credit the memoir with all that creative production? That is so fantastic.

MACINTYRE: I cannot escape the fact that up until that book – you know, I cleaned the closet – I was pretty well stuck and since then, I've just sort of gushed out. Four novels and I have one underway. *The Bishop's Man, Why Men Lie, Punishment,* and then the fourth one, *The Only Café,* will be out soon. It'll be ten years. Four novels in ten years.

SIMMINS: And what a thought – that the memoir cleared the decks for the novels.

MACINTYRE: I think it did, I think it did. It took me down into places that I'd been hiding from, places I'd been avoiding and once I confronted all that stuff, then there was nothing in the way of invention, nothing in the way of exploring feelings. I got away from myself to a certain extent.

SIMMINS: So if the memoir opened you up emotionally and spiritually, then you brought all that impetus and energy and, frankly, courage, into fiction. And hence the Giller. Imagine – *memoir gave you a Giller.*

MACINTYRE: I think so. I give it a lot of credit. Maybe it was as simple as just finding a voice, maybe it was the cathartic experience of really getting into yourself and sort of laying it all out there and going to people who were directly affected by it and saying, 'Look, what do you think?' And they say it's fine.

Linden MacIntyre
Craft

Private Lives and Public Events

As mentioned earlier, some memoirists, such as Linden MacIntyre, choose to tie their private lives to public events, for example, the story of growing up in Port Hastings, Nova Scotia, in the 1950s, coupled with construction of the Canso Causeway, during this same period. This not only gives the memoir a more universal angle, it also provides setting and a historic timeframe, which, in turn, provides specific details and atmosphere.

But that's not all. MacIntyre, a brave and gifted writer, knew from page one of his story that he could not hide from the more personal aspects of the memoir. These included parts of his own father's life story, and the challenges and disappointments therein, and MacIntyre's relationship with his father, which, due to time apart and the attitudes of time, place, and Celtic culture, was not a close one.

For your memoir:

Consider a major event in your own lifetime, and how it changed your life or outlook or both. The event can be on a local scale, or national, or international. Now make notes on the personal events in your life which happened at this time. Can you see an interconnected story here? If it helps you see a structure for a possible memoir, give the public event a title. Is there a *Causeway* in your life, around which you can write a memoir?

The Audrey Edit

Audrey, as you recall, is MacIntyre's ideal reader – and lives in his own editing mind. Audrey is smart and sophisticated and unflappable.

She also likes everything done right, and that includes every aspect of writing intended for publication which MacIntyre may be planning to do. "Right" means serving the story, and serving the writer, as well as can be done. So while Audrey doesn't mind the occasional expletive, she'll shake her head no, if the language doesn't suit the character, or slows down or interrupts the narrative. She'll also fight for more meaningful character development, snappier dialogue, or more evocative details about food, clothes, music, language – and everything else that sets the reader in the decade he's supposed to be visiting.

For your memoir:

Create an Audrey or Luigi or Wang Li or Saoirse or John Angus to edit your work. And here's a tip: you may find that Audrey can hear your work better if you read it aloud. When you trip over a sentence, you can be sure that Audrey will say, "Too long, break it in two." Similarly, if you're throwing swear words in the manuscript simply to show the world that your parents "are not the boss" of you, or the world needs to lighten up and be less formal – Audrey will almost certainly shake her head, and not even comment on the matter. Trust her; she'll do you proud.

Voice

Linden is known as a stylist, with a clean, punchy delivery, which raises the subject of "voice." The common perception is that a written work cannot proceed without establishing a voice (this dictate could stop a lot of people cold). Voice is often used as a synonym for style, as well. I think there is a third dimension to voice – and that is energy. We often enjoy a writer's style because it's energetic. The words are like a strong and shining current, carrying the reader along. (Diane Schoemperlen and I talk at length about voice, later in the book.)

For your memoir:

Take a page of your writing and parse the sentences. Yes, that's right, parsing is a great old-fashioned pastime and a helpful one, too. It means you are going to "analyze a sentence into its parts and describe their syntactic roles" (Dictionary.com). Are the sentences simple (one subject and predicate) or compound (more than one subject and predicate)? *Simple sentences read well.* But too many in a row can make prose sound choppy and uninspired. Are your adjectives and adverbs as precise as they can be? It's always such a pleasure to see unambiguous language. Are you enjoying yourself, with the story moving along smartly – or is the diction flabby and wandering? And so on. You might even play some driving music as you read over your writing – rhythm and blues, rock and roll, dancing fiddles, a blazing twelve-string guitar, a soaring symphony. Can you make your writing do that? Give it a go.

Chapter Two
Who writes memoirs?

Who writes memoirs?

Anyone who wishes to write one. You don't have to be famous or infamous; you don't have to be a former president or child star. You don't even have to put words on paper.

By all means write, if that's your preferred form, but you can also tape a story – yours or someone else's; print out recipes, along with illustrations and text; paint a memory; take new photos, or arrange historic photos – even create a DVD of songs.

As Linden MacIntyre said, he had to deal with feelings of immodesty and discomfort at the idea of writing about his own life, with himself at the centre of the narrative. How he found the way forward was to narrow the focus, and to find facts to guide and contain his story. (Yes! This was a memoirist's impulse, even before MacIntyre became a published memoirist. Remember that he widened the focus first, by choosing to write about the causeway, and then narrowed it to his part in that world: perfect.)

Even still, his psyche had other plans. *Finally*, it said, *focused time to consider the events of our past ... the people of our past, who we loved, even if we didn't totally understand them. Can we find some understanding – can we at least seek it? Can we find compassion and broader understandings of family – can we forgive ourselves for wasting precious time, which might have been spent in their company? Can we think about the shocking banality of tragedy we encountered in our youth, and salute those whose hearts would not heal?*

All of which is exactly what MacIntyre did.

Never underestimate the wisdom of your subconscious. It's as important as your imagination (which you will need, to unearth and augment early memories), and your motivation to write (without that, your pen will never move across the page). But you can't boss that psyche around, either. It will present gifts in its own way and own time. Again, what is the "Causeway" event of your life? This may or may not be the story you have to tell, but finding a large, universal happening in your life and the lives of the people you lived among may help you tell your own, more personal story. And it gives you *setting*, blessed, powerful, lingering setting.

Conversation with
Edmund Metatawabin, author of
Up Ghost River: A Chief's Journey Through the Turbulent Waters of Native History

Edmund Metatawabin, CM, former Chief of Fort Albany First Nation, is a Cree writer, educator and activist. A residential school survivor, he has devoted himself to righting the wrongs of the past, and educating Native youth in traditional knowledge. Metatawabin now lives in his self-made log house in Fort Albany, Ontario, off the reserve boundary, on land he refers to as 'my Grandfathers' Land.' He owns a local sawmill and also works as a consultant, speaker and researcher.

Sometimes called the "Nelson Mandela of the Cree people," Metatawabin received the Order of Canada in 2018.

***

SIMMINS: Could you tell me when you first decided to write the memoir, and why?

METATAWABIN: I think it started a long time ago, about 1970.

SIMMINS: So long ago?

METATAWABIN: Even before that, in high school. I hated high school because we never learned anything about ourselves as First Nations people in elementary school. The nuns used to laugh at us for not knowing that we were red, the 'red race,' and they made fun of that. All through high school it was just cringing and trying to disappear every time the savages attacked the wagon train or burned the settlers' cabins and you know, I was supposed to be that savage. And even my friends, the white friends, they were very, very uncomfortable when we went to history class because they knew that I was going to be made fun of. And they did a lot to try to get me out of it, or at least there, with that kind of treatment in the history books, they said, 'I wish I was in your shoes. I wish people would look at me because here I am the white guy and everybody ignores me and I'm invisible to everybody. But here you are, you're walking with us and you're the one people notice. They look at you, so you have some presence. Even though it may be negative but you still have a presence. They still notice you.' And then afterwards, I went on to university. Now it's getting to be 1970.

SIMMINS: Yes, tell me more.

METATAWABIN: I was struggling with identity, struggling with the memories of what I went through in elementary school and also what went on in high school. It always seemed to be a struggle to try and find out who you are. The good thing was sports. That's what got me through high school. I played a lot of sports.

One time in high school, about grade twelve. We were young boys heading to manhood. There was a white kid who was merciless in reminding me, in full hearing of the other students, either the hallway or classroom, that I was 'just an Indian!' Very embarrassing to say the least and I could never be comfortable being with the others. After lunch I left my boarding home to arrive at the school in time for the bell to call everyone back in the respective homerooms.

In grade twelve, my class was in the gym. The gym was divided by a flexible wall. The boys were on one side and the girls on their own side. It was a big school, Kirkland Lake Collegiate and Vocational Institute, between 1963 and '68. About five classrooms together. The teacher said, 'We're playing murder ball, two sides! Everyone in!' Towards the end of the game, I saw my tormentor carrying the ball, heading my way. He veered towards the flexible wall and I went to meet him. He speeded up. As we got close to each other I feinted to the right and immediately went back left. Seeing me go to his left he went right. I met him as he leaped up to get past me on my left. My elbow dug into his left side underneath his ribs. My momentum slammed us against the flexible wall. The ball dropped and I hit it to the other side of the playing area. Everyone went with the ball and the game went on.

Everyone saw what happened and they knew why. The game went on. Nobody ever mentioned it, but I was satisfied. Another time, another day, some time later. It was late spring. Track and field time with other schools. Competition time! After elimination, the last four runners were me, my friend Bruce, from Kirkland Lake, and two others. Bruce was faster than me, but we always trained together. As we lined up there was a lot of trash talk. But not the usual kind. These ones were meaner – 'That little Indian can't run!' 'Go back to the reserve!' 'First and second place for sure!' and so on. Bruce just gave me a smile.

Bruce was way ahead in the 400-metre race. I was running third. Towards the home stretch, at the last turn, I saw him turn his head right to see if anyone was making a move. As he turned his head, I sprinted on his left side, just barely having room, and passed him. The one behind us was making his move at the same time. But I was ahead of them. Bruce and I took first and second spot. No more catcalls; I was satisfied.

SIMMINS: I can see how these experiences would motivate you to start thinking about writing a memoir. I can also see how sports were your lifeline, as they are for so many young people. Were there also early readings that affected you in your young years?

METATAWABIN: The first book I read in 1970 was called *Man's Search for Meaning*. The author was Viktor Frankl and he wrote about the Holocaust. He was in the concentration camps and he's talking about being incarcerated, being behind the fence and coping with the other inmates and struggling with that kind of thing. As I kept reading the book, I just kept saying, 'That sounds familiar, that sounds familiar,' and that's when I started to think about the residential school in the same kind of way that he was talking about it in *Man's Search for Meaning*. I started to lean towards psychology, sociology and I read books on total institutions, identity, and asylums, books like that. I just kept on working, kept on reading until I saw direction. I knew that one of these days I would have to write a book on my experiences. Viktor Frankl was the one that kicked the idea into motion. It wasn't a long book.

SIMMINS: No, some memoirs are very short and quite wonderful.

METATAWABIN: Yeah, yeah, it had a real impact on me. I'll never forget it.

SIMMINS: It was as though you were looking for a context or structure of sorts. You had had these experiences and then when you saw similar experiences in a very different world, it was as though it all became possible for you to write about. You think, He's done it, I can do it, too. What were your thought processes after that?

METATAWABIN: The immediate one was that, Oh, another tribe suffered, another group of people suffered and now we were not the only one. So you start to read about other people's sufferings and it seems to be a common theme in the world that certain people suffer at a given time and they go through it and they come out stronger. And so I thought, Well, okay. I remembered the prophecy that I was given by the elders in their ceremonies. They saw a person, an entity in a white collar that spoke of hardship to come. They said, 'Your children will undergo a severe trial, a severe test and it'll be very hard.' The elders wanted to know if there was anything they could do to try and stop that from happening for the young people and the entity said, 'No, no, this is the only way to make your people strong. After this experience they will become stronger and shine for the world.' I remember that and as each trial that comes along you always think, Oh, this must be it, or this must be it. After a while you just learn to live life and deal with hardships.

SIMMINS: Edmund, do you see strength being gained now by the upcoming generations?

METATAWABIN: Oh, yeah. I see the young people. They're taller than me; they're giants.

SIMMINS: They're giants! I love it. I actually didn't mean physically strong, but I know what you mean about the size of the younger generations.

METATAWABIN: Yeah, well, tall compared to me. Yeah, they're playing basketball and they're bringing home their trophies and they're hanging them up on the gymnasium walls for everybody to see. And the young ones, they want to be playing basketball too, they want to win. They're passing that on.

SIMMINS: Sports are a great way to do so much, to develop our strength, our patience, and so many good things.

METATAWABIN: It equalizes everybody.

SIMMINS: Yes, exactly, it does. Are you working with young kids with writing at all? With indigenous kids?

METATAWABIN: I'm just passing on the stories. I want them to know that they have a long, long, long history and they come from a long line of people and I think they are characters that they should be proud of. And so hopefully they produce books with these stories. I say to them, 'Remember the story for young people.'

SIMMINS: What about the people in your generation, the people that you would have gone to school with? Are there more people writing about their experiences?

METATAWABIN: Not with us; it's very few. Most of them are saying, 'You know, I'm glad you wrote the book.' They're letting me carry the torch, so to speak.

SIMMINS: I wondered about that. Please correct me if I am wrong, but wasn't part of your motivation to write a memoir to give voice to some of the students at St. Anne's [the residential school in Fort Albany, Ontario, 1902-1976]?

METATAWABIN: Yeah. Many in my age group are still on the streets in Toronto, North Bay, and Timmins. They haven't been able to recover. I was just lucky because I went west and met elders who were really, really solid. Not old men or women but real elders who showed substance, who showed power, and who showed a lot of caring. These were very, very gentle people. I'm glad I saw that and because I saw that and I knew for sure, definitely, that they were elders, and that's an aspiration for everybody.

I wish they could go see these people and sit with them and talk to them and feel their presence and power. It means they can just touch you and say, 'Oh, yes, yes, we know what you have. We call that such and such a disease.' For example, there was a young man who came to see them. Within two minutes they said, 'Oh, yeah, okay, you got what we call sand in the brain.' And they said, 'You have to go to a sweat lodge at least four times and that should fix that.' And even now I know another friend, an elder medicine man who comes from Manitoba. I talked to him about my symptoms. He's grabbing medicines from his trunk and putting them in a bag and then he says, 'Okay, here's your medicine. I gave you several herbs, now here's how you take them.' And the other one is Albert Damon from Arizona, a Navajo, and he's the one who showed me real power among our people. Clearly seeing through me as an individual and saying, 'There are a couple more weaknesses that you have there,' and without him judging me about it.

So I grew up thinking that yeah, yeah, there is a certain way to live and you have to pursue that as much as you can. I went to the cultural side, I went to see what was there and that we were not just savages mindlessly doing things according to the books. Even now, the books I read demean the First Nations all the time, all the time. Even without maybe a plan or a purpose; it's just the amount of knowledge they have. The authors show me their weaknesses, they show me about what they write, what's missing in the books and so I try and recover that missing information and find the real story. If I read about a certain family in 1760 starved in the bush, well, I go back and try and find out what happened there. And usually it's contained in the stories of the people that, yeah, that family starved because of these circumstances, that's what happened to them. So this is sort of filling in the blanks kind of activity. Something we were never given in the school system.

SIMMINS: No, that was not given to you. I wanted to talk with you about the differences in oral histories and written histories and the idea of writing about one's life. That would not be a traditional First Nations way to keep history. Could you tell me about a more traditional way of keeping the life stories from one generation to the next?

METATAWABIN: First of all, the written form is abused a lot. Even the Bible is not real; it's been put together with stories from different tribes all along the Mediterranean coasts, from the rural people. Their stories, the teaching stories. Somebody collected all these and put them into a Bible. So that was put together by men; probably by men, yes, and stolen from these other tribes. Even today's authors, David Suzuki, let's say – he writes books and makes a killing out of writing these books, but he takes ideas from the First Nation people. He's the one getting money for that. And then you will read something about a tribe in Africa who were saying that this certain animal's behaviour was in this way. It was many years later that doctor so-and-so from England observed the same behaviour with that tribe on this animal and therefore that's when it became real. It had to be a white man observing it and then it becomes real [see *Wisdom of the Elders*, by Peter Knudson and David Suzuki, page 94, second paragraph], but just because the First Nation people say it, it's not real yet.

But in our communities the oral stories are judged more harshly than the written form, so if you tell an oral history and you try to change it for your own sake, there are many elders who will jump on you and say, 'That's not right. Correct that version; otherwise, don't say anything anymore.' And the oral history goes a long way back, too. We know who brought us from the upper world into the lower world and we have that name and we call that entity Ehip. That's who brought us from the upper world into the lower world. And if you look, like you're on Earth and you look up, everything is upper world and we are in the lower world. We have stories of the somewhere else and being delivered here by Ehip. We know that we were placed here by somebody, by an entity. And we have our stories that we keep. It's pretty well engrained if you say the Seven Teachings of the Grandfathers. You cannot change that and this started thousands of years ago. That is what the Seven Teachings of the Grandfathers are and no one has been able to change that. It's very, very constant.

Look at the map of America. Can you see the figure of the turtle? Why do we refer to that continent as Turtle Island? This name is thousands of years old. We had the name long before contact. There are legends that contain the name Turtle Island. The history books do not give us too much credit, not too much technical knowledge or skill but, let me ask, who went that high up in the atmosphere, long, long ago, looked down at the world, and noticed the shape of the turtle in what we call North America?

SIMMINS: And would all your kids know the Seven Teachings of the Grandfathers?

METATAWABIN: Yeah, everybody knows these.

SIMMINS: Everybody who listens, right?

METATAWABIN: Yeah, and they will say, 'Not that one,' even the little ones, they know. 'It's not that one, it's this one.' You know they know them. So it's a very harsh way of keeping the knowledge. It's very strict and it has to be accurate. But books are not accurate; they're written without the referee, without somebody there to pay enough attention to say, 'Oh, that portion, I don't think that's right.'

SIMMINS: So was it your parents who gave you the Seven Teachings of the Grandfathers?

METATAWABIN: No. It's a grandfather's role and grandmother's.

SIMMINS: Oh, I see.

METATAWABIN: Yeah, your parents – they're giving food and sustenance and shelter. Spiritual teachings come from the grandparents.

SIMMINS: How much time in the life of the community is given to oral stories? It's a rich, rich part of the culture, is it not?

METATAWABIN: We have a radio station, a regional radio station. We have a morning show, a ten o'clock show, a lunchtime show, and then we have a five o'clock show, so we have four hours every day where the elders are encouraged to come and talk on the radio and talk about their history and their legends and any information that could be useful for the young generation.

SIMMINS: That's wonderful. Is it popular?

METATAWABIN: Yeah, we listen to it a lot, but it's not popular with the young people anymore because their language has gone. English is very easy to learn and the young people have gravitated towards the English rather than the Cree. And it's going to hurt the content but for those of us who can speak the language, and English, we try and translate everything for them so hopefully they retain these stories.

SIMMINS: I wonder how to get to the younger generation if they're being so influenced by all forms of media, which comes in English, not to mention schooling, and so on. Is there more teaching of traditional languages now?

METATAWABIN: Well, we're using families now. Not so much the language; we use the language, those of us that can teach, and the families are coming back so we have the Sundance, the sweat lodge and the night lodge and shaking tent, so those have come back. And so the young people are there; they're sitting in the family so that means a lot.

SIMMINS: Yes, it would.

METATAWABIN: So they're back.

SIMMINS: Good, good. Could you tell me about the expression – and I couldn't possibly pronounce it – but it means you have been listened to?

METATAWABIN: *Nahihtamowin*?

SIMMINS: It was in your book, yes.

METATAWABIN: *Nahihtamowin*. For clarification, *nahi-tamowin* is the root word or noun. If we use the word as a verb, it changes to *ki-nahi-tatin*, meaning 'My behaviour will attest to my respect for your words.'

SIMMINS: Did you feel that you were listened to when you wrote the book?

METATAWABIN: Yeah, yeah, definitely yeah. Especially the young people maybe eighteen, nineteen, twenty, those are the ones who find it really, really helpful. They're the ones that say, 'Now it makes sense, now it makes sense,' meaning all that crazy parental, adult behaviour when they were very small … behaviour acquired because the adults were survivors of the residential school system. All the turmoil that was happening in their houses when they were four, five, six years old – the partying, the drinking, and even just the confusion among the older people. Now the young ones say, 'Yeah, yeah, that's makes sense.' They say thank you for that.

SIMMINS: That's such a gift.

METATAWABIN: I hope they will know that the confusion they experienced while they were young is not the life that they want to give to their own children. I hope it stabilized them. That kind of knowledge is very helpful. So I'm glad they say it helps.

SIMMINS: That would make you walk tall. I've been talking with other memoirists and there's been quite a bit of talk about catharsis –

how people felt before they started the book, while they were writing it, and when they finished. How did you feel when you finished *Up Ghost River*? When you realized it was really happening, it was getting published, it was going to be seriously considered by many readers?

METATAWABIN: Well, you feel like you rest at the plateau that you were trying to get up on. I thought publishing a book was going to be like a measure for me to reach, a goal, and once I got there, everything would be fine. So you struggle with that. This was my third book and the struggle was behind the other two and then finally this one, dealing with a major publisher. That was a goal, that was an achievement.

SIMMINS: Indeed it was.

METATAWABIN: And so I felt good about that and now I have publishers giving me their business cards. A door has been opened and that's good. So now I can just relax a bit and say, 'Okay, what's my next book?'

SIMMINS: Just now, you gave me a professional response, as in, here you were as a writer, and you were having these reactions from people and it was good. I also meant how did you feel inside, having told the most difficult stories of your life?

METATAWABIN: Well, of course, you're scared. Everybody is thinking of self-preservation and you're standing in the world and other people feel particular emotions about you. So you don't want to expose yourself to that, or to show any kind of weakness, but if you're going to be an author, you have to be an author. And so I said, 'Okay, I'll do that,' and it was hard. It was a lot of pacing around my house. My wife said, 'Okay, I'll go to work, you write the book; I'll go to work and leave you alone during the day.' So I started to work during the day and I wore my heart out and I played Pink Floyd to get back on track.

SIMMINS: Did you feel slightly less burdened by the memories, once they had been pulled out and put in to the book? Was there any lightening to your spirit?

METATAWABIN: Well, you know, I get bigger hugs, longer hugs, I guess, so that helps for me personally. And just people saying, 'You know, we like your book. We read your book.' And they're passing your book around; that's very rewarding. But it's finished and, it's not really finished, the story continues. It hasn't changed, so that part, it's still going on. It's not as if you complete something. You've just torn a page out of your history and you've showed that to the world, but there's still a big book that still has to be told. So that's not done yet, not finished.

SIMMINS: Tell me what you're working on now with your writing.

METATAWABIN: We have been fighting the government for documents showing the abuse of the kids, the children of St. Anne's, and the police investigation. It happened in 1994 for four years, a four-year police investigation. The government had those papers in 2003 and had been saying – while people are trying to resolve their issues – that no, no, no, there was nothing going on, there was no sexual abuse, there was no physical abuse. They have the documents in their hands and they're trying very hard to hide these documents. We've gone through to the court three times now to get these documents to the public. Finally, they are public and so we continue.

Now we have encountered another problem. We find that it's the legal profession that has been siding with the churches and the government to hide this part of history. We have legal firms playing both sides, representing the church and also helping the survivors in their search for justice. But telling the survivor, 'Oh, that's not true, that's not true, so-and-so was not present at that school at the time that you mentioned,' but they knew what the contents of the investigation were. I suppose you could say their intention, their plan was to minimize everything, even denying things that happened in that school. The independent assessment process which is going on now is for survivors to get some compensation for pain and suffering without going to court.

And the lawyers are doing their best to minimize that and say, 'No, no, you didn't suffer, there was no priest by that name.' So it's just playing both sides, which I think if you remember Paul Bernardo and Karla Homolka – the lawyer who had tried to hide evidence was disbarred. The same thing is happening right now. So it's very bad, very bad and I ask myself, 'Is that the law?' I thought the law was all about justice and equality, but I find that it's not really about justice.

SIMMINS: My heart's getting heavy listening to you. I think, Why can't there be change, why can't there be justice?

METATAWABIN: As long as you can, put yourself in the mindset of that's not my life. This is just something that I am encountering, but I'm able to say, 'Well, that's a separate room that I can leave at the end of the day.' And you know, my space is good, my space is clean here, my home and community and the region, the people that I'm hearing, they know they are suffering but they still know how to have a good time. They still can separate themselves from what they know is the injustice and the unfair conditions that they're placed in. They're still trying their best. They still see that's something that they will have to overcome. It's work in progress.

SIMMINS: Yes, it is. Indigenous writings are richer and stronger all the time. And there are more new and gifted young writers each year, added to first ranks such as Lee Maracle, Eden Robinson, Tomson Highway, Richard Wagamese, Thomas King – so many. I wonder if there might not be people your age or the kids looking at your book, the way you looked to books before you started your memoir and saying, 'Ah, you can do it this way.' Tell me about your teaching.

METATAWABIN: I teach class in one of the communities here. I teach first-year and I have tapes from 1968 from the elders and they talk about a particular incident that happened in the community where I'm teaching. So I have two tapes. I brought them into class. I think about the third meeting in, we were talking about colonization and the effects. I played those tapes and I said, 'Bring your tape recorders,' before I played these so they were prepared for that. They captured the words of their elders who talk about this incident and they turned it into a research assignment. They also wanted to do it as a group assignment. Now they have big ideas about what it could be eventually, a book or a movie or things like that. I think you're right, there will be more writers.

SIMMINS: I am a writer, you are a writer, so we're talking about words on paper, but there's many, many, many ways to record stories, but the important part, especially with the elders who are truly old, is to get the stories. It doesn't matter how that's done. What matters is to stir up the enthusiasm for keeping these precious stories safe. You don't want them to disappear.

METATAWABIN: No, I don't think they will disappear.

SIMMINS: Good, that's what I like to hear. Edmund, I've got your book right here, and I'm looking at it as I sit at my desk. I've been looking at the cover photograph. There's the young boy in the centre of the row there looking right at the camera. Tell me about this photograph.

METATAWABIN: The hardcover edition, with the photograph of the girls?

SIMMINS: Oh, I misunderstood. It's a small girl.

METATAWABIN: If I had braids, if I had long hair in braids and somebody cut my braids off from behind and very short, that's what you see. Somebody's braids have been cut. So you are looking at the girls in the classroom, reading. That's on the hardcover book. The stoic nun is standing at the back, but we can't see her face. On the soft cover edition, the little boy of four is yours truly. I am looking at the camera and obviously scared of the photographer.

SIMMINS: I see.

METATAWABIN: On the hardcover edition that's a sign of anger on their faces and the sign of, 'You're not going to put me down' kind of thing. It was taken about 1940 by a priest who turned out to be a serious pedophile. He had the camera and took many, many pictures. He abused the people of his age when he was a young man. These people are now grandmothers and he continued abusing the young children as he was getting older. So he was a priest. Priests are untouchable. When we say, "Father so-and-so, you know, he did something,' the elders would immediately say, 'Shush, don't say a thing, that's a priest.' So he won't be charged.

At the time of their power, 1940, and before and after that, the powers of the Catholic Church were very, very large in Fort Albany. They influenced the Hudson Bay Company for business dealings. They have trappers, so you don't want to do anything to influence the way a trapper was treated. Criticism heard from your family could mean the difference between life and death. As a member of the community, you were very careful what you said. The Minister of Lands and Forests was in charge of granting permits so again, that's a lot of power. If you don't have a tag on the fur you could not do any trading, you're outside the law. And another one was the Indian Agent, as they were known by Aboriginal Affairs then. He was the one who granted yes or no kind of treatment on everybody. He'd say, 'This is a good prospect or this is a bad investment,' about each individual. He could break many people and he did break a family of ten because he denied them any kind of assistance when they wanted to go out on the land.

That's when the economy was on the side of the colonizers. But this family starved one by one, beginning with the mother, the oldest son, and then the next son, and then until only two of the youngest ones were left, plus the father. And they were found by that man's brother very close to death, and they were able to save them. So that's the kind of power that the Indian Agents held. If I mentioned the sweat lodge, my mother would say, 'Don't say that word, don't say that, or the priest will hear you.'

Now if the priest hears you, then they know your parents or your grandfather has been talking about traditional teachings to you. Cultural teachings were against the Church and therefore against Canadian law. They would come and visit you and if they found that you'd been saying that, then you could no longer deal with the Hudson Bay Company business-wise and even maybe, you would not be allowed to do any trapping. That's the kind of fear that the parents had. That's why they chose not to pass on traditional teachings to their young.

SIMMINS: I feel overwhelmed hearing these stories. I know it's not yesterday, it is today. I think about the pernicious, long-lasting effects of colonization that so many people are dealing with. Again, that makes my heart heavy. Can we talk about something that brings you great joy right now?

METATAWABIN: My grandchildren; just like you, just like everybody. That's where the future is. You make sure they have a good beginning, that they have a good foundation, and that they have happiness. That's all you can do. We tried to encourage our children to go to school and at the same time, we were not really overly concerned about their attendance at school. We took them on the land, we taught them education and not lessons in the classroom. Classroom learning was secondary. We did try and think about that, but we thought traditional educating was the main thing.

SIMMINS: I wish you every good outcome in your current battles, and I am so glad you have a wonderful, supportive family.

METATAWABIN: I want to encourage anyone reading these words, the history we've been talking about is about colonization, but we have the power to change things, beginning now. There's nothing we can do about the past. The past is done, but we can make changes for the future. If we start now, based on new information that we have and to the Canadians we keep telling them, 'Settle down, settle down, don't keep looking for something too high or too far away, just settle down.' For example, if we can eat twice a day, that should be enough. Right now we are eating too much, we're consuming too much and we may even be eating nine times a day, every chance we get we swallow something and that's too much. So eating twice a day should be sufficient. Have a good breakfast in the morning and then have a substantial supper, then that should be enough.

That way we can save what we have for our great-grandchildren. Using less will save more for them. They're the ones we're living for. We are preparing the world for them. It's not about us anymore, you know. We're okay. We're alive and well. It's assurance that we are looking for. It's for our children to have the same as when they're raising their kids. That's the only advice I can give the Canadian public. You know, just settle down; relax and have some fun!

Edmund Metatawabin
Craft

Overcoming fear. "Shining for the world."

There is no getting around it, writing a memoir takes courage. One way to deal with this negative emotion is to turn it into a positive. Edmund Metatawabin's memoir is honest and heartbreaking – and he wrote it as much for all the children with whom he was incarcerated at residential school, to give them the dignity and healing of voice, as he did for himself. He also desired to speak out against the dominant settler society, which either overlooked First Nations in their own lands entirely or presented false images of every kind, from intellect to customs to culture.

Whenever I had trouble reading about the abuse of the children – often, my breath would catch, and I wept; other times I felt sick at my stomach and in my spirit, for days after reading – I reminded myself how much harder it was for the children to have endured the abuse, for the other children to have witnessed it, or to have been forced to take part, and I would read on, to honour the writer, his family, and his childhood friends. If they could live it, I could read it.

Edmund Metatawabin was motivated to overcome his fear of personal exposure in a memoir, and to record the story of his harrowing childhood, by his need to honour his indigenous brothers and sisters, and find some peace for his own troubled soul. By creating the memoir, he would, in his own way, "shine for the world," as prophesied by elders.

Motivation is the fire in your belly when you write your memoir. Few fires burn more brightly than those of love and honouring.

Metatawabin is also pragmatic about the exposure that writing of any sort, especially memoir, will bring to the life of the writer. It's part of the deal. This is a true writer speaking.

For your memoir:

Besides yourself, think about for whom you are writing a life story. Is there someone in particular you'd like to honour in your stories? Is there some impossible-to-repay figure in your life you wish to write about – to immortalize, in the way only a memoir can? Make a list of names of people who are important to you. Does one name jump out just a bit faster than the others?

This is not only a question of showing love and respect to someone special in your life, who themselves may be alive or dead. It is also your artist's soul resonating with certain ideas, images, and memories connected to this person, about which you may feel compelled to write. Honour the stories your heart already knows; hunt out the deeper ones, their voices, like music in the distance, seeking ingress to your story.

Speaking out against the dominant culture: Writing your own history

There are dominant cultures around the world. In Canada, it is the European Christian settler culture which has dominated for the past five hundred years. Yet the Aboriginal peoples have been in Canada for millennia. When Metatawabin went to elementary and high school, he was taught a version of history that made no sense to him, as it pertained to his own people. Not only that, but the version was condescending, insulting, and provably false. Indigenous history was presented as though it had no value at all. Metatawabin has spent a lifetime resisting the dominant culture's derision, secrecy, and abuse. Part of this resistance was writing his memoir, *Up Ghost River*. Metatawabin has also fought hard to bring the historical records of one of the most notorious residential schools in the country, St. Anne's, in Fort Albany, Ontario, to light. The fight for transparency, justice, and restitution continues in the highest courts of the land.

For your memoir:

You may be coming out of another culture and language, to write a memoir in English. If so, you will need familial and professional support on your creative journey. I need to underscore the idea that having writing professionals help you craft the book is not giving power to someone else; it is giving more power to yourself, to make sure the story you intend to convey is in fact the one you do convey.

Simply stated, rally your troops.

Obviously you must trust the individuals you work with. People's reputations tend to follow them, so you shouldn't have trouble finding the right editors, writers, and even proof-readers, to help you create and polish your story. This is easier if you are dealing with an established, traditional publisher, as Metatawabin did, but not too difficult, either, if you choose to self publish. Consult with your provincial or territorial writers' federation or guild for recommendations. Failing that, you can consult with The Writers' Union of Canada, which can also suggest professionals you can contact.

As for your family – their emotional and actual support is crucial, especially if you are a survivor of wrenching and scarring life circumstances. This goes all the way along the line, from first discussions of your memoir, to work on it, to finishing it. If, however, your family was the source of your pain and hardship, you will have to find a secondary support system, by way of friends, colleagues, teachers, or whomever.

For anyone, writing a memoir is a complicated, protracted, and sometimes exhausting process. This can be doubly true for someone working in a second language, against the grain of accepted historical timelines and "facts." Sure, there's joy and satisfaction at the far end of writing a memoir, but it takes time and gumption to get there.

All writers do best with loving, non-judgemental support along the way. Think of Edmund's wife, Joan Metatawabin, who said, "I'll go to work and leave you alone during the day," and did just that, to support his writing journey. Other ways to support a writing spouse or partner might include providing child care, making meals, doing housework, or even walking the dog. All of this frees up the writer to have time, blessed time, to work. If you believe in what you are doing, chances are, people who care about you will, too. Allow them the privilege of supporting someone they love, to help them create art, and present truths they themselves would give much to see.

The story continues ...

Like MacIntyre, Metatawabin did not view the end of his memoir as the end of the story. How could either of them see it that way, or any of us, either? A memoir is a chapter of life, not the full life. Long after we write "the end" on the last page of our memoir, our lives, with luck and good fortune, continue on. Some writers are even known as "serial memoirists." And there are many: Maya Angelou, Diana Athill, Maxine Hong Kingston, Frank McCourt, Jamaica Kincaid, Linda Greenlaw, Annie Dillard, Ian Brown, Patrick Lane, to name but some.

For your memoir:

Identify three major themes in your life. Examples could include good versus evil, coming of age, power and corruption, parental love and loss. For me, the three themes might be the complexities of the word "home"; a deep love of animals, horses and dogs particularly; and early loss, by both death and divorce (which, yes, sometimes seem one and the same). Can you see yourself writing complete memoirs about all three subjects? Does one theme in particular push to the head of the line? (If so, that's the one to grab!) Could all three be contained in one memoir? (Probably not.)

Canadian indigenous writers, in all genres

Around the world, it's an exciting and robust time for indigenous literature of all genres. In Canada, First Nations and Inuit men and women are creating memoirs, fiction, poetry, screenplays and drama, performance art, and children's stories. As well, their work is being gathered together in anthologies. If you are an indigenous person, hoping to start or expand your writing, or a mainstream writer or reader looking for new voices, wisdoms, and beauty, there is a wealth of titles for you to read, in every genre. Among the writers are Christy Jordan-Fenton and Margaret Pokiak-Fenton; Alootook Ipellie; Zondra M. Roy; Terese Marie Mailhot; Cliff Cardinal; Marilyn Dumont; Sherman Alexie; Louise Bernice Halfe; Joanne Arnott; Billy-Ray Belcourt; Janet Rogers; Leanne Betasamosake Simpson; Waubgeshig Rice; Andréa Ledding; Michelle Sylliboy; Joshua

Whitehead; Wanda John-Kehewin; Cherie Dimaline; Alicia Elliott; Tanya Talaga; Darrel J. McLeod; Thomas King; Eden Robinson; Jesse Thistle; Jordan Abel; and many, many more.

For your memoir:

Read outside of your direct life experience and personal knowledge of other cultures and their histories. Your readings will enrich your own life stories. Remind yourself of human commonalities: our need for love, respect, support, and kindness; our deep cherishing of family, friends, the natural world and its animals, along with meaningful work, connections to community, and spirituality. Note the differences we can have, too. How do you feel when you begin to grasp new, layered, even ancient belief systems, and new ways to move through the modern world, on into the future? Is it exciting? Or do those new-to-you beliefs and traditions make you feel uncomfortable, more entrenched in the validity of your own ways? Why? Can you explore all these feelings in your own writings?

Remember, a memoir is like extending a hand to a stranger. You, the writer, are not sure how that stranger might react, but if your own hand is extended in an inclusive, unthreatening way, you can certainly hope for a similar response. Your ways may not be another person's ways, and vice versa. But in the same way most of us enjoy travel, and learning about new foods, customs, art, architecture, language, religion, and so on, we all benefit from learning about other people's experiences and cultures by "visiting" their life stories and, for a while, being a part of that landscape.

And always, in the process of reading and in life, we grow as spiritual beings when we understand anew human needs and desires common to all nations and all peoples. When your reader laughs, cries, draws a sharp breath in shock or dismay, feels a red surge of fury, on your behalf – then she is a member of your world nation. Best of all, with true life stories, feelings of kinship don't dissipate when the last page is turned. The reader, after all, can never again say, "I didn't know …"

Chapter Three
When do we write a memoir?

Traditionally, memoir is a middle-aged person's pursuit; having a bit of life to actually write about comes in handy. That said, when Malala Yousafzai wrote her inspiring memoir, *I am Malala: The Girl Who Stood Up for Education and was Shot by the Taliban*, she was seventeen – and subsequently became the youngest recipient ever of a Nobel Peace Prize. (Yousafzai's memoir was written "with Christina Lamb," so she was aided by a professional writer.) Other young people, such as Canada's singer/songwriter extraordinaire, Justin Bieber, now twenty-six, have written memoirs as well. In the then sixteen-year-old Bieber's case, as in many others, young or old, the book was ghost-written.

Ghostwriting is a fine and traditional way to produce a memoir. Ask former New Democratic Party (NDP) Member of Parliament and Toronto city councillor Olivia Chow, now a Distinguished Visiting Professor at Ryerson University, who wrote about her early life, and about the period after the unexpected death of her charismatic husband, Jack Layton, leader of the federal NDP. Or ask beloved Canadian superstar singer and recording artist Anne Murray. Both well-known and capable women went with non-fiction writer and ghostwriter Lawrence Scanlan. How he captured their voices so perfectly, I will never fully understand. I suppose hours and hours of tapes and talks can do that, along with an unflagging desire to "get it right."

And before you ask, no, it's never too late to pen a memoir. Centenarian Bertha Wood, from the United Kingdom, was born in 1905 and had her first book, *Fresh Air and Fun: The Story of a Blackpool Holiday Camp*, published on her one hundredth birthday, on June 20, 2005. The book is based on her memoirs, which she began writing at the age of ninety.

It is also traditional to "write one's memoirs" when one retires, or at least steps back from full-time public life. This has meant a goodly number of people writing the stories of their lives (more commonly in the form of an autobiography than a memoir) in their sixties, seventies, and even eighties.

The short answer to "when" is probably … whenever the time is right for the individual.

Which sounds vague, but isn't meant to be so. Believe me, you'll know.

In my case, I was fifty-five when my first memoir was published – and I couldn't get the words down fast enough. Some days I thought I'd get wrist-lash at my keyboard. There were many factors at play in my need for speed, but certainly wanting a book published after twenty-five years of freelance journalism was one, as was a desire to "have a voice," in a place where I was neither born nor raised. Once, after a long discussion on motivation, I had a student in one of my workshops turn to me and innocently ask, "Why did *you* write a memoir?" Before I knew the words were out of my mouth, I said, "Because I was afraid I'd disappear." We all blinked at that one. But it was true. I needed to write about my life in a new and slightly foreign place, in the new and slightly foreign condition of marriage-in-the-late-thirties. I also longed to review earlier times and events, right back to my childhood.

So it was my time to write a memoir. I loved every desk-flying moment.

Others may only feel free when their parents are dead. They may find freedom in that reality, and they may not. Voices from beyond the grave can be strident, as can related, living voices, such as siblings, or aunts and uncles. Some writers, such as Pat Conroy, even write about the death of a parent – after writing fully about their lives in other books. Hence Conroy wrote *The Great Santini* in 1976 (a novel, but closely based on life events and real "characters") and a memoir, *The Death of Santini*, in 2014. In the first book, the father character, based on Conroy's own father, is a brute and a sadist. In the second, non-fiction book, Conroy, with work, finds aspects to admire about his father, while remaining clear-eyed about his unapologetically violent nature.

Interestingly, Conroy, who claims to have written more about his own family than any other American author/novelist, is candid, even relaxed, about the differing memories he and his six siblings have about, for one example, their mother. While the tendency in such cases is to believe the older or oldest sibling in a clan (Pat), who has collected up memories longer, Conroy's obvious devotion to his mother, along with his abiding, mostly uncritical love for her, makes me guess that the other siblings likely have, at times, the truer recollections. Of course, all the memories are "true," as we can only go with our hearts' and minds' deepest searings, and our most cherished interior tapes and movies.

"When" is a yearning and an imperative, which may even ebb and flow, depending on the complexities of your life circumstances. It may take you several years or longer to work up to the work of memoir. And by "work," I mean words on paper/words on the screen. So many people love to talk about their lives – all of us, usually – yet not everyone has the courage, resolve, work ethic, and humming creative and emotional need to create permanent stories about their lives. They think, perhaps, if they just fend off the concrete form one more month/year/decade, their clearest understanding of it will come to them. And that brilliant understanding, of course, will be accompanied by the finest, most beautiful words – right?

Maybe. In the same way we can only live one day at a time, we can't know what tomorrow might bring, in terms of greater understandings, or deeper insights in to past behaviours and events – or the quality of our writings. Today, as my father used to say, I see myself as a "fine and flawed human being," who may yet turn out to be one of those "serial memoirists."

And how many books does it take to become one of those?

Not sure. Am thinking (she is smiling) maybe with memoir number ... three.

Be bold. Own your when. Tomorrow's epiphanies can go in your next memoir.

As for the when of finishing ... you might blister through your story in a year, or you might take ten long years to pen the precise story you want to share with others, or perhaps only with family.

You are, right now, the ... perfect age to write a memoir. The effort will take the time it takes. If you stall, get professional writing help. The right professional will be as pleased to see you succeed as you are.

The when of memoir is always now.

Conversation with Donna Morrissey, author of
Different Dirt: A Memoir

Donna Morrissey comes from The Beaches, an outport on Newfoundland's northwest coast. She is published by Penguin Canada and has written six nationally bestselling novels, has been published in *The Walrus*, *Canadian Geographic*, and *The Globe and Mail*. She has received awards in Canada, the U.S., and England and her novel *Sylvanus Now* was shortlisted for the Commonwealth Prize.

Donna's fiction has been translated into seven languages. She was nominated for a Gemini for her screenplay, *The Clothesline Patch* (which won a Gemini for best production). Her latest novel, *The Fortunate Brother*, spent six weeks on the bestseller list, and won the Arthur Ellis Award for best crime novel of 2017. Morrissey's new novel, *The Unclaimed*, is scheduled for release by Penguin Canada in 2020. Her memoir, *Different Dirt*, comes out in 2021.

In her spare time, Donna mentors an online writing program with Humber College, Toronto, and teaches occasionally at Dalhousie University in Halifax, Nova Scotia.

﹃

SIMMINS: When your publisher asked you to write a memoir, what were your first thoughts?

MORRISSEY: I knew I wanted to write the story of my mother and my mental illness, the grief of my brother, and how that all happened. I've completed six novels now, and I've never been able to completely tell my mother's story. I had just finished my seventh novel, *The Unclaimed*, and was getting ready for editing. Penguin, my publisher, offered me a two-book deal for *The Unclaimed*, plus the memoir. I hadn't yet started the memoir. But they wanted it first. Memoirs are hot right now. Their question to me was, how somebody goes from isolation, as I did in my early life, to becoming an internationally-selling author. They thought it was a good story to hear. So it's a timing thing or fate, I don't know.

SIMMINS: So had you thought to do one before this suggestion? Had it ever crossed your mind, as in, 'One of these days I'd like to do that'?

MORRISSEY: Yes. I intended to start after this novel I'm currently working on was published. So my agent put forward a two-book deal. Penguin said yes, but, and again, they wanted the memoir first.

SIMMINS: Interesting they wanted the memoir first. I like the phrase, 'You want the completed story of your mother,' because there's been a little bit of this and a little bit of that and so on, but you wanted the full circle.

MORRISSEY: Yeah, she's been a character in all of my books and her story, even fictionalized, doesn't really tell it. It's an entwined story, my mother, our grief of losing my brother, my subsequent descent into Post Traumatic Stress Disorder, her cancer. Writing this memoir was like taking a big ball of wool and pulling apart the strands that detail our combined stories, and leaving aside those things that didn't fit into our story.

SIMMINS: I'm excited for you. How far along are you?

MORRISSEY: I'm done.

SIMMINS: Congratulations! You weren't working on the novel and the memoir at the same time, were you?

MORRISSEY: No, I can't divide my attentions like that. It's *so* engrossing, writing a novel or a memoir. It takes all of me to sink into the emotions of either my characters or me, and bring them to the page. It's mentally exhausting, and exhilarating.

SIMMINS: You didn't do personal essays over the years or anything like that?

MORRISSEY: No. I did one magazine piece on my PTSD years ago, a medical magazine.

SIMMINS: Interesting. So it sounds very much like you knew what you wanted to do. Did you know where to start?

MORRISSEY: I knew I had to start from the beginning. That means, establishing my family, my roots. So important, how we are formed in our earlier years. All stages of our journey through life, all the different strands weaving into who we are, start with where we're from.

My earliest memories are of love and the passing of my baby brother. That has hugely influenced me. But other things weigh just as important – the love of family, my fascination with 'away.' I had a huge imagination and wanted to travel 'away' someday. Our wounds follow us. That is the pathway that took me through this memoir – my earliest wounding, and my curiosity for 'away.'

SIMMINS: It's a powerful idea to be starting with those huge themes. Very powerful. So you knew where you were starting and you had a pretty good idea of where you're going to be finishing. It sounds as though you didn't struggle for the circle of the narrative.

MORRISSEY: Yeah. Unfortunately I don't get to write the endings I'd like to write, as I do with fiction, so it's following the path of how it all came to be that my brother got killed on my watch, how I became ill as a result of that. And I went to university as a result of the illness. It's all entwined. [In the early 1980s, Donna Morrissey and her younger brother Ford left Newfoundland for the oil fields of Alberta. They hoped to earn their fortunes and send money to help out while their father was ill. Ford was killed in a workplace accident.]

SIMMINS: Yes. It's wonderful that you can see that now, that you didn't have to go searching through the weeds to find stories. It sounds like there's a very clear narrative here.

MORRISSEY: I've been telling this story for a long, long time, you know, but just bits and pieces of it along the way. Looking back on our lives, we see those big moments where great joy or tragedy struck. And they light up, are brighter than the others. I see them as little fires leading the way back through our beginnings. Those conscious moments that always live big within us. Mapping who we've become.

SIMMINS: That's a beautiful image of small fires, because fire is a cleanser, fire is a threat, fire brings light, fire brings warmth, fire brings danger. In your writing experience to date, what are the major differences between fiction and non-fiction?

MORRISSEY: The difference is I'm not the creator with memoir as I am with fiction. With memoir, I'm relating what life gave to me. Times when I have written real life moments in fiction, I've created endings that are perfect. With memoir, I don't have perfect endings, I have the rawness of what really happened. Not all actions are glamorous, or have symbolic or metaphorical meaning. Sometimes it's just a blah ending that just runs into something else. So you gotta figure out how to write those moments and layer them with meaning. Because even the most ordinary of moments carry huge meanings.

SIMMINS: I love the way you said that because you're 'presenting, not creating,' and so you might be dealing with the banal instead of the symphonic. You know, something comes to a whimper instead of a large ending but you still have to find the beauty in it.

MORRISSEY: Yes, that's right, you have to muscle those inane moments and a good narrative can do that. You can bring in a theme, then bring in the theme of family or love or whatever your work is about. You need the banal to catch up to the drama.

SIMMINS: You're enjoying yourself.

MORRISSEY: I'm a little scared. It feels indulgent, you know, writing totally about yourself. So to me it's always a matter of deflecting the attention onto others in my story – onto my family. Even my own PTSD, I sometimes deflect it onto the illness as though it is a character. It's about thinking 'one's self' is not exciting enough to be the subject of a story. And given how I'm speaking of 'my' personal journey through mental illness, and the suffering it evoked. Eh, you might say I'm feeling vulnerable about this memoir, about putting it out there for everyone to read. Memoir is *so* personal. There's no buffer of a character carrying it for you. I have become the character.

SIMMINS: You're absolutely right and there will be times before the book comes out that you'll be pulling your hair out and then those around you who love you will say, 'It's good; if you've done what you needed to do, it's a fine book.' There's a vulnerability to memoir, a nakedness.

MORRISSEY: Yes, there is vulnerability. Funny, there is so much of my real life put into those novels, moments that are close to the bone, that carry the rawness of truth, that it's challenging to rewrite them. Sometimes I just want to copy them and paste them into my memoir.

SIMMINS: Could you not do that?

MORRISSEY: I tried, but the mood and tone were off, the rhythm. Each piece of writing has a different voice, pacing. I was constantly surprised by how much of my real life I injected into the fiction.

SIMMINS: Well, how many authors can say that, that their fiction and memoir are so closely related there are sections that are almost interchangeable? I'll be interested in reading your memoir, and seeing how it differs from your fiction. As a memoir teacher I say, 'Yeah, I want those books in my library because there's *nothing else like it.*' This will be fabulous, reading the memoir, then reconsidering the works of fiction that spun off from the memoir.

MORRISSEY: I hope you continue thinking that. It might've been easier for me had I started with the memoir first, then followed the fictive path. Feels like I'm swimming against the river, finding my truths in fiction.

SIMMINS: What is the major difference for you in memoir versus fiction?

MORRISSEY: I think I might've mentioned earlier, with memoir, I'm not a creator, I'm presenting my truths.

SIMMINS: Great phrase, 'I'm not a creator, I'm presenting it.' So do you find the creative process feels different?

MORRISSEY: Yes, it feels totally different in that number one, I don't have to research, I know everything. Number two, I don't have to rework dialogue so much. I'm a big dialogue person in fiction. Dialogue's not as intricate because I know what was said, or the essence of what was said. I don't have to create every scene at every turn. Fiction is much more demanding.

SIMMINS: I'm enjoying the elements of this discussion – though I wouldn't necessarily agree that fiction is more demanding than non-fiction; just very different. So, obviously, you're enjoying yourself. Getting more personal, do you worry about the responses of your siblings or people from your home village?

MORRISSEY: No, because I'm treating everybody as the princess; I don't have any axes to grind.

SIMMINS: Axes to grind?

MORRISSEY: No, I don't have any axes to grind. When I do touch on sensitive relationships, I hope it's with grace. With regards to my siblings, you know, I have love, pure love for them; they were as devastated as me by the tragedies that took place in our family. I can only cradle them as I go through, just hope that I portray them in a way that they deserve to be.

So it's done with respect and love and no axes to grind, none. You can't, not when you've done the work because in the end, it's all about you. It doesn't matter what anybody did, it's all about you. It's how you interpret a situation, how you react, and what you do with it. Nobody is to blame for anything. Even the accident that took my brother, you can't blame the work crew because they were negligent. It wasn't just 'one thing' that killed him. It wasn't just that the brakes weren't on, on that truck, it wasn't the fault of the nineteen-year-old kid who sat behind the wheel. It's all the things that brought us all together in that moment. So many things coming together that you can't separate it; it's too arbitrary. These things, the moments in our lives, were all heading to this one moment from the day we were born.

See, that's what happens when you go into the real. When you're doing fiction, your characters carry it, but when you sit alone with it and you go into in the personal, that's when – it's not even pain; it's just the emotion of it.

SIMMINS: I never thought of characters carrying anything; that's an astonishing thought for me. It makes perfect sense when you say it. You're used to good and supportive company; now you're alone on the stage. You know what I mean, that you've got all the characters around you carrying the load, carrying the emotions to a greater degree.

MORRISSEY: To refine that idea more, in fiction, characters carry those bits of you that are so real. It's like lending bits of yourself to the character. Now, with writing a memoir, I'm more up close. I'm wearing them myself. It's like taking back the pieces of me I put into fiction, and putting it into my real story.

SIMMINS: Amazing. Bless your publisher for pushing for the memoir. Though you said you wanted to do it anyway. Are you a reader of memoir?

MORRISSEY: No, but I am now. Well, I can't say that I haven't read any memoirs. *Angela's Ashes* by Frank McCourt was a huge book that I read and *The Glass Castle* by Jeanette Walls and *Educated* by Tara Westover, so I've read all of those, certainly. You know, the bestsellers, but I have more of an interest now because a lot of my friends are reading memoir. I have this interest in it because my attention has been turned there. Doing a class on memoir with you has introduced me to more memoirists. I've heard a lot about Richard Wagamese's work, but I've never really heard anything from him until you read his essays from *One Native Life* in class. As I'm listening I'm thinking, I want that book, I want more. So yeah, I think I'm a little more intrigued by memoir.

SIMMINS: It is huge. Such a fascinating genre.

MORRISSEY: Yeah, I'm a lot more intrigued by memoir.

SIMMINS: Glad to hear it! How old were you when you wrote your first novel?

MORRISSEY: I was forty.

SIMMINS: Forty. So was fiction always your first choice or you did you stray off into poetry or anything else?

MORRISSEY: No, nothing like that, no.

SIMMINS: When did you know you were going to be a novelist?

MORRISSEY: I have no idea. I had written a couple short stories and one that I couldn't finish because I know now that they were meant to be novels, right? Because the back story just kept pushing. I was like, 'Wait a minute, you don't belong here, this is supposed to be an eight-page short story,' but it just would never stay within the boundaries. And so I would think I was failing. I didn't realize, you know, that I just needed a bit more space than eight pages. For some reason, I had eight pages as the count. And then I did a screenplay from two of the short stories and I got nominated for a Gemini for one of those screenplays. Then the film itself won a Gemini for Best Production. So that was crazy and that was the beginning. From there, I started writing another short story that again shed its boundaries and went into *Kit's Law*, which was the first novel.

SIMMINS: That's fascinating. I can't think of another writer who has said that to me. I know Alice Munro was known to have said that she only had time to write short stories because as a mother, of a relatively big family, of four children, I believe, she only had time to do the short stories; she didn't have the time to produce a novel. So I've heard that before, but I haven't heard anyone say that they basically sat down to do short fiction – and a novel came out.

MORRISSEY: I remember the moment, I actually remember the moment. I was at the end of this story, which is now the novel *Livvy Higgs*, I was at the end of this story and we were waiting for the cat to die in an old woman's lap and I didn't know how a cat died, you know? I was thinking about how does a cat die? Jesus, does it close his eyes and meow his way into heaven? How does a cat die? And as I was figuring out that, or somehow I just became that old woman and my eyes lit upon a picture on the mantel of a young man, wearing an army uniform (which wasn't in real life), and the words just came out of my mouth, 'He used to say he loved me. Back then I didn't know what love was. I used to be a girl in the gully; my mother had red hair.' And that was the beginning of *Kit's Law*. I had no idea what I was doing, no idea, and it just took off in to that novel and it got rid of the old woman in the rocking chair and the cat came back six years later to *Livvy Higgs*.

SIMMINS: Isn't that something? Extraordinary.

MORRISSEY: Yeah, talk to me about synchronicity and meaning and the universe and fate.

SIMMINS: Nothing wasted.

MORRISSEY: Everything. Even you and me sitting here right now, having this coffee.

SIMMINS: Wonder what book that will end up in? Oh, yeah, that's right, mine, *Memoir: Conversations and Craft*! On a book tour with a memoir, do you think it will feel different than with a novel?

MORRISSEY: I think I'm going to have to give more of myself on the stage. Every time I write a book, I go on tour and always it's with fun and laughter. I don't know how this is going to be. It's a whole new ball game for me; I have no idea. I'm going to stand up there and talk about me. I never talk about me. I always talk story. I talk about my characters and story and things that happened. I hate indulgence and then my agent says something the other day that really made me skittish towards memoir. I had sent her something. I said, 'Well, what do you think of this?' and she goes, 'Well, I don't know, Donna,' she said, 'this could be a great part of your story or it could be just a discursion. Just write until you know it's done.' I'm thinking, A discursion? There's two chapters on that bit she says *might* be a discursion. It can't be a *discursion*. And then I'm thinking, Oh, my God, everything is a discursion, life is a discursion. I don't know what a discursion is.

SIMMINS: It's an odd word. I wonder if she meant digression – that you were digressing?

MORRISSEY: Maybe. I think they're both the same.

SIMMINS: You're a morning writer, are you not?

MORRISSEY: Yes.

SIMMINS: So even when you're teaching, you're guarding your morning writing time.

MORRISSEY: Very much so.

SIMMINS: I'm sure you've never missed a deadline in your life but …

MORRISSEY: What, writing deadlines? Are you crazy? Try a year or two. Writing deadlines are meant to be missed. Everybody signs the two-year contract.

SIMMINS: You're talking to a journalist. I don't miss deadlines.

MORRISSEY: No, it's common that you sign two years for a manuscript and you produce it in three; everybody knows that.

SIMMINS: I did two books in two years; didn't miss a deadline once. But we'll see what happens if I ever try fiction.

MORRISSEY: You journalist, you.

SIMMINS: Yeah, yeah. So anything you'd like to say to fiction writers who are considering doing memoir? Anything at all?

MORRISSEY: You gotta take it on like a story. You know, you just don't sit and indulge in memories. There has to be a hard theme. There has to be a hard heart and you have to open it, somehow, as you would fiction. In a sense, you have to treat it like fiction in that it's got to have the one thread going through it – unless you're going to do a series of short stories of your life. In which case then you treat each short story like a short story of fiction with a thread carrying it and it's gotta have a little arc before you end it. It just can't be a run-on. It's boring.

SIMMINS: Absolutely.

MORRISSEY: There has to be an arc.

SIMMINS: You might have to ramble in the beginning to get going, that's fine, but at some point you're going to have to say here's the real beginning, and boom! In you go. How did you feel when the memoir was done?

MORRISSEY: Ohh, I was exhausted. Emotionally and mentally. Going back through those hugely devastating moments, reliving them. Bringing them to the page, some days were torturous. Especially the parts about the PTSD, those first days. And my brother's death, of course. And then my mother. Times I walked the house with my arms wrapped around myself, hugging myself. It was tough.

SIMMINS: What kept you going through those tough parts?

MORRISSEY: Walking. I walked a lot. There are lovely wooded trails in my neighbourhood, I walked and walked. Then, after dinner, I sprawled before the tube. I gorged on Netflix. I just needed to be totally mindless till I went to sleep. Having said all of that, there are hugely loving moments in my past and my present. I am blessed to have a loving family. I had pictures of them all around me while I wrote. I kept looking at their faces, loving them. Thank God we had love.

SIMMINS: Any other tips for a fiction writer coming into memoir?

MORRISSEY: Mmmm, well, there are lots. Remembering that the memories must tie together. That we are creating a story. That this memoir has a heart and everything we write is supporting that heart. There are times when I wrote a beautiful memory, but, in the reread, I was forced to acknowledge that it didn't belong. That it played no role in supporting the heart of the story. At one point, my word count was 85,000 words. During the third draft, I had it whittled down to 70,000. That's when I started to get scared ... and I knew I had to pass it over to my editors before I whittled the whole thing out of existence.

SIMMINS: Can you be sure that what you edited out didn't really fit?

MORRISSEY: It's all about intuition. But it's hard to be objective. I'm hoping my editor will come and say, 'Hey, Donna, we want more from your life on The Beaches, do have any more yarns about your grandmother?' Oh, cripes, do I ever. I haven't lost anything I cut out. It's all sitting there, hoping for a chance to hop back in the story.

SIMMINS: Hop back in the story. I like that. What is your biggest fear?

MORRISSEY: Of boring the reader.

SIMMINS: Do you think you have?

MORRISSEY: (Grins) I'll let them decide. I've done enough damage with my edits already. I'll not do more by pronouncing it boring before it gets into a reader's hands. But, of course, that is everyone's fear, that the reader won't like me.

SIMMINS: I sure know that fear. What did you enjoy the most about the process?

MORRISSEY: Mmm, I really enjoyed the childhood stuff. Going back and bringing to life those poignant moments that mapped my later years with regards to curiosity, imagination. Our first children's books, our first movie. We were so isolated that I remember my first everything. Felt like I'd gone on a beautiful journey during those first days of immersing myself into those early days. Made it feel so close to me again. I smile now, just thinking about it.

SIMMINS: Are there any important writerly insights you have derived from writing a memoir?

MORRISSEY: Actually, yes. There is one, a very important one. When I look back now, I see mostly those things that I have written. It feels as though there is a spotlight shining on them, and I have to peer hard beyond that light to see the things I didn't write. It's as though, having written the memoir, I created myself. And that's not fair to those many, many things that I didn't include. Who was it – Marco Polo – said, on his deathbed, *I have not wrote the half of what I saw and did.* And so, it's to remember, a life holds many things; this memoir is a pathway through certain aspects of my life.

SIMMINS: Why did you choose to write this particular pathway?

MORRISSEY: I feel I have quite a lot to say about mental illness, grief, love. It has been a hugely challenging part of my life. And I hope that others will connect with it, perhaps not feel so alone if they're fighting the same dragons. We need each other. I gave of myself in this memoir. I hope it serves more than being just a Sunday read.

Donna Morrissey
Craft

Fiction versus non-fiction: less freedom, as much – or more?

As a novelist, Donna Morrissey brings a unique, supportive set of skills to the task of writing a memoir. No one needs to tell her about pacing, or tension, or character development, or story arc, or climax; she has those skills down pat. As you've read, she'll be the first one to tell you that she has mined her own life for stories, or the plots of her novels, and that her family members, particularly her mother and siblings, have been "characters" in her novels from the beginning of her writing career.

But Morrissey is now facing a new writing challenge: memoir. She can't rewrite the endings, to make them symphonic or triumphant, or jazz up the regular, banal bits that are a part of each and every life.

Or can she?

My bet says she can. It's all a question of focus. So while Morrissey can't change the truth of an event, she can choose which parts of it to focus on, and challenge herself to find beauty and meaning in any landscape in which she finds herself. That's what writers do. They find beauty beneath the horror. They see the holy in the humble or scorned. Most of all, they peel back layers of the discernible and obvious, to find more complex offerings for their readers.

Morrissey also believes that our deepest wounds are inflicted in childhood or our teenage years, and that we battle these ghosts and memories throughout our life. I agree. I further believe you, the memoirist, should be mining this period ruthlessly.

And finally, Morrissey says, "Little fires leading the way back." To my mind, this is a fruitful way to think about the "plot points" of our lives. It is these we will be thinking about, when we sit down to write our memoirs.

For your memoir:

Take a true-to-life event from childhood or teenage years. It's always had a certain cast-in-stone quality. If it is commonplace, your job is to make it riveting reading. If the event is so frightening your heart still pounds to think about it, identify the one moment when you experienced pure bravery and resolve. Perhaps you remember a time of harrowing humiliation. Think about that, and see if there wasn't a small, shining ribbon of dignity and strength, which enabled you to walk away, or in some way deal with the situation. Whatever event you choose – surprise yourself! Turn the idea on its head, shake it around, pierce it with words, shatter it with humour, or warm it with love. It's all in the point of view …

"I can only just cradle them as I go through, just hope that I portray them in a way that they deserve to be."

Like Edmund Metatawabin, Donna Morrissey writes with great love and respect for those dearest to her, both alive and dead. She has done this in her fiction, and vows to do it in her memoir. She has, she says, "no axes to grind." One has the strong feeling that if, like most of us, Morrissey in fact does have one or two axes she could grind, that she won't be doing it in print. You could call it "the rule of Thumper." It was Thumper's mother, actually, who suggested to Thumper, when he said something uncomplimentary about the newly born, spindly-legged Bambi, "If you can't say something nice, don't say anything at all."

Memoir, however, is not big on rules, and certainly not ones set down by animated Disney bunnies.

While there are no rules about the tone of a memoir, there are true life tales so one-note unpleasant, that's all anyone remembers about them. I've referred to this type of book earlier as "revenge memoirs," but it usually earns the extra moniker of "exposé." The title that often comes to mind is *Mommie Dearest*, written by Christina Crawford, the adopted daughter of Hollywood star Joan Crawford. In 1978, Christina wrote unflinchingly about her appallingly dysfunctional childhood. But if she sought pure sympathy and across-the-board support, she did not receive it.

Christina's hobnail-boot approach remains controversial. And yet and yet – perhaps she spoke the truth, perhaps she couldn't see any other way to write about all that pain and suffering. We seem so quick to blame the victim, disbelieve the wounded.

The problem with "misery lit" is that it starts to grate, even bore a reader. Reading on, you can even feel grimy and wretched. By its end, even the brilliant *Educated* (2018), by Tara Westover, takes a toll on the reader. You want her – or, really, her savage and sick family – to go far, far away.

For your memoir:

I am going to presume you are not writing a revenge memoir, that you have loftier goals. But all memoirists will at some point write about people they don't understand or respect, or who they dislike, or even hate. (As mentioned earlier, Pat Conroy, in his fiction, did this over and over again, pertaining to his fighter pilot father, Don Conroy. In the younger Conroy's memoir, he achieved an astonishing level of forgiveness and acceptance – while still tormented by the violence and cruelty that he, his mother, and his siblings experienced in their early years as a family. It rang uneasily true for me. Often, tormentors hold a beyond-the-grave power over those they have tormented, who, in my experience in this life, simply want peace and quiet, within and without.)

Write a short story – a page, two – about someone you have strong, negative feelings about. This person may appear in your memoir. Include all the aspects of character that trouble you most about that person. Do not hold back. If one adjective is good, use two or three. Vent your spleen, as the saying goes. Show no mercy. Take no prisoners. (Marine Don Conroy would approve of all of this.)

Two, chuck that story. You know the writing isn't worthy of you, or your memoir. But you're feeling a bit cleansed from the venting, and it was all worth it to use so many nasty adjectives in one place (sorry, Audrey).

Three, rewrite the story. No cuss words, few adjectives. Pause to consider why this person behaves as she or he does. Think about what they receive back, after behaving badly – even if it's only horrified silence. What could that possibly mean to them? Shut your eyes tight, and think back to see how you behaved in these difficult circumstances.

Is there a small nugget of forgiveness in here anywhere? Did the person not spare you, perhaps, but did spare a younger sibling? Failing forgiveness, is there a deeper understanding of one complex human by another? Failing even this, and perhaps most interesting of all, do you feel some feral-level recognition of what the person was striving for, what they hoped to gain? One of evil's most wretched manifestations is banality. But even that can be fascinating, in the hands of a good writer.

For your memoir:

Just one more exercise on the subject of difficult people who may need to be written about in our memoir. Write whatever it is you need to write about a particular person, probably a family member. Now, read it aloud, slowly. I guarantee – you will find words that make you uncomfortable, and don't actually need to be there. Omit nothing that adds to the perfect pitch of themes in the overall story. All the other extras, all the other … discursions/digressions … have to go.

Option:

Many authors choose to show family or friends the sections they appear in in the memoirs, and check with them if they are comfortable with the wording and presentation. If not, out she comes, to be followed by a rewrite. Some family members of authors, as we'll see shortly, in the conversation with Plum Johnson, even ask not to be involved in the memoir at all – not included, not named, not made identifiable. And yes, people can be written *around* in a memoir. It all depends on the storyline. Are they a major part of it, or not? If not, no worries, mate.

Chapter Four
Why do we write memoirs?

The following list was created by participants in one of my workshops – yes, they were amazing, as always! Other participants and I have added to it since its first iteration.

And of course the list is infinite. For one of the funniest bits of prose on why anyone writes, I heartily recommend the introduction to Margaret Atwood's *Negotiating with the Dead: A Writer on Writing*.

You can write a memoir to:

- create something one-of-a-kind
- bear witness – for yourself/for others
- create a record of your life
- understand your life; to heal; experience catharsis from trauma
- express compassion for others
- experience self-forgiveness
- set yourself a challenge/to meet that challenge, with the discipline of daily or regular writing
- leave a legacy/to note your presence in the world
- enact revenge (hint: this is *not* a good idea)
- find truth, justice, and restitution
- add to the historical record
- enjoy the pleasure of storytelling
- revisit and explore memories
- make atonement
- write about the meeting place of public and private worlds
- experience clarity at leisure
- get the last word
- feel pride in an accomplishment

- give credit in a public manner
- further personal agendas or promote personal causes
- correct a story you feel was badly or incompletely told
- offer your alternate version of the truth/a truth
- uncover injustices
- shine a light on addictions/what is hidden/in the dark/considered taboo or tragic
- "debunk" a myth or misconception
- carry on a culture
- pass on knowledge or experience

Whatever your motivation may be to write, at the core there must be fire. Memoirs take determination to start, and guts and heart to finish. You may be heated by "good" motivations, even altruistic ones, or you may be heated by "bad" (selfish and hurtful) motivations, such as settling a score or two. It's your book. Do as you wish to. But remember, you will have to live with it … for years to come. Words, either written or spoken, can't be "taken back." Make sure yours are as accurate as you know how to make them – and that your story has beauty.

Conversation with Claire Mowat, author of
The Outport People; Pomp and Circumstances; Travels with Farley

Claire Angel Mowat was born and educated in Toronto and is a graduate of the Ontario College of Art. Originally a graphic designer, she switched to writing during the 1960s when she lived in Newfoundland.

Mowat has written three non-fiction titles. The first, *The Outport People* (1983), details the five years she and husband Farley Mowat spent at the start of their marriage in Burgeo, an outport community in Newfoundland. Her second book, *Pomp and Circumstances* (1989), arose from her experience as a lady-in-waiting, and witnessing protocol behind the scenes at the Governor General's residence in Ottawa. A third memoir, *Travels with Farley*, first published by Key Porter in 2005, and reprinted by Pottersfield Press in 2015, describes the couple's life in the Magdalen Islands.

In addition to "candid, friendly and concise" personal narratives (*Miramichi Reader*), Mowat has also written a trilogy of young adult fiction: *The Girl From Away* (1992), *The French Isles* (1994), and *Last Summer in Louisbourg* (1998). Widowed in 2014, Claire Mowat continues to divide her time between a small town in Ontario and a country farmhouse in Nova Scotia. She is currently working on a new book.

SIMMINS: You've written three memoirs. I'd like to talk about each of these memoir writing experiences, starting with *The Outport People*. How did this time in your life, when you and Farley were living in Newfoundland, become a book?

MOWAT: Well, I think happenstance. I trained to be a graphic designer and illustrator and the idea was that we'd go off to this little community [of] Burgeo and Farley would write books, and I would illustrate them. Somehow it didn't come out that way at all because the only person in the community who knew how to type, I think, was me. Farley needed things typed out for whatever he was writing, so there I was, typing away. I did that for two or three years and there was never any time to draw anything. Then I started answering the mail and so on and then finally after we had left that community, I was still typing, because I thought that I was making notes for him, things that he would use in whatever books he was going to write. And Farley just said to me one day, 'You can do this, too. Just sit down and work at it.' So to make a long story short, I did.

SIMMINS: Now when you talk about notes, these were notes you were taking in your journals.

MOWAT: Yes. I'm a compulsive journal keeper to this day. Every once in a while I sit down and type out something. I don't keep it in a little book with a lock on it; I just do it by three-hole-punch paper and put it in a binder. Of course I realized when I lived in an outport in Newfoundland fifty years ago that I was witnessing a culture that wasn't like the one I grew up with in Toronto. People would come in with funny little things that they would say that I'd never heard before, such as 'Candlemas Day dark and glum, worst of winter yet to come,' and I didn't even know when Candlemas Day was. It's Groundhog Day. Originally it was called Candlemas. So right in my own kitchen, neighbours and neighbours' children were always telling me things and I would write them down.

SIMMINS: So you'd had the prompt from Farley to do some of your own writing. Had you already said to Farley, 'You know, I think one of these days I might just start writing myself'? Or was it that initial prompt from him that made you think, Oh, okay, I can do this?

MOWAT: I would say it was the initial urging from him. He could read what I had written, notes and letters and things, and thought, in his opinion, that I was capable of writing a book.

SIMMINS: So you brought to that first book [*The Outport People*] a bit of an anthropologist's eye. I mean knowing that you were in a very different place with a very different language and very different history and so on. Was that the source of the curiosity that prompted you to write?

MOWAT: Yes, I do think so.

SIMMINS: Which is a great prompt, isn't it, because it's so fresh and original.

MOWAT: Yes. Now I didn't study anthropology ever, though I may have read the odd article or book, but I was just interested in what was going on around me.

SIMMINS: How did it feel when that first book came out?

MOWAT: Oh, wonderful. That was 1983. Yeah, because I think up till then, most people wondered what I did all day.

SIMMINS: You had the art training and when that didn't actually turn out to be a life choice in terms of your vocation, you must have felt a sense of relief that writing came to you.

MOWAT: Well, yes, the fact that the book was good enough to be published and it got wonderful reviews and sold very well, that certainly was a moment of triumph.

SIMMINS: So we have *The Outport People* in 1983 and *Pomp and Circumstances* in 1989. Tell me how *Pomp and Circumstances* came together.

MOWAT: Well, there's another whole chapter in my life that I never thought I would experience, the world of protocol and the fact that a friend of ours, Edward Schreyer, turned out to be the Governor General of Canada. That was another huge surprise. We knew him as the Premier of Manitoba and when he was defeated in government we thought, Oh, well, maybe he'll get a seat in the Senate or something'll happen. Lo and behold, there he was, Governor General. The Schreyers didn't have a lot of friends in Ontario. Everybody that they'd known all their lives was in Manitoba so we were constantly invited up there to take part in dinners. I guess Farley was the token representative of the arts or something like that. Yeah, because when they first got there, I was just finishing *The Outport People*. It was published while Ed and Lily Schreyer were in Ottawa in Rideau Hall.

SIMMINS: What were those early days together like?

MOWAT: They invited us on a State visit and we had travelled with them to various places.

SIMMINS: So you knew you all got on well.

MOWAT: Yeah, we travelled well together and then of course this strange world of protocol and diplomacy, I never thought I'd be part of that. You know, having to get dressed up in the morning instead of slouching around in my jeans. You'd have to be well turned out.

SIMMINS: You were a lady-in-waiting, correct? I mean, that was the job, wasn't it?

MOWAT: Yes. In the protocol of the day that was the title. When you go to events, especially overseas, there's a listing with the king at the top or the prime minister or whatever, and then there's all these other people who are *aides-de-camp* and so on and so on. Then there's a position, lady-in-waiting, which just means that you're accompanying the principal woman of this visit.

SIMMINS: I had images of you doing, you know, doing more personal caretaking for Lily, and I thought that must have been hard.

MOWAT: I think we get that from Shakespeare because in Shakespeare the ladies-in-waiting are always sitting on the stage doing embroidery or something.

SIMMINS: Or doing the lady's hair.

MOWAT: No, I didn't do anything like that. There's a dresser and that's the person who looks after the clothes of the principal woman, whether she's a queen or a wife of a prime minister or something like that. And yes, that person is a full-time position in Ottawa and when the lady in question travels that person travels, too. And she's the one who presses the dress and puts it on, and so on and so on.

SIMMINS: You were more of a companion, were you not?

MOWAT: Yes. That's much more of what it would be and you know, in a way it's supportive; you're there so that the principal lady doesn't have to walk into a crowded room all by herself. And then I always made sure I found out where the bathroom was and stuff like that.

SIMMINS: That was for a period of three years, was it?

MOWAT: No, five.

SIMMINS: Five?

MOWAT: Well, I wasn't there all the time; this was intermittent occasions. The Schreyers were there for just over five years because the incoming Governor General, Jeanne Sauvé, was ill, so Ed Schreyer agreed to stay on for another six months.

SIMMINS: Where did you and Farley live then?

MOWAT: Oh, same as now. We lived here in Port Hope, Ontario, and spent the summer in Cape Breton Island.

SIMMINS: How much time was it doing the duties?

MOWAT: They were just done on occasion.

SIMMINS: I see. And they visited you and Farley, too?

MOWAT: Yes. But when the Schreyers used to visit us in Cape Breton, of course, it was far from the world of protocol and formal dinners. Then they were just themselves.

SIMMINS: So over a period of five years you were doing these intermittent duties and again, it's a whole new world, a whole new cast of characters who fascinated you and prompted you to write the book.

MOWAT: Yes.

SIMMINS: And also the originality of it; I mean, no one else had written about that.

MOWAT: Well, I don't think they had in Canada, maybe in Britain; there may have been things like that there. [Claire was correct. The latest book on this absorbing subject is *Lady in Waiting: My Extraordinary Life in the Shadow of the Crown* (2019), by Anne Glenconner, who was lady-in-waiting to the late Princess Margaret, Queen Elizabeth's sister.]

SIMMINS: How was *Pomp and Circumstances* received?

MOWAT: It did well, but it didn't have the appeal of *The Outport People*. I think in Canada, people are more interested in the farthest corners of the country.

SIMMINS: Yes, remote and unknown.

MOWAT: Yeah, and there're a lot of them in Canada. Think of all the indigenous people and Hutterites and the many different cultural groups of people in Canada who you don't run into every day, if you're a middle-of-the-road Anglophone person.

SIMMINS: Did you have to do quite a bit of research for *Pomp and Circumstances*?

MOWAT: I did talk to quite a few people who worked at Rideau Hall and I found out, for example, what the *aides-de-camp* were expected to do and the *maitre d'*, the guy who was in charge of all the footmen, and they would tell me exactly what they were expected to do. I interviewed a lot of people really.

SIMMINS: I am thinking that the processes for writing the first memoir, about life in a Newfoundland outport, and the second, about the life of a lady-in-waiting for the wife of the Governor General of Canada, were quite different. The second book is more of a non-fiction memoir, because you're providing so much information about a system and a government and so on. This included doing interviews, as a journalist would. I presume you didn't do interviews for *The Outport People*.

MOWAT: No, I didn't do interviews for *The Outport People*. In fact, I changed people's names in *The Outport People*.

SIMMINS: I didn't know that.

MOWAT: Well, protection.

SIMMINS: That's a part of memoirs ... a choice that people can make to change names of people involved. In my own memoir, *Coastal Lives*, I sometimes chose to give no name at all. I used "the fisherman," or "misguided angel," and other monikers. And that was fine; that was as far as I wanted to go. I didn't want to use some names. People's privacy is important.

MOWAT: Yeah, you don't want to walk on somebody's toes. In *The Outport People* there were a few unlikeable people in the book and so, I just gave them different names. But I was told later that when the people in Burgeo got hold of the book, they all knew exactly who I was talking about.

SIMMINS: My oldest sister wrote a memoir about commercial fishing in B.C. when she was a very young woman. It was called *Harvest of Salmon*, and the fishermen just pounced on the book. They had more fun trying to figure out who was who because, again, she'd given them different names, but to the inner crowd, it was quite obvious. Oh, well, we do what we can, eh? And she wrote with enthusiasm, no malice. Now, after *The Outport People* and *Pomp and Circumstances* there were the novels.

MOWAT: Yes, and then I wrote the young adult novel, *The Girl From Away*.

SIMMINS: The trilogy.

MOWAT: Trilogy, yes. *The Girl From Away, The French Isles,* and *Last Summer in Louisbourg*.

SIMMINS: You started with two memoirs, moved on to fiction, and then latterly came back to memoir with *Travels with Farley*. But first, I wanted to say you must be so very pleased that the memoir about Farley was recently reprinted.

MOWAT: Yes, yes I am. It got some very good reviews when it first came out.

SIMMINS: I loved it, Claire. I thought it was a perfect balance of love and truth.

MOWAT: Oh, thank you.

SIMMINS: You were very real. It gave me a fuller understanding of how your lives came together and then unfolded and I really enjoyed that. And I loved Farley's *Bay of Spirits*, too.

MOWAT: Yeah, that's lovely, too.

SIMMINS: Now, tell me about coming to the third memoir, *Travels with Farley*. What was the process there? I believe Farley's memoir, *Bay of Spirits,* came out in 2006, the year after *Travels with Farley*?

MOWAT: That's right.

SIMMINS: So you wrote the story of your lives before Farley did. I find that interesting. I guess in a way, we all want our version of events to exist. You're going to have your strongest memories and the things that were more important to you or whatever. I don't know – you're going to have your version.

MOWAT: Yeah, I will. They're not exactly the same.

SIMMINS: So how did Farley receive that? How did he feel about the book?

MOWAT: Oh, well, he was always happy for me when I got a book published and it was well received.

SIMMINS: Yes, but this is a bit more personal. He didn't stub his toe on anything or say, 'Really, is that how you saw that?' He was fine with the book how it appeared?

MOWAT: Yes, I'm sure he was and now, thinking back on it, he must have been working on *Bay of Spirits* at the same time I was working on *Travels with Farley.*

SIMMINS: The dates were so close you'd have to think that.

MOWAT: I guess we were both working away on memoirs at the same time.

SIMMINS: And memoirs of how you met! You probably had some fun saying, 'Well, do you remember that? And what about such and such, what year was that?' You probably had some back and forth about events and so on.

MOWAT: We did talk to each other about what we were working on. That was a great advantage of two writers living together.

SIMMINS: Absolutely. I know when *Coastal Lives* came out and I was, obviously, wanting Don to like it, and his first response, which I thought was very funny, was to say, 'I thought you went very easy on me.' And I said, 'Hmm, what *should* I have said?'

It seems to me that there's not going to be too many writerly couples that are going to have memoirs of their lives together like you and Farley do. Scholar's and historian's gold, when you think about it.

MOWAT: I hadn't really thought about it.

SIMMINS: So, all together, you've written three memoirs and a trilogy of the novels. Did you find the writing experience from memoir to fiction different, similar – how did you find it?

MOWAT: I found it a lot easier to write fiction because you don't have to keep looking things up and do as much research because fiction comes out of your head, or my head. No, I remember the first one I wrote, *The Girl From Away*, I remember thinking, Hey, this is easy. I'm going to write a couple more of these.

SIMMINS: Funny, I've had other writers say the opposite! I am working up to fiction. I keep thinking, Oh, I can't do this, I can't do this, and Don says, 'Oh, you'll do it, in your own sweet time.' So I'm finding it very reassuring to be talking to all these memoirists who came to memoir first and then did go on to fiction.

MOWAT: Yes, Linden MacIntyre did that.

SIMMINS: Exactly. He had done one non-fiction book before the memoir and that was *Who Killed Ty Conn*.

MOWAT: Now I've never read that.

SIMMINS: I hadn't, either. It's investigative journalism, his speciality, of course. But interestingly, in fairly short order after that he wrote *Causeway*. Back to your journals. I want to know more about them. You said you've written those all your life?

MOWAT: Well, the first one, yeah, the year I was twelve …

SIMMINS: What did twelve-year-old Claire Angel Wheeler write about?

MOWAT: ... I was given a little red diary, twelve and thirteen years old, and you know, I wrote something every day. Well, you can imagine, a twelve-year-old girl.

SIMMINS: Oh, yeah, lots to say.

MOWAT: A huge thing in my life was that I had my hair cut! Anyway, then after that it was occasionally that I'd sit down and write something. When I learned to type when I was only fourteen that helped a lot because I could just sit and type away and put my thoughts on paper.

SIMMINS: And did you collect all those typings up into a binder?

MOWAT: I'm not sure where they are. Maybe my mother threw them out. I don't know.

SIMMINS: I'm just wondering, because if you start with a journal, that's a handwriting process, and apparently, it's quite a different experience than typing. You can be just as productive or more so with typing, but scientists say it's a very different creative process in our brains. There are still authors out there, like Budge Wilson, who handwrite their work.

Let's talk about voice. When you sat down to start the memoirs, do you think you were using almost the journal writing voice? Because there's a lovely immediacy to it.

MOWAT: God, I don't know.

SIMMINS: You just sat down and have the voice you needed, or did you have to struggle for it?

MOWAT: No, I guess it just came to me.

SIMMINS: I just wondered how much that might have to do with someone who kept journals and wrote letters – having an immediate voice.

MOWAT: I guess I did. I hadn't really thought about it.

SIMMINS: I just would feel sorry for the person who's sitting down to write who had never done any journals or letters and so on because they're kind of coming to it cold if, you know what I mean.

MOWAT: I really don't know how somebody like that would get started.

SIMMINS: Get started, exactly. Seems like one of those things where you have it, but you don't really know you have it. You had the voice because you've been using it; you've been doing the letters and doing the journals. So you sit down to do something a little different, but you can still hear your voice. You can still get from A to B to C and on with the story.

MOWAT: I suppose so. Maybe it's like that with people who become opera singers. One day they sort of open up and they can sing.

SIMMINS: So obviously, you had no struggle with voice. You simply sat down, had the impetus from being excited about whatever the subject was, thought, I can do this, and off you went.

MOWAT: I'm just remembering that when I went to school I was quite good at writing what we called composition, English composition. I always found that easy to do and I did well, whereas, I would fail miserably at arithmetic. I'd be fine writing a story. We're all given a different kind of brain.

SIMMINS: Yes, and that story supports the notion which I pretty well agree with, that serious writers are born. Every writer improves or tries to and many challenge themselves trying different genres and all the rest of it, but there's a certain ease with words that writers are born with, don't you think?

MOWAT: Oh, I think so, just like singers are born. And natural athletes. There has to be something there and then you do something with it.

SIMMINS: When I'm teaching memoir classes there are obviously going to be people in the class that basically are there to talk about memoir and writing generally, and that's fine. We all learn something, we share, and we enjoy ourselves. There are others who are really keen to get words on paper. Those are the ones I really hope to inspire and help along with their writing journeys. Of course it's legitimate and often inspiring to talk about writing. But there are people that come to the workshops on fire to create. They just want a little bit more information about how they might put their ideas on paper. You can inspire someone to some degree, but they've got have something burning inside too.

MOWAT: Oh, yeah. That's one thing Farley always told me. He said, 'Don't talk it out,' you know, whatever it was I was going to say in my book. He said that if you talk about it, maybe not to him so much, but if you talk to other people or give a little talk at your local church group or something, that you then have told the story and you're less likely to write it down.

SIMMINS: Good advice! Do you read memoirs?

MOWAT: Yes, I love them. I'm crazy about them.

SIMMINS: What have you read lately that you've been crazy about?

MOWAT: I'm currently reading Bill Bryson; he writes travel memoirs.

SIMMINS: Oh, yes, he's wonderful. So funny! What's this one?

MOWAT: *The Road to Little Dribbling – The Adventures of an American in Britain.*

SIMMINS: Isn't it a fabulous title?

MOWAT: Yes, and it sounds so English. I also read the memoir by Anna Pottier, who lived with Irving Layton for quite a few years.

SIMMINS: *Good as Gone: My Life with Irving Layton.*

MOWAT: I must say I wasn't crazy about them, but it was a good story nonetheless.

SIMMINS: Pottier did a good job, then?

MOWAT: Yes. We had met Irving Layton a few times; I wouldn't say we were friends or anything but in the early days of CanLit, especially the McClelland and Stewart crowd, we would all be at the same dinner parties or promo parties or something. So it was interesting in that sense that they were talking about situations and people that I knew.

SIMMINS: What particularly do you think it is that draws you to read memoirs more generally?

MOWAT: I guess the fact that it's not an invented story. It's somebody real, something that happened to them. I remember when I was in high school and reading a book called *Land Below the Wind*, by Agnes Newton Keith. She had gone off with her husband to British North Borneo, though I can't remember why. This all took place a very long time ago. Even when I read the book in high school, it was at least ten years old, but I loved it. [Over the course of five years, American Agnes Newton Keith documented her observations and experiences in a highly personal series of articles that comprised her first non-fiction book, *Land Below the Wind*. It went on to win the *Atlantic Monthly* annual prize for non-fiction in 1939. Readers felt she captured the essence of colonial life from the perspective of an American expat with humour and grace, describing the local people – Chinese, Murut, and Malay – with affection and sympathy.]

SIMMINS: Beautiful title.

MOWAT: Yes, well again, that was apparently part of British North Borneo, but *Land Below the Wind*, that was what the people who lived there referred to their own land. I guess whatever sort of monsoon wind in the area passed them by. I couldn't have been more than about fourteen or fifteen when I read that book and I loved it.

SIMMINS: With non-fiction, and memoir, there is an extra imaginative tingle when you realize that this isn't made up, this is real. And yet, there's a long, long, long and honourable tradition of dishonourable or fake memoirs, such as American author James Frey, and his fake memoir, *A Million Little Pieces*.

MOWAT: No, I don't know that book.

SIMMINS: Well, Frey wrote a fake memoir about his life with drug addictions and being in prison.

MOWAT: Oh, yeah, now I do remember. I didn't remember the name of the author or the book, but I remember the story.

SIMMINS: Why do we feel so betrayed if someone says, 'This is a true story,' and we find out they've made it up? Why the indignation and fury?

MOWAT: Well, nobody likes to be lied to.

SIMMINS: I guess that's it, isn't it? Just seems so over the top at times.

MOWAT: Well, if somebody comes along with this preposterous story and claims, 'This is what I did and this is what happened to me,' and then you find out he was lying, you get mad. You feel used, and betrayed.

SIMMINS: And also, if you've bought into it and gone through all sorts of emotional levels and then it turns out you've been made to feel a fool, I guess the sting is there.

MOWAT: Yes, I think that's it; you've been duped and tricked, as though by a con artist.

SIMMINS: I want to talk about memoir's after-effects. I think memoir can make you a better human being, make you more open to others because you've finally dealt with some of your own huge sources of pain and you're not just travelling through life, you're seeing life and pondering on it. And, if you're lucky, your heart has healed in some way. That's a wonderful gift for a memoir to give a human being, don't you think? Compassion, and healing. Linden said memoir opened him right up. And I thought, Well, yeah, you can't write with one hand pushing your heart away. Do you agree?

MOWAT: Yes. And memoir makes you dig for things and unearth things.

SIMMINS: Things you might not even have known you were looking for, in the first place.

MOWAT: Absolutely.

Claire Mowat
Craft

Journals

I wasn't surprised to learn that Claire Mowat came to memoir writing after a lifetime of writing journals. Daily or regular writing from our young years on is so helpful for developing a confident voice in a published memoir, which Claire has done three times over.

For your memoir:

If you're lucky enough to have kept journals over a lifetime, gather them up and devote some time to rereading them. No matter how sharp you think your memory is, you'll be amazed at the details you've forgotten, even about the big events in your life. These details, of course, are memoir gold. See if you can find a particularly rich period of joy or change or upheaval in your life (marriage; moving; children; divorce; an affair; illness or disability) and study the journals which come from this time.

Opportunity

Another idea that jumped out at me during the interview with Claire was the fact that she was always alert to writing opportunities in her life. She moves to a new home with a culture, landscape, language, and traditions that are all new to her as well? She takes careful notes and writes *The Outport People*. She is offered the unusual position of Lady-in-Waiting to Her Excellency, the Right Honourable Lily Schreyer, wife of the Governor General of Canada, Ed Schreyer? Claire talks it over with her husband Farley and they see it as a wonderful opportunity for new experiences and adventures, with two people whose company they already know and enjoy. The outcome is *Pomp and*

Circumstances, which Claire yet again experienced and wrote about at the same time (which I also did, by living and writing *Year of the Horse* at the same time), proving that memoirs don't have to be written in retrospect, but on occasion, in real time.

Did Claire know how her time as a lady-in-waiting would all pan out? Absolutely not. And that was part of the fun. I know it was for me, with that second memoir. I certainly wanted a triumphant ending, and with luck, hard work, and support from others, got one.

But Claire or I would have written about whatever ending had come along to our lives, perhaps even have found triumph in defeat, because that's the writer's way, to see more than one dimension in any one circumstance, and to find jewels amidst the dross.

With her third memoir, *Travels with Farley*, Claire saw another opportunity to write a captivating story of her life – and in that case, it was the most central story of all: her nearly fifty-year marriage to author and environmentalist Farley Mowat, one of the bestselling authors of all time, whose books have been translated into fifty-two languages and sold over 17 million copies around the world. The world knew a fair bit about the irrepressible, unpredictable, brilliant, generous, short-tempered, and complicated Farley Mowat (who died in May 6, 2014, just shy of his ninety-third birthday).

They did not know nearly as much about Toronto-born-and-raised Claire Angel Wheeler, who, they would learn, was far more strong-willed and of firm opinions in her own right than the "Golden Girl" of Farley's own memoir of their life together, *Bay of Spirits,* might suggest. Did Farley shortchange Claire in this way? No, he did not. He simply told the story he needed to tell about the love of his life, his version of their life together, as did Claire, in her own memoir. Even within marriages, couples have different memories of the same time periods, and different needs and desires to revisit and write about these memories. It's all in the selection …

For your memoir:

Have a look at your calendar for the year ahead. Do you have events planned that could form the basis of a memoir? Or does your spouse or partner? Could those events be stretched out, added to, and shaped, to form a longer story?

I had always wanted to write about the many and marvellous horses who have graced my life. The opportunity to do so came via a "hell blessing" (credit to writer and comedian Bill Carr for this term), when, in 2011, I was badly injured in a horseback riding accident. As I healed, I thought about all the good horses I've known, and I vowed to come back to riding, guns blazing. As I had to teach myself to walk again, my dream took some time to realize (2015). But once I'd made the decision to ride again, all sorts of new dreams and plans opened up for me. I knew I had a memoir in my hands!

Care and consideration of others

Claire talked about not wanting to "step on people's toes" with her first memoir, *The Outport People*, and so she changed some people's names, to guard their privacy – and, as importantly, to protect herself and her husband, writers of all things, who were also "from away," and would always be treated with some mild suspicion in the Newfoundland community in which they found themselves. Claire's decision on this was immediate and sound. Trust yourself to do the same, should circumstances warrant it.

For your memoir:

There's no sidestepping the matter – when you write about your view of a particular time or place, others will disagree with your memories, or, possibly, feel hurt and misrepresented by your descriptions of them. To expand on the point above – trust yourself to say and do what is needed, and no more.

One strategy I found useful with my first memoir, *Coastal Lives*, was to reread the sections that pertained to certain people – and pretend I was that person. I also read the sections aloud. I removed a lot of unnecessary adjectives, and even "happy talk," by which I mean burbling on about something that truly isn't germane to the story. When I got to the nitty-gritty of some descriptions, I would ask myself if anything could be softened, or better yet simplified, and still make the point or points I wanted to make? Often, it could.

Please don't misunderstand: if your writing style has a bit of an edge to it – or a lot of an edge – then the way you write about everything will be different from other people who are gentler. Edge can also be stylish – as can very contained and precise – and should never be modified just to sound "nicer," or more palatable. People even trust and enjoy edgy; it's the anti people-pleaser, seeking mostly to please itself, in all the good creative ways (e.g. *Let's Pretend this Never Happened*, by Jenny Lawson). Readers are smart. They know a writer's style is only one aspect of a person's character.

Back to soft pedal. I am not talking about being dishonest or dodging hard truths or realities. I am always talking about considered choice. In the end, you will write the story that's in your heart and head, and accept whatever consequences come along. My further advice would be not to let harsh descriptions of others distract the reader from the main story. You may also lose the reader's trust by being constantly critical and judging.

Chapter Five
How do we write memoirs?

I Structure

The structure of memoirs is open-ended – whatever you want, whatever suits you best to use. Use your imagination. Here are a few examples.

Chronological: When in doubt, write a beginning, middle, and end, using a chronological structure. This often works well for complicated or time sensitive stories, such as Diane Schoemperlen's *This Is Not My Life*.

Non-chronological: While a popular choice, you have to be careful not to lose your reader as you bound hither and yon – and you still need a plot, or main narrative. This choice also lends itself to using past and present tenses, and/or a mix of narrative and essays, or other genres.

Thematical: Many memoirs are thematical: cuisine or food-related; travelling; a love story; our forebears' histories; addictions; difficult childhoods – and so on. You can, of course, have several or many themes – the trick is to have them mesh well (not to worry, several rewrites will take care of this). Again, your central story should lead the way; it is the path beneath the writer's feet. Themes enfold the story, like the sky above, and the rivers beneath the earth, waiting to be "daylighted."

Mixed genre: The sky is the limit. You can mix photographs and prose; poetry and essays; narrative and maps; prose and ink drawings or collage. You can even use previously published work, such as personal essays or even articles.

"Book-ends": You know your beginning and end, and you let the middle work itself out as you write.

Dual-focus: The stories of two people at once, such a Holocaust survivors, perhaps a husband and wife, or sisters and brothers, or friends, who experienced the same shared story or chapter of a life. You can even have a multi-point-of-view memoir.

Point of view: first-person (I); second-person (you); third-person (he/she). First-person is recommended for your own memoir. Second-person is wearisome. Third person works well for fictionalized memoirs, and, sometimes, when writing a memoir for someone else.

Writing for someone else: This deserves more than a casual mention. Writing professionals are often approached by prominent people from every field of endeavour to help them write a memoir. The writer, or "ghostwriter" as they are often called, does all the work for this, and is paid by previously arranged contract. Ordinarily, the writer amasses hundreds of hours of taped conversations and works with these to create the book. Some ghostwriters, such as Lawrence Hill and Lawrence Scanlan, are very conscientious, and will check on each and every paragraph in the book with the main player to ensure it sounds like their voice. The best of these memoirs are a treat to read, as they are carefully, even beautifully, constructed and the reader is confident in the veracity of the voice.

Tenses: Past; present; or start in the present, change to the past, or start in the past, change to the present. Again, keep that narrative strong. Readers don't like to turn in circles too much, no matter how lovely the writing may be. *Story* is what we want. Turn to the past when it's needed to explain later events.

Inciting incidents: Start your memoir with an inciting incident, which is an episode, plot point, or event that hooks the reader into the story. This particular moment is when an event thrusts the protagonist into the main action of the story.

Here are some examples of inciting incidents:

- the sudden and shocking death of a mother, father, or family member on their birthday
- the day you got fired from work and then discover your spouse has left you
- you overcome your fear of swimming in deep waters – and you see a shark fin coming towards you

This is how Robert McKee, author of *Story: Substance, Structure, Style, and the Principles of Screenwriting*, describes the device: "The inciting incident radically upsets the balance of forces in your protagonist's life." An easy way to think of it is that prior to the inciting incident, you had been living a normal life, but afterwards, nothing is ever the same again.

Fictional: Remember, memoirs can also be fictional. Many writers chronicle the lives of family they know, a grandparent, perhaps – or, sometimes, a relative they've never met, such as Sally Armstrong's memoir for a long-deceased relative, *The Nine Lives of Charlotte Taylor*. Another well-regarded fictionalized memoir, written in post-modern style involving aspects of magic realism, is *Running in the Family*, by Michael Ondaatje. The story deals with his family, and his return to his native island of Sri Lanka, also called Ceylon, in the late 1970s.

Letters: This can work well with either an entire collection of letters (one person's, or the collected correspondence of two people, or even an entire family), or just a few letters scattered within the main narrative. Nowadays, e-mail correspondences can be voluminous and just as compelling as paper letters. These can and have been called "epistolary memoir" (e.g. *Dear Boy: An Epistolary Memoir*, by Heather Weber).

Non-paper: Memoirs don't have to be stories on paper. They can be film or videos, or collections of photographs and letters.

For your memoir:

Take six memoirs out from the library and read them, one after another.

1. Make brief notes as you read, as to which book you liked, and why.
2. For each book, condense the "likes" to a list of qualities, such as style, setting, humour, language, pacing, and so on.
3. Then number the qualities from one to ten, to indicate which is most important to you.
4. Next, consider the title. Did the book live up to what the title indicated?
5. Last, consider the Table of Contents and chapter titles. Can you see a way forward for your own memoir, by considering the structure of these memoirs?

II Elements of Storytelling

There are many elements of storytelling, depending on the particular type of story being told, and the person who is telling it, but among the common elements are:

1. Setting
2. Characters
3. Plot/Action
4. Conflict
5. Themes
6. Narrative Arc

Exercise I: For the first five elements, write at least a paragraph that pertains to your potential memoir.

III Identifying and Working with Themes

This is a large part of the magic of writing. Themes resonate long after you've finished a book. Themes are (mostly) not apparent until you finish a work. Then they appear like threads in a dress or a shirt. They give your work colour and interest. Themes in memoir/literature include:

Good vs evil (*Night*, by Elie Weisel)

Coming of Age = classic (*Coming of Age in Mississippi*, by Anne Moody)

Power and Corruption (*The Inheritance of Shame*, by Peter Gajdics)

Survival (*Acid for Children: A Memoir*, by Flea)

Courage and Wisdom (*The Honey Bus: A Memoir of Loss, Courage, and a Girl Saved by Bees*, by Meredith May)

Prejudice (*I Know Why the Caged Bird Sings*, by Maya Angelou)

Love and Loss (*Elegy for Iris*, by John Bayley)

Death and Loss (*The Year of Magical Thinking*, by Joan Didion)

Individual vs Society (*It's What I Do: A Photographer's Life of Love and War*, by Lynsey Addario)

Appearance vs Reality (*Run, Hide, Repeat: A Memoir of a Fugitive Childhood,* by Pauline Dakin)

"The Outsider"

Most of us think of ourselves as outsiders of some sort. It might be in our community, country, families, places of work, or schools. Other things that may set us apart from the mainstream society include: language; culture; health and mobility; religion; identity and immigration; character; class issues; gender and orientation issues; occupier vs occupied territory; incarcerated vs free; young vs senior or infirm; and guild vs non-guild.

Exercise II: Write a page about your experience of being an outsider.

The Happy Outsider

Being an outsider isn't necessarily a negative experience. When we travel to a new country, we are, in many ways, outsiders – and yet we can have splendid, pleasantly isolated times. If we are a new student at a school, we are certainly an outsider. But in this instance, too, we can enjoy our separation from "the pack," and the lack of drama and complexity this can mean.

Exercise III: Write a page about being a happy, or at least an intrigued, outsider.

IV Narrative Arc

Don't allow yourself to be intimidated by the terms "arc," "story arc," or "narrative arc," all of which refer to the chronological construction of plot in a novel or story. It is simply the ups and downs of the tale.

As you can see, a narrative arc typically looks something like a hill, with one side steeper than the other. It has the following components: exposition, rising action, climax, falling action (also known as "denouement"), and resolution.

Story arc

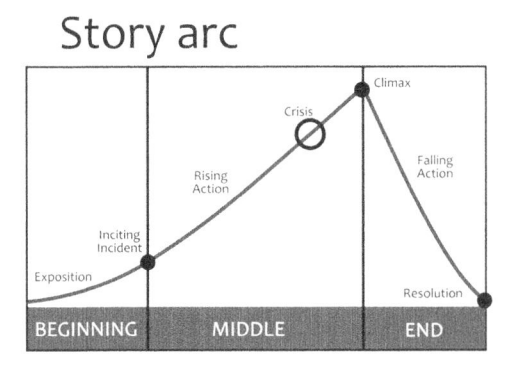

Design by D. J. Saulnier

Let's have a closer look at those five classic elements.

Exposition: This is when you first grasp the reader's hand and pull him into your story. Most readers don't want to be dropped into the middle of a chronicle with no clue about where they are, or who they are seeing, moving about their lives. The exposition offers background information to ease the reader along. Here, they meet the main character or characters. That takes care of the "who." Said people or animals live in certain places, circumstances, and time period, and that takes care of the "where" and "when."

Rising action: Like bread rising, this is when conflict begins to grow. Often, a writer will use an "inciting incident" to get that loaf plumped up. This is the triggering event that puts the main events of the story in motion. At this point your reader should be having some *aha* moments as to the story you are telling them. The driving pace now has the reader engaged, or committed.

Climax: That loaf can't get any bigger. Your reader may even wonder if you added so much yeast that your floury creation is about to burst. If you've been smart enough to add different subplots and characters, they'll be converging at this point. Typically, the climax requires the main character – you, in the case of memoir – to face hard truths or to make a life-changing choice.

Falling action: At last, time to eat the baguette. This component could also be called consequences or aftermath, as it covers the time after our heroine's decision. As the action falls off, the conflict gives way to resolution. This is also the time to tie up loose ends, and when all the heightened emotions begin to simmer down.

Resolution: -30- as the journalists say. It means "the end." You may choose a happy ending or you may choose a sad or ambiguous one. Any old way, your reader knows the story has finished. He's also seen how you and other characters have changed internally and sometimes externally, and how the world may have changed, as well.

Exercise IV: Using the template provided, can you draw a possible story arc for your own memoir?

Conversation with Lawrence Hill, author of *Black Berry, Sweet Juice*

Lawrence Hill is a professor of creative writing at the University of Guelph. He is the author of ten books, including *The Illegal, The Book of Negroes, Any Known Blood,* and *Black Berry, Sweet Juice: On Being Black and White in Canada.* He is the winner of various awards, including The Commonwealth Writers' Prize, and two-time winner of CBC Radio's Canada Reads. Hill delivered the Canada-wide 2013 Massey Lectures, based on his non-fiction book *Blood: The Stuff of Life.* He co-wrote the adaptation for the six-part television miniseries *The Book of Negroes,* which attracted millions of viewers and won eleven Canadian Screen Awards.

The recipient of ten honorary doctorates from Canadian universities, as well as the 2017 Canada Council for the Arts Molson Prize, Hill served as chair of the jury of the 2016 Scotiabank Giller Prize. He is a volunteer with Book Clubs for Inmates and the Black Loyalist Heritage Society, and is an honorary patron of Crossroads International, for which he has volunteered for forty years and with which he has travelled to Niger, Cameroon, Mali, and Swaziland.

A 2018 Berton House resident in Dawson City, he is working on a new novel about the African-American soldiers who helped build the Alaska Highway in northern British Columbia and Yukon in 1942-43. He is a Member of the Order of Canada, has been inducted into Canada's Walk of Fame, and in 2019 was named a Canada Library and Archives Scholar. He lives in Hamilton, Ontario, and in Woody Point, Newfoundland.

SIMMINS: I'm interested in how you came to your memoir and what the motivation behind that was. I loved the structure of *Black Berry, Sweet Juice*, beginning with personal stories and then sharing interviews with Canadians of black and white parentage, and their experiences of growing up and their thoughts on racial identity.

HILL: Thank you. I wasn't looking to tell the story of my life up to that point of writing. I just wanted to meditate on one specific angle of my life: growing up in a family that was black and white and coming to terms with a sense of mixed racial identity.

SIMMINS: Yes, this theme guided the book well.

HILL: At the time that I was writing it, there wasn't yet a single-authored book in Canada that examined how black and white identity is formed. Americans had been writing about it, but I felt that conditions were quite different in Canada and that it merited its own book. So I was motivated by the need to express myself and to work through my own identity evolution as a child, adolescent, and young man, but also I wanted to make a mark on Canada and to offer something that hadn't been written before.

SIMMINS: That strikes me as fabulous motivation. To think that you were on ground that was new for Canadians would really be exciting.

HILL: I don't normally think of writing for a specific audience. However, with *Black Berry, Sweet Juice*, there was something unusual in play. I hoped that I would attract some readers of mixed race – people who might find an extra reason to meditate on the book and to find in it something that they perhaps hadn't seen before in print.

SIMMINS: I don't believe I've had another memoirist speak to the subject of motivation and audience. I'm glad you are addressing that idea, as though the audience was pulling you on in a way, in terms of your motivation and wanting to do the book in the most thorough and interesting way you could.

HILL: Because of my own experiences, I feel deeply about racial identity and how it is construed. What does racial identity mean? How is it formed? Who gets to be what, and how might self-perception be challenged by others? But traditionally, Canadians have been loath to examine this subject.

Many of us feel that it's a dirty question and if we just don't talk about it, we're not as bad as those nasty Americans who've done so many dastardly things. I'm saying that playfully, because I don't believe Americans to be uniformly nasty and dastardly. Canadians tend to think that we're superior and if we just don't think about these things, then we're cleaner in a way. And so I wanted to smash that to smithereens and go to a place that was *verboten*: who are you, how do you see yourself, and how did you come to be seen by others?

SIMMINS: If you're going into areas that are considered *verboten*, did you find that you were apprehensive at all?

HILL: Yes, I was apprehensive. Although I found certain issues interesting, I worried that others might find them trivial, superficial, or unimportant. For example: how do people of mixed race deal with their hair.

SIMMINS: I was just reviewing that. It was a new subject for me.

HILL: I worried that people would think, people are being shot and put in jail and segregated, so who cares about their hair? When I did write that chapter about my own hair and about other people's experiences around hair and identity, it turned out to be the most popular chapter in the book.

SIMMINS: You must have loved how that turned out. I really enjoyed that chapter, too. One thing I must tell you – when you did the chapter on 'Where do you really come from?' I couldn't stop talking about that for days. I think my husband, Don, said, 'You know, honey, I get the point,' but I was absolutely fascinated by that observation of yours. Because it's something everyone seems to do in this country. I do it, and everybody I know does it. We know we're being chatty, you know, fun Canadians by saying, 'Oh, well, tell me about where you really come from, who you really are.' And maybe that's what we feel inside, that we're just being innocent and friendly, saying that to someone of colour, or a visible minority, but it's just so wrong. You rocked my boat on that one.

HILL: Thank you.

SIMMINS: Yes, that was very, very special. Just to return to an earlier point, I've had a number of American friends tell me this, and I don't know quite how to feel about it, but they basically say that racism that they've encountered, being American-born, that the racism they have encountered in the States is so out front and unequivocal. Yet they come to Canada and they find that Canadians are much more sly and much more hidden about it, but it's there, you know, as bountifully as anywhere else. I don't know if that was ever your experience because of course you have Canadian and American family. Do you have any response to that?

HILL: I've found that Canadians tend to be more sneaky and reticent in terms of how they might talk about identity and how they might express racist views. It might be, 'Sorry, that job's not available anymore,' even though it's not really been taken but the person just doesn't say that we're not going to rent to a black person, or give the job to a black person. That seems to be par for the course.

SIMMINS: Can you tell me how your background in journalism served you when you came to write this memoir?

HILL: First of all, I learned as a journalist how to interview people. So I didn't feel shy conducting interviews and that was helpful because I had to ask all sorts of intimate questions, such as what were your dating preferences and were your dating preferences affected by notions of racial identity? Or how about your hair, or when did you first start becoming aware of who you were racially, when was your first perception of race for yourself or for others and when did you first start to ask questions about your own racial identity? It takes a certain kind of boldness to ask that kind of stuff. You have to establish a trusting relationship and you also have to be kind and unthreatening. I felt that having been a journalist helped me approach people confidently, but also with kindness and in a way that would seem disarming.

SIMMINS: Yes, and I presume you told them that you did have this background, and did that develop a little extra trust too?

HILL: Absolutely. Being a journalist helped me understand how to organize the story. I didn't want to write a memoir that was only about me. Perhaps deep down I didn't feel that I was important enough to write about me and me alone. And so to address that insecurity, I chose to interview other people and then to work their observations and their life experiences into the book. It helped broaden the scope of the writing and it made me feel more confident that I was writing something valid because I was exploring the experiences of other people who also had one black and one white parent.

SIMMINS: Yes, the broader range was key, I think, to the book's success. I was interested, too, that you interviewed your own siblings and they were kind enough to come right in on the project with you. In a way, you're almost standing with them. Did you feel supported in their support of your book?

HILL: Oh, 100 percent. Yeah, they were great. It was wonderful. They were very supportive.

SIMMINS: Were you surprised by anything they said?

HILL: Well, you know, some of the things that my brother experienced weren't quite the same as the things I experienced. We have the same father, but that didn't mean our father acted the same way toward each of us.

SIMMINS: Tell me more.

HILL: Dan was older, so he bore more of the brunt of aggressive parenting, even in terms of trying to shape racial identity. [Singer/songwriter Dan Hill is Lawrence Hill's older brother.] So I was surprised by how much more aggressive our father was in saying things and acting in ways that were racially demeaning toward my brother. He made us both wear stocking caps in a ridiculous attempt to straighten our hair at night, but Dan got a lot more of that sort of thing.

SIMMINS: Yes, I just reread that part and was uncomfortable with that, definitely.

So there was a space that you filled by writing that memoir of yours. The book was well received and so many people responded to it in a wonderful way, in a big wonderful way. What did you learn about yourself by completing that book?

HILL: It was the first time that I gave myself permission to meditate in a happily obsessive way about who I am and how I have come to form my own identity. It's one thing to imagine a fictional, mixed-race character – I'd done that before, in a novel called *Any Known Blood* – but it's quite another to lie back on the operating table and say, 'Here, everybody, examine me.'

I discovered in writing that I actually felt part of a broader, mixed-race community. And before writing that book, I thought of myself sometimes as black or sometimes as white but coming from a mixed-race background, but I never actually sought out a mixed-race community before. I'd never said I'm going to go boldly and confidently introduce myself to dozens of strangers who are of mixed race like me, and start asking a bunch of questions and form a bond with them. Then after asking a bunch of questions I'd then write about them and feel that I was communing with them. And I'd never really intuited a sense of mixed-race community before writing the book, but I did begin to acquire that sense of community in the course of researching it and writing it.

It's not like Toronto, where I was living at the time, had a mixed-race community. I mean, you know how it is: people are just spread out everywhere but I still felt a sense of community in Canada and I hadn't really sensed that before in that particular regard. So I felt a kind of a kinship with people of mixed race, which I hadn't felt before. So that, I guess, is what emerged from the process of researching and writing the book. Because of all the people the book introduced me to.

SIMMINS: I want to dig a little deeper on this subject. If you now feel kinship to a particular group or you feel a sense of community where you hadn't necessarily felt one before, what are the other, surrounding gifts you walked away with?

HILL: One of the things I walked away with was friendship. Several people that I'd never known before who are now – that book came out eighteen years ago – who are now my friends.

SIMMINS: What a huge gift that is.

HILL: So that book has given me a whole lot in terms of emotional sustenance, one of the biggest forms of it being new friendship.

SIMMINS: That's great. And that was what I was hoping you'd say, in terms of the aftermath of the memoir. It's been eighteen years since it came out, but how wonderful that you can say it wasn't short-term friendships that were created, but long-term, durable friendships.

During the course of writing this book, I've basically chosen favourites from my memoir library, which just gets bigger and bigger. I started off talking to Linden MacIntyre. One of the things that came out of that conversation that I've just been so interested in and now ask of each of the writers I talk to is the writer's journey they had, in coming to memoir. You are a fiction writer and a non-fiction writer and when I spoke to Linden he basically suggested to me that he would not have come to fiction as strongly as he did without having the experience of memoir first. I found that fascinating. Can you give the timeline with your fiction and non-fiction writing? You started first with fiction, did you not?

HILL: Yes, and so for me it's the opposite of Linden. I would never have come to that memoir as strongly or as vigorously if I didn't have the novel writing background first because that's what taught me about drama and story. Even though the details are true, I tried to work on narrative and on story development.

SIMMINS: Now isn't that interesting – it's the direct opposite experience, isn't it?

HILL: I tried to tell stories that would have an arc to them. It helped me to be a novelist first, and to understand how to locate memoir in story.

SIMMINS: I think this will be an excellent point to drive home for writers who want to write a memoir. Narrative, story, and arc, these are key to a good memoir.

With Linden, I thought it was interesting, because he was thinking to himself that he sure as hell wasn't going to bare his soul or anything embarrassing like that – that was not the journalist's way. And of course he came to it and he bared his soul like crazy; there was no other way to do it. Then, when it came time to do fiction, he told me that he'd learned from the memoir that you can't write with part of your heart hidden or anything else. If you're going to be writing these books you can't hide, you can't. The heart has got to be wide open. He felt very strongly that the memoir had given him that first.

Now you're saying almost the direct opposite – that when you sat down with arc first in your mind to create a novel that you were thinking about pacing and drama and all the rest of it. That for you, it was crucial to write the fiction before you wrote the memoir. And both experiences are 100 percent valid and true.

HILL: Both of them make perfect sense.

SIMMINS: Onto something a little different. *The Deserter's Tale*, published in 2007, is the memoir of an Oklahoma-born soldier by the name of Joshua Key. He was deployed to Iraq where he describes the horrific conditions the Iraqi civilians were subjected to, along with his forced participation in raids on accused terrorists whom he believed were innocent. He ultimately sought asylum in Canada. Did you ghost-write this memoir?

HILL: Yes, I wrote every word.

SIMMINS: Can you tell me about that experience?

HILL: Well, it's funny. I didn't count that as a memoir because I was writing about somebody else. On the cover it says, 'By Joshua Key, with Lawrence Hill,' so my role was open and acknowledged. It's Joshua's story, but I was the writer so I had to collect his story through interviews and then find a way to find his voice and to tell it and to keep checking with him, to make sure that every paragraph was right and rang true to him. I read every paragraph aloud to him on the phone. He was still suffering from Post Traumatic Stress Disorder and the easiest way to have an immediate conversation that held his attention tightly was to talk, as opposed to have him read something. And because we weren't together very much – we only got together about three times – in terms of reading things back to him, the talking was done on the phone.

SIMMINS: I'm lost in admiration for the writers who do this and do it well.

HILL: I loved writing that book; it was fascinating.

SIMMINS: There's something else I'd like to circle back to, as well. We are talking, you and I, about your memoir from eighteen years ago and you have said things along the lines of, well, I didn't want it to all be about me, so I took my journalist's background and interviewed others and entered into new communities that I hadn't had contact with before and so on. All of which leads me to ask – it is eighteen years later, you have had a fabulous eighteen years, one writing and filmmaking triumph after another, sensationally busy and receiving marvelous acknowledgements for all this work – do you think there might be another memoir?

HILL: I don't think so. I have zero desire to write another memoir. I'd rather keep writing fiction. It's a lot safer emotionally to make up a story than to expose yourself in a memoir. I'm proud of the memoir and of the fact that people still come up to me today and talk about it. But my heart is with fiction.

SIMMINS: And you can't deny the writer's heart.

HILL: That doesn't mean that my heart was not with *Black Berry, Sweet Juice* when I wrote it, it was, but my heart has moved on.

SIMMINS: I believe it was Annie Dillard who said that even during the course of the time it takes to write a memoir, the person who started it and the person who finished it are very different people. That really resonated for me. So if we're talking about a period of eighteen years passing between when your memoir was done and your life now, we're talking about two different writers.

HILL: The other thing is that long ago I came to easy terms with my own racial identity. So I don't feel I have any more to say or work to do.

SIMMINS: Yes, I see. Although, when it comes to serial memoirists – and you're speaking to one – the subject or focus of different memoirs is often very, very different. But there might have been another area of your life that had come to the forefront of interest for you. Although it doesn't sound like this at the moment.

HILL: No, not right now, but who knows what's around the corner? I won't say never, I'll just say it's not part of my five-year plan.

SIMMINS: Sure, sure. Did you find that when you had decided on your structure of *Black Berry, Sweet Juice* that you were away and running?

HILL: Well, that's interesting. I guess that depends on what 'away and running' really means.

SIMMINS: At some point, the memoir was simply an idea. You're poking at it and considering the parameters, and thinking, Okay, how am I going to get started on this? I guess I'm interested in the moment when you did decide on the structure. After that, did you feel that you could move along at a very steady workman-like pace?

HILL: It didn't work like that for me. I didn't decide on a structure and then fill out the pages of the blueprint. I just started writing and started exploring as I went, and the structure emerged after I'd written about two hundred pages.

I started writing and coming upon a bunch of different themes and essays and bits and bits of journalism and then I started to ask myself how I could stitch it all together. So the writing itself sort of drove the elaboration of the structure, as opposed to the structure fitting into place and then the writing following.

It's not a moral principle. It's just how I work, and how I discover my material. I write novels like that, too.

SIMMINS: Interesting. Across the board, then.

HILL: Yes. I just start writing and I begin to see what is revealing itself to me. My first drafts are messy because I haven't got it all figured out yet. I don't know how it will all hang together. Writing is my way of discovering what I'm trying to say.

SIMMINS: This should be very reassuring to somebody who's obviously not as experienced a writer as you are, when they first start a project. If they make one hell of a mess, just carry on with it. To have someone such as yourself say, 'Don't sweat it, that first draft is pretty messy, it won't ever be all tidy and straightforward, but from it, you get the roadmap to wherever you're going to.'

HILL: Yes, that's very true.

SIMMINS: It's almost a skill to trust yourself like that, not to fuss but to just jump in, make a mess, scribble and cross out and put arrows backwards and arrows forward and simply trust in your own creative energy.

HILL: It's called blind faith. And you do have to trust that you'll find your way. I never tell anybody else how to write, but it's how I like to write. And when I do try to approach it more intellectually by scratching my chin at the kitchen table, I never come up with anything that I end up using. I never have and I probably never will.

SIMMINS: It's as though that first draft that is so messy and almost violent in a way is more piped in to your psyche than your intellect, right into the maelstrom of the creative process.

HILL: You said it perfectly. I've never quite said it that well but that's exactly true.

SIMMINS: I think I have a foot in either camp when it comes to messy and tidy drafts. I do a bit of the messy and then quite a bit of the fussing on the other side and the fussing never serves me well. I'm glad you've told me about the way you write. I think I'll give myself more permission to take the short-cut right down into the psyche.

HILL: I do a lot of fussing, but that's on the second or third or fourth or fifth draft.

SIMMINS: Oh, yeah, that's the fun part, rewriting, but really, in some ways, the hardest part is giving yourself permission to create.

HILL: Yes, for me the first draft is always by far the hardest.

SIMMINS: I love the idea about the maelstrom that can be creativity. I'm certainly going to remind emerging writers who I talk to not to be so controlling, to really give themselves permission to create, whatever messy form that might take.

Lawrence Hill
Craft

Audience

When Lawrence Hill began his first and only (so far) memoir for himself, he had a very specific audience to whom, about whom, and for whom he was writing, the mixed race Canadian. Knowing this made his writing task so much easier. He never once had to scratch his head and think, Yes, but will 'they' (the mystical, mythical they, comprising comprising any writer's reading audience) be interested in this, in reference to the particular subject I am focusing on? He, a mixed-race Canadian, was interested in frank discourse about a wide range of subjects related to race, culture, and identity, and he was pretty sure his self-same audience and his broader reading audience would be, too.

There is no theatre production without an audience. And in the same way, no book can be fully enjoyed without an audience, or reader.

Acknowledging your audience, writing directly to them, may be one of the best decisions you make about your memoir. Your writing will sound authentic and personal. You will know how to do it. Is your reading audience:

- yourself?
- the general public?
- a specialized group?
- your whole family?
- adults or children?
- an "Audrey" figure?

Once you know for whom you are writing, your story will start to fall into place. Your language might be profane – or not. You may focus on the milder parts of your life – or the harder ones. You may choose to include some details and not others. You can see the face, and you know the heart of the person you are writing for. They will help you guide and finish your story.

For your memoir:

Try a simple exercise. Put a photograph or illustration on your desk that represents the individual or community you believe may be your intended audience for your memoir. Write a paragraph or two, no holds barred, to that person or those people. Write as though no one in the world but them could understand your stories. Now, read it back to yourself, aloud. Does it ring true? Do you feel excited and ready to write more – or a bit lost, and maybe even embarrassed and self-censored? If the latter, then change the photo or illustration and try again, with a slightly different but related subject.

When you feel safe and limber and motivated, you are writing to the right audience. (This is such an important aspect for all writing, memoir very much included, that the next chapter will contain more information on the subject.)

The practice of writing, and structure

I was fascinated to hear Hill say, in relation to the practice of writing and structure, that "the writing itself drove the elaboration of the structure, as opposed to the structure fitting into place and then the writing following."

This is the way writing works for Hill. He's in the minority – and in my own more modest realm, I am with him in that group. I do like to lean into a single, strong narrative line, so perhaps my heart and psyche know where to start, which is always helpful. But thereafter, I am dashing and darting and digressing, all the while taking my reader very firmly by the hand, alongside. If they squeak that they are getting lost, or I feel that I am, I just look around for that narrative line, and pounce back on it. It's like the train that rides the tracks of the story.

For your memoir:

Like Hill, you may be interested in writing about a single, central aspect of your life. Perhaps you are a para-athlete, preparing for the Olympics, or perhaps you grew up with three moms, and no dads. Maybe you were raised as a single child – and only just found out that not only were you adopted as an infant, but you also have a twin brother. In a heartbeat, the world is completely different. Is this an A to B chronological story, or will you need to write the passionate stream of the story first, background mixing with current day, without worrying yourself about what happened when?

The short answer to this is … see what happens. If, having decided on an aspect or a period of your life you wish to write about, you then sit down at your desk and take off like a rocket, I'd say not to worry about an outline. If, on the other hand, you feel stuck and awkward, sketch out an outline and see if that frees you to get started. I'd offer the same advice if you get stuck midway, or even towards the end. What is the story you really want to recount? If you, that para-equestrian, actually want to compete on the *Great Canadian Baking Show*, but three-quarters of the way along, your story remains stuck in the barn, while you yearn for the kitchen, you're going to have to decide on the most important story, and change your structure.

The good news is … story always comes first. So no matter how you get to a completed memoir, ride the story train first.

Unexpected gifts

An unexpected gift to Hill when he wrote his memoir was the creation of several significant and lasting friendships. Now as this was the first time I'd heard of that happening to a memoirist (though, really, why not?), I was intrigued. How lovely!

My larger point to you would be that you simply can't predict what gifts can come to your life, after having written a memoir. Friendship, peace, clarity, healing, family rifts closed, love renewed, love expanded, new life paths chosen, and much else. We don't write in expectation of these miracles, because memoirs have their own mysterious ways and paths, and timing, but nor do we close our eyes and turn away if gifts do arrive in our lives.

For your memoir:

What is the best gift that memoir could give you? Quickly, without second-guessing, write a list of ten gifts you'd love to receive by completing a memoir. Choose one from the list. Write that one word on a recipe file card. If you wish, cover the card with stars and stickers, notes of music, or colourful doodles, anything that catches your eye and makes you smile. Keep the card and the photo or illustration of the person or persons in your "audience," the ones for whom you are writing. May as well open the door to unexpected gifts. You never know ...

Chapter Six
Life Before and After Memoir

Life before and after having written a memoir depends on so many factors. Perhaps most important of all is the writer's motivation. And so, if you are an ambitious professional writer looking to add to your *oeuvre*, or if you are a young or middle-aged man or woman keen to share a remarkable time in your life, or if you are a determined ninety-year-old man who has finally self-published his "campfire stories" for his six grandchildren, you'll likely feel the same degree of satisfaction and pride in the final product. As these two emotions can't come often enough to most of our lives, put pen to paper, says I.

On a personal note, I was dithering just prior to the publication of my first memoir, worried about it on every level you can think of. As an artist and a professional, I worried if it was "good enough." If not, would I be sliced and diced in reviews? As a gentle woman in a tough old world, and as a home-loving introvert, I felt alarmingly exposed and wondered if I'd thrown all sense of safety and self-preservation out the door. As a human being who enjoys connection with others, I hoped other human beings would want to read the book and find some inspiration in the choices I made, or even small wisdoms, as they dealt with some of the universal passages and losses I did at the middle point of my life. And, of course, being the youngest child and a major goofball, I prayed they'd laugh out loud, often, from the deepest regions of their bellies.

Mostly I wanted my heart to stop thumping so erratically and return to its regular beat.

Which, of course, it did – but after more time than I am willing to tell you. Seriously, I have my own anxious ways at times, so my period of adjustment after my memoirs were published was likely longer than yours will be. Do not use this as an excuse not to write! You'll be just fine. Better than fine.

But even still, life is different after memoir. It is an artistic and emotional journey to write a book of any kind, let alone an honest, considered life story. Along with your motivations, you will have their hairy cousin in your midst, a.k.a., expectations. These, too, will vary in number and intensity, according to the makeup and character of the writer. In brief, I'd say, and with respect and caring, a memoir isn't establishing world peace or discovering a cure for cancer. It might not necessarily even be one of the best things that ever happens to you. Those are more likely to be your family and friends, and for so many of us, our animal families. They are certainly your good health, which includes mind, body, and spirit, and your adventures and personal delights in this world.

For the majority of us, who are not Michelle Obama or David Sedaris, memoirists who sell millions of books and make a corresponding income in return, our lives will not change significantly after we have a book with our name on the front cover. Not richer, not better known, not breaking new records for Instagram debuts, or crowned a new Twitter king or queen.

But you will be an author, and you will feel different inside. Good different. Changed different. A bit more ... well, there. You have sat down with your history, your good, bad, and terrible memories, and looked for themes, patterns, and yes, sense, and beauty, and then written a story. You've striven to create art – something that touches the reader on many levels, in many ways. You have also, I hope, looked for ways to stitch your stories together with the stories of the wider world.

Tell me a story, I could say to you, *tell me your story*. And now, you could.

Conversation with Diane Schoemperlen, author of *This is Not My Life: A Memoir of Love, Prison, and Other Complications*

Born and raised in Thunder Bay, Ontario, Diane Schoemperlen is the author of fourteen books and winner of the 1998 Governor General's Award for English Fiction for *Forms of Devotion: Stories and Pictures*. Her books have been published in the United States, the United Kingdom, Germany, Sweden, France, Spain, Korea, and China.

In 2007, she received the Marian Engel Award from The Writers' Trust of Canada, given to an exemplary female writer in mid-career. In 2012, she was Writer-in-Residence at Queen's University in Kingston, Ontario, where she has lived since 1986. A *Toronto Star* review of her 2017 collection *First Things First: Early and Uncollected Stories* named her "one of our most interesting and iconoclastic writers." Diane is currently a mentor with the Humber School for Writers Correspondence Program. In January 2019, she was appointed to the board of directors of McGill-Queen's University Press.

Published in 2016, her book *This Is Not My Life: A Memoir of Love, Prison, and Other Complications* takes a close and candid look at her six-year relationship with a federal inmate serving a life sentence for second-degree murder. Her memoir was longlisted for the British Columbia National Book Award, shortlisted for the RBC Taylor Prize, and appeared on numerous "Best Books of the Year" lists, including *The Globe and Mail*, the *National Post*, *The Hill Times*, and the CBC. In 2017, Diane was the recipient of the Matt Cohen Award: In Celebration of a Writing Life from the Writers' Trust of Canada. In 2018, she was awarded the Molson Prize in Arts by the Canada Council for the Arts "in recognition of exceptional achievement and outstanding contribution to the cultural and intellectual heritage of Canada."

SIMMINS: You came to memoir after many years of writing fiction. How did you start your book?

SCHOEMPERLEN: I began by reading many reference books on how to write a memoir. One of these that still sticks out in my mind was called *The Art of Time in Memoir* by Sven Birkerts. He emphasized that writing a memoir chronologically was always a mistake, because it would be boring for the reader, and there would be no narrative arc. In fact, many of the books about writing memoir that I consulted agreed with him.

SIMMINS: That must have been discouraging.

SCHOEMPERLEN: Yes, it was, because I couldn't imagine how to tell this story any other way. It is a complex story and we had many different stages in our relationship. I felt the reader wouldn't be able to follow at all if in one scene there I was visiting Shane in prison, then in the next scene we were shopping together at Loblaws, and then in the scene after that he was back in prison, but this time it was a different prison. Much too confusing!

Another thing that kept coming up in these reference books was the idea of starting with what they called the 'initiating' or 'inciting incident.'

SIMMINS: Tell me more about that.

SCHOEMPERLEN: Generally speaking, this means starting with something that actually happened *later* in the story and then telling the story in a way that works back to that.

SIMMINS: A prologue could also serve in this way. But I am still curious why these authors of books on memoir were so intolerant of certain structures.

SCHOEMPERLEN: Not all of these books were completely prescriptive in that way but when I kept running into these ideas over and over again, it was very discouraging.

SIMMINS: It seems to me that with your readings and in part because you were coming to memoir for the first time after twelve works of short fiction, you wanted to find the best way forward. But did you not take a year in those first musings?

SCHOEMPERLEN: Yes, I spent a whole year trying to figure out how to do it. In addition to those reference books, I was also reading a lot of other people's memoirs because, to be honest, I had never been much of a memoir reader. Most of what I had read was fiction, either novels or short stories.

SIMMINS: Did you have a particular memoir that really you thought, Oh, sure, that's well done?

SCHOEMPERLEN: There were several that helped me figure out how I might write mine. Some of these were prison-related, but most were not. One of the most helpful was *Between Gods* by Alison Pick. In fact, I used a quote from her memoir at the beginning of the epilogue in mine. Although there is certainly no connection between the subject matter of our books, hers was very important to me, in helping me to discover how I could best tell this story.

SIMMINS: Motivation. I want to know your primary motivation for writing your memoir. I'm always interested in that spark, that moment when a person says, 'Oh, I need to write to about this.' So when was your spark?

SCHOEMPERLEN: I probably felt it all the way through the relationship. I am a writer, after all. What's a poor writer to do with a story like this? How could I *not* write this story? I didn't keep a journal or take notes during the relationship, but the idea of possibly writing about it someday was definitely there in the back of my mind.

SIMMINS: But even still, there must have come a moment when you started thinking, Maybe I need to collect up some books, do my research to see how I might do this. So was there a particular moment that you just went *bing*, I'm going to do this now?

SCHOEMPERLEN: No, there wasn't a particular moment. It was more like a kind of sliding into it, I think. As a fiction writer, I knew I could've turned it into a pretty good novel.

SIMMINS: Indeed yes.

SCHOEMPERLEN: But I wanted to write it as a memoir partly because I felt this was an opportunity to educate Canadians about our own prison system. Like most people, what I thought I knew about it came from American movies and TV. As I discovered, our prison system is quite different. I wanted readers to know that what I was saying about our system was not fiction. Then, through no fault of my own, three weeks after Shane and I first met, the Harper government got in with their first minority. For the entire length of our relationship we watched their "Tough on Crime" agenda being put into place. I had quite a lot to say about that as well, none of it positive.

SIMMINS: How did you find the writing process?

SCHOEMPERLEN: I was quite deluded about the whole project at first. I was so sure I could do it. After all, I'd written all those other books, obviously I knew how to write a book, and in this case, I already knew the story. So part of me thought, Well, yeah, I got this. I know how to do this. How hard could it be? As it turned out, it could be hard, very hard, extremely hard.

SIMMINS: Was that good or bad?

SCHOEMPERLEN: I suppose it was a good thing because maybe if I'd known beforehand how hard it was going to be, I might not have tried to write it at all. Who knows, right?

SIMMINS: I think it'll be reassuring for readers of *Conversations and Craft* to realize that even accomplished writers can struggle with the memoir writing process. But your struggles and your ultimate victory are their gems of wisdom. Let's return to structure. You ultimately decided on chronological, correct?

SCHOEMPERLEN: Yes, and it did work for me, despite all those reference books advising against it. One of the comments that I've had the most about this book, and which I absolutely love, is, *I couldn't put it down.*

SIMMINS: Very nice! And I agree.

SCHOEMPERLEN: I think this has something to do with the chronological structure. It just keeps going forward. I think that's part of what makes people feel like they can't put it down.

SIMMINS: Yes, that, and your fabulous pacing and your beautiful prose.

SCHOEMPERLEN: Thank you. But as far as that forward momentum goes – we've all had that experience of reading a book where we just keep going and going because we can't put it down. It thrills me no end when people say that. It's my favourite compliment. Nobody's ever said that about any of my other books!

SIMMINS: No wonder you cherish it! That's good for me to remember as a teacher, too. People say, 'What's the particular benefit of chronological?' And I can say, 'That it can give you a nice galloping pace.'

SCHOEMPERLEN: Yes. Even with sections in it where I write about things from the past – my past, his past, and so on – still the story is moving forward all the time. Just like real life.

SIMMINS: I've learned over the years that writers make the creative choices they are most comfortable with. I think it's got a lot to do with people's learning styles – divergent, convergent, accommodative, and assimilative, and how their brains operate.

SCHOEMPERLEN: That's a good point.

SIMMINS: I was interested by a comment you made about flouting some of the conventions that were, you know, being pressed upon you – as regards structure. Beyond this, what other conventions did you not follow that the instructional books pushed you to do?

SCHOEMPERLEN: There was the question of where to start, the matter of the inciting incident that I mentioned earlier. This just flummoxed me, because I could think of a dozen different places that might have been workable that way, but I could never decide which one would work the best. That's why it ended up by accident with that first sentence which is, by the way, my favourite sentence of any of the thousands and thousands of sentences I've ever written in my entire life.

SIMMINS: It is brilliant.

SCHOEMPERLEN: It was not written to be at the beginning of the book; it was actually written in the scene where Shane and I spend the night together for the first time at his mother's apartment. When I wrote that sentence I was so excited! I thought, Wow, this is truly the best sentence I've ever written! So I typed it up in an e-mail and sent it to my editor, Jennifer Lambert, and said, 'Look what I just wrote.' I thought, Poor Jennifer, how many writers is she working with and does she need all of us sending her one sentence at a time? But I did it anyway and she wrote back immediately with, in capital letters, 'Wow, what a great first sentence that would make!'

SIMMINS: May I read it aloud now?

SCHOEMPERLEN: Of course.

SIMMINS: 'It is safe to say that never once in my life had I dreamed of being in bed with a convicted killer, let alone one with his teeth in a margarine container in the kitchen, his mother in the next room, and the word HI! tattooed in tiny blue letters on his penis.'

If you got that sentence out of all the initial confusion about how to start and write your memoir, you can say thank you, don't you think?

SCHOEMPERLEN: Definitely. And if it hadn't been for Jennifer suggesting that it could be the first sentence, I don't think I would have had the idea or the nerve to do that. So I put it at the beginning, but then I left a blank because I still didn't know what to say after that. Then there was the first actual scene at the soup kitchen when Shane and I met, but for the longest time there was a large blank between the two. I didn't know how to get from one to the other. I also don't think I was trying to make that moment at his mother's apartment the inciting incident – I just truly loved that sentence!

SIMMINS: The thing about teaching memoir – any sort of writing, of course – is that there are always so many aspects one can teach. It would be fantastic to do a first-sentence or first-chapter workshop, getting people started like that. Wouldn't I just love the opportunity to say, 'Listen up, here's a first line you'll never forget. Diane Schoemperlen worked like a demon for that incredibly brilliant sentence. Then she left it there on the page, with nothing following it –' for how many weeks?

SCHOEMPERLEN: Months. I left it like that for months. I didn't want to put the whole scene of spending the night together at his mother's place at the beginning of the book because even that one scene, without chronology and explanation, wouldn't have had the same impact. He was still in prison at that time but, because of the way the Canadian prison system works, he had weekend passes once a month to go and stay with his mother. Without the background of why we, two people in our fifties, were having our first night together at his mother's apartment, it would've made little sense.

SIMMINS: Now I'm interested in the fear and apprehension that you must've felt at various times in various degrees of severity. How did you push through that?

SCHOEMPERLEN: Perhaps what I've called my self-delusion was a factor in that, and perhaps not thinking too far ahead was also part of it. I was just trying to get it written and not worrying about what was going to happen when it went out there into the world and the people who were in it would read it. Did you ever know the writer Alison Gordon?

SIMMINS: No, I did not.

SCHOEMPERLEN: She was a journalist who also wrote some wonderful mysteries and she was a lovely, lovely woman. Once we were both reading at the Prince Edward County Authors' Festival in Picton, Ontario, and we were commenting on how we'd been invited to this thing so far in advance. Alison, who had a really wicked sense of humour, said, 'I just said yes because I thought, Oh, what the fuck, I'll be dead by then.'

I often thought about that when I was writing my book. I could put the prospect of having finished the damn book so far in the future that I didn't have to think about it. Another bit of psychological trickery on my part, I suppose.

During the writing of this book, it seemed that the actual moment of having finished it was so far away that I wasn't worried. When I did occasionally feel anxious and fearful, I would think about what Alison Gordon said and I'd laugh out loud. I wish she was still alive so I could tell her how much she helped me. I could decide not to worry about it until the time came. I could tell myself, *Everything will work out fine.* Now, that's not something I normally say in my daily life – I'm a person always leaning more towards the side of catastrophe at any given moment!

SIMMINS: I'm curious, Diane, because there's such a complementary and enriching aspect of the factual information in the book. Did you at times of distress and worry think, Oh, well, I'll just disappear into this bit of research for a while. That'll bring my pulse down.

SCHOEMPERLEN: Yes, there was that. Originally, I had some idea that those more factual researched parts would be separate chapters alternating with the narrative. I decided that wasn't a good idea because it would keep stalling the story while I went off to talk about the prison system. At one point in the first draft, I had ten whole pages about all the acronyms used by the Correctional Service of Canada. They have the complete list of them on their website: at that time, the list included over 800 acronyms!

SIMMINS: Good Lord above.

SCHOEMPERLEN: Being a language person, I had so much fun with that list, but in the end, I realized that it might not be as interesting to everybody else as it was to me. So there are bits in the book about the acronyms, but only when they are actually part of the story. Generally speaking, I decided that I had to find ways to incorporate the factual information *into* the narrative rather than having it appear as separate chapters.

Now when I hear so many people telling me they couldn't put the book down, I think, Oh, I'll bet you would have put it down if I'd done it that way! Or they might just as well have skipped those chapters.

SIMMINS: That's true, and you certainly didn't want that.

SCHOEMPERLEN: I think it was a good decision on my part. I enjoyed doing the research because, as you say, it was a kind of respite and it was also a good lesson in deciding how much I could put in before it was just too much.

SIMMINS: One of the lovely things about memoir and the reason people consistently seek it out, I do believe, is they want to go somewhere with you, they want to go on a journey with you and if you can literally open doors that very, very few people get to open or might not even want to open but nonetheless are curious about, then that puts a bit of magic dust on a book.

SCHOEMPERLEN: I think that's true. I think that, in addition to the personal story being told in a memoir, readers also do want to learn things.

SIMMINS: Yes, and the trick with your book, which you did so well, is that you have to have complementary information in there, but it has to be deftly done, well placed, and you did that.

SCHOEMPERLEN: There were places where I knew I could go on and on, but I needed to remind myself I wasn't writing a textbook. For example, there is a scene when I was in California at a conference about the Virgin Mary. One of the Brothers who'd organized the conference was extremely educated not only about medieval art but also about the origins of prison systems around the world. We talked a lot about the word *penitentiary*. The original concept was based on the monastic system. The word itself comes from the root word *penitent*. I wanted to put so much of this history in the book, but again, I knew it would be too much. So it's there, but it's only mentioned in a couple of paragraphs where it could be part of the narrative, rather than an aside or possibly a tangent.

SIMMINS: It seems to me that there are benefits to writing a memoir as a senior writer. It's not like you dawdled about and said, 'I really have to stretch my wings on this, I really have to pontificate.' No, you don't, and you know it. So I imagine those decisions were, to a degree, fairly cut and dry. Though I'm sure there was some regret, too.

SCHOEMPERLEN: Yes, there was some, but, having had a lot of experience, I knew there were times that I'd go off on something and then look at it later and think, *Well, you don't really need to say* all *of that.* I learned how to be careful in this way when I was writing my novel *Our Lady of the Lost and Found*, about the Virgin Mary. I did a lot more research for that book than for this one. In fact, it was the first book I'd written that required a lot of research. I learned then about the perils of research and how sometimes you can use it as a way of not actually dealing with the matter at hand, and how sometimes you can give into the temptation to put in much more than is necessary.

SIMMINS: How did you deal with the privacy concerns in the book?

SCHOEMPERLEN: Certainly in memoir this is an important consideration. Privacy is quite a different matter in fiction. After all, I did write a whole novel about the Virgin Mary and the Pope never called to complain! But when you're writing about ordinary people, especially ordinary people who are still alive – privacy is a huge concern. This was a big weight on my mind, especially because I wrote the book without consulting him – essentially I wrote it behind his back. So yes, all the names have been changed except those of myself, my son, our pets – and also those of Stephen Harper and other politicians whom I felt didn't need to be protected.

SIMMINS: You put this in the front pages of your book, did you not?

SCHOEMPERLEN: Yes. That's another thing I learned from reading other memoirs. I liked the idea of putting the Author's Note at the beginning. In fiction there's usually some kind of Author's Note at the end. But when reading a memoir, I found that I liked knowing from the beginning what they had done about changing the names and so on. I decided to put my short Author's Note at the beginning, where I could explain a few things.

For example, there were some people, mostly members of his family, who I left out altogether because I was afraid they would sue me no matter what I said. In fact, I felt my author's note was very clever, especially the last paragraph, which says: 'For reasons of both privacy and length, I've had to leave a number of people and events out of these pages. For those who are disappointed not to find themselves here: I'm sorry. For those who are relieved: you're welcome.'

SIMMINS: That strikes me about as perfect a way to do it as one could do it.

SCHOEMPERLEN: Thanks! I thought so, too. I knew there were people who were expecting to be in the book, in a good way, but again, for privacy reasons, I decided not to include them. For example, I mention the potluck suppers I went to, run by Kingston Community

Chaplaincy for the families and loved ones of prisoners and ex-cons. There were so many interesting people in that group. I could've written a whole book about any single one of them, but I didn't put in anything specific about any of them for privacy reasons. Quite honestly, I didn't want to have to be running around checking with everybody. I didn't want to have to gather that much input from other people. Generally speaking, that is just not part of my writing process. Also, I originally intended to include some of the people I'd met in the prison visiting rooms – I met so many interesting people there!

SIMMINS: Yes, I bet you did.

SCHOEMPERLEN: Other prisoners and their families – there were so many things that I wanted to say about all of them, but in the end, I didn't. Again, it was for privacy reasons. Whereas, if it had been a novel, I probably would have included a lot more about that, in a more specific way. There were also things I wanted to say about some of the staff, some of the ones I really liked, but I had learned during my prison years that you have to be careful about saying *good* things about them as much as if you were saying bad things about them. For example, there was one female guard we were very fond of. She was always kidding around with us, joking and teasing, but then she was reprimanded for being too friendly with us.

There was another guard, the dog handler, whom I did mention briefly in the book. He was very interested in writing, including mine. We often talked about books as I was going into the prison, but he worried that he'd be accused of giving me special treatment. There were all kinds of issues with this book that were specific to this book.

I checked with only two people about what I was saying about them. One was my son, because as far as I'm concerned, he's the most important person in the world. There were a couple of things in earlier drafts that he asked me to leave out – which I did with no hesitation.

The other person I checked with was the woman I've called Dorothy in the book who in real life is the woman to whom the book is dedicated: my friend Joanne Page, who died in 2015. While working on the book, I often talked things over with her. Joanne was diagnosed with terminal cancer in 2009 during the time that Shane and I were apart, and in my early drafts that was in the book. But one day I was talking to her on the phone about this and I said, 'You know, Joanne,

I don't know what to do about that. Do you want me to include your cancer in the book or not?' And she said, 'Well, it might be nice to be in a book and *not* have cancer,' and I said, 'You got it.'

SIMMINS: I've never heard of a choice like this before. I think it's the right choice, personally, and professionally.

SCHOEMPERLEN: It was right for her and it was right for me. When I tried to put it in the book, the fact of my best friend having terminal cancer was so big that I couldn't possibly make it some kind of side story along with the main story of my prison relationship. So I left it out altogether. She's in the book all the way through. She doesn't have cancer. Then at the end, in reality, she died in February 2015 before I was finished the book. I was even more glad then that I'd left the cancer out, because I sure didn't know how to write about her dying. I still miss her every day.

When I had my book launch at Novel Idea – the same place in Kingston where you launched *Year of the Horse* – there were many people there who were also close to Joanne. She was a very beloved person in Kingston. I knew I had to explain to these people why Joanne didn't have cancer in the book. I got a little weepy while talking about it and then I looked around and half of them were crying, too. I felt that I had done the right thing because they all loved the idea that there she was in the book, but she wasn't sick and she didn't die.

There are so many very personal and individual decisions that the writer of a memoir has to make. You have to think long and hard about two important questions: who do you care about the most, and how is your book likely to affect them?

One of the things I talk about whenever I give memoir writing workshops is the matter of intention. If you're writing a memoir with the intention of somehow getting revenge, that's not going to be a very good book.

SIMMINS: Yes, I agree. I talk about 'revenge memoirs' a lot when I'm teaching. If you've got a black heart when you're writing, it's not going to work.

SCHOEMPERLEN: It's not going to work in the end, but it's fine to get all that stuff out in your earlier drafts. I certainly did, but then you have to step back from that. I know there was a *lot* of revenge I could've taken with this book. But I didn't, and I feel proud of that. Not just concerning Shane, but because there was something else I skimmed over in the book. I did lose some friends because of my relationship with him. I didn't throw them under the bus in the book. I wrote about that part of the experience in very general terms. I didn't write this book to hurt or upset anybody – except maybe the Correctional Service of Canada! But as for individual people in my life, I didn't want to hurt any of them and I think that's really important.

SIMMINS: There is a question of pride when one produces a memoir. I imagine that one of the moments when you felt proudest was when Shane phoned you and said he loved the book. Can you tell me about that?

SCHOEMPERLEN: Yes, that was really something! I always knew he would get in touch with me after the book was published. At some point I was worrying out loud about that and somebody said to me, 'How will he even know you've written a book?' I said, 'For God's sakes, he lives in a halfway house in Ottawa, not in a cave! He's free to come and go. He can go to a bookstore and buy the damn thing just like anybody else! And they do have radio, TV, and newspapers there. They just don't have the Internet. Oh, he'll know.'

I had my Kingston launch on May 4, 2016. The next afternoon when I was going out the door – to do some errands and to take my son to the doctor, not for anything serious – the phone rang. For some reason – I never do this – I went back into the kitchen and looked at the call display. It was him. I thought exactly what he used to always say: 'Here we go.' I knew I was going to hear from him, but I didn't think it would be quite so soon. I didn't answer the phone because we had that doctor's appointment to get to.

We got in the car and went downtown. I had about an hour and a half of seeing the doctor and doing errands to prepare myself for whatever Shane was going to say. When we got home, true to form, the phone was already ringing. I picked it up, said, 'Hello?' and he said, 'Do you know who this is?' Obviously he'd forgotten that I have call display. I said, 'Yes, I know who this is,' and he started to cry. I went into what I think of as 'mommy mode.' I said, 'It's okay, it's okay, you say whatever you need to say and we'll figure it out, everything's going to be all right.' After a few minutes he pulled himself together and he said, 'I really love your book.' I said, 'Oh, thank God.'

SIMMINS: What a moment.

SCHOEMPERLEN: That wasn't the only phone call; we had several more calls after that. We talked about it at length. I think part of the reason he loved the book was because it was fair. He said, 'You didn't make me out to be a monster.' I said, 'You're not a monster, I never thought you were a monster.' He said, 'Well, you could've really thrown me under the bus.' And I said, 'You're damn right I could've, but I didn't, so be thankful.'

One of the things I'd thought ahead of time was that if he contacted me and was furious and making a big fuss, I would have said, 'Listen, there were a bunch of other things I could've put in the book and I didn't, so maybe you should be thankful.' I don't mean things that he had done to me, but there were things he'd told me about that he'd done in prison that he shouldn't have … things that the Correctional Service of Canada might have been very interested in hearing about.

SIMMINS: You must've been one relieved person.

SCHOEMPERLEN: I was. By the end of that first conversation I was crying a bit, too, because it was all very emotional. We had not spoken at all in four years. At one point in these phone conversations, he said, 'I know you wrote this out of love and pain.' Indeed. For me, this was the best personal outcome.

SIMMINS: How it worked out for you – it absolutely couldn't be better, but it brings up a huge point that I would say to anyone who picks up a pen to do a memoir and that is, be fair and when you think you're being really fair, be more fair.

SCHOEMPERLEN: Be more fair, yes.

SIMMINS: And so if you have to swallow a whole bunch of things that you think, But he did this, and she did that, keep swallowing, because people who know you, they know the finer details of things or not, but you're the one that picked up the pen, so you have the greater burden to be fair, I believe.

SCHOEMPERLEN: Yes, I agree. When I was close to finishing the book, I read the whole thing over, trying to read it from his point of view. I tried to imagine what it would be like for him to read it. I tried to shut all the other voices out of my head, including my own, and I tried to be him. I think this was a very helpful exercise.

SIMMINS: That's a fabulous thing to do. I've suggested similar things to people in my workshops. I've said to people before, 'Okay, so you're worried about the bit about your sister, read it with your sister's mind.' But I've never heard of anyone reading an entire manuscript through one particular person's eyes.

SCHOEMPERLEN: I would also say, 'Don't underestimate the therapeutic value of writing a memoir.' When I started writing the book, I was angry, I was hurt, I was still in a lot of pain. Writing about it helped me to understand him in a way that I didn't when he was actually in my life because I could step back from him. He wasn't a monster and I did love him. Writing the book and then trying to read it from his point of view made me understand that that's okay. It's not okay what happened, but it's okay that we went through all this together and yes, I truly loved him. It seems to me that when we have a bad relationship it's easy to say afterwards, 'Oh, but it wasn't really love. It didn't work out so that means it wasn't really love.' I don't believe that. I believe that there's healthy happy love and then there's *other* love and you don't have to deny loving somebody just because it didn't end happily. Writing the book has given me a much more peaceful feeling about the whole experience.

SIMMINS: I'm very glad to hear you address the issue of catharsis, because when it comes to memoir, it's such a big one. Often when people talk to me about their expectations of writing a memoir, they instantly believe it's going to be cathartic. I tend to put the brakes on a bit with that because I say, 'You know, it may bring you peace and it may not, but with great respect, if that's your primary motivation for writing a memoir, I would suggest getting a therapist, too. Because feeling better is really not the sole or central reason to produce art, and I presume you do want to produce art.'

SCHOEMPERLEN: Yes, and I did make good use of my therapist while writing the book. There's no reason why you have to do just one or the other. You can write the book *and* have a therapist. My therapist became very important in the actual writing of the book. In the year when I was trying to figure out how to do this, I took a workshop about writing memoir from Shannon Moroney at Kingston Writers-Fest. That's where I got the idea of including my therapist in the writing process. Shannon's workshop was called Writing What Hurts. The truth is most of us don't sit down to write a memoir about all the happy parts of our lives. We have these big difficult stories we want to try and grapple with and some of it hurts an awful lot. Shannon's own memoir is called *Through the Glass*. She had a similar relationship which unfortunately ended quite tragically.

SIMMINS: I would like to read that.

SCHOEMPERLEN: One of the things Shannon talked about in her workshop was creating what she called a 'support onion.' As she explained it, there are layers of different kinds of people who can give you support while you're working on something that hurts. And one of the people who can be most helpful is a good therapist.

I had already been seeing my therapist Louise for years before I started writing the book. We had worked our way through all the shit of the whole thing. Following Shannon's suggestion, for most of the last year that I saw Louise, we talked about the book. I went to her with a book problem each week, asking, 'What do you think?' After all, she already knew the whole story, she'd been there for most of it. So I would ask, 'How do you think I could write about this part?' or 'How do you think I could deal with that part?' It seemed that because she wasn't a writer sometimes the answers were very simple for her. For instance, there was that problem of what to say about some of his family members. I wrestled with that for a long time and then I went to Louise and said, 'What am I going to do about this?' Without hesitation, she said, 'Leave them out.' And I thought, *Oh, right, you're right. I can leave them out.*

SIMMINS: Simple, and brilliant.

SCHOEMPERLEN: She could cut through some of the complicated writerly overthinking that I was doing and go straight to the simple solution. So if the writing hurts and you have a good therapist, I think you can go to them and say, 'I need to talk to you about what I'm writing, as opposed to what I lived through.'

SIMMINS: Yes, that's fascinating. I'm also very interested in your thoughts on voice because voice is so huge. If you don't have voice you don't have anything. And you have referred to the voice you employed in your memoir as 'plainsong.' Can you tell me about the discovery of voice and how this particular choice worked for you?

SCHOEMPERLEN: My fiction has a very literary voice and a lot of what I think of as jazzing around and playing with language and form. Every time I tried to write any of this memoir in my more literary voice, it sounded wrong. It felt wrong, too, as if I was trying to make things prettier than they actually were.

Eventually I realized that the voice I wanted in this book was just *me*. It's me and you sitting at the kitchen table talking and I wanted it to be that simple. It's a much plainer and more straightforward voice than in my fiction. Once I realized that was the right direction to take, then I found the writing moved along much more smoothly. This memoir is me telling you what happened just the way I would if we were sitting down drinking tea or coffee and laughing. Even in some of the most difficult scenes there's humour, because that's me. That's part of how I get through life: being able to laugh. I think that's true for a lot of people. Once I gave up the idea of trying to make the voice sound a certain way, then it just rolled on. Once I stopped fighting, it was as though I could hear the voice that was there from the beginning. It took me a long time that first year to finally understand that this was the way I needed to tell this story.

SIMMINS: This is a wonderful story to share with other, emerging writers – to listen hard for the prompts about voice. Imagine someone of your experience taking a year to find the voice for memoir. So intriguing that the plainsong was there all along, yet every time it came up you said, 'Uh, no, you know what, you're not sparkly enough.' By sharing this, other writers might find their memoir voices a bit faster than you did. And I love the idea of explaining this story by saying, 'Listen, this experienced writer really didn't know how to find her voice for memoir, then she listened very carefully and she said, Oh, the voice is me.' So at that point, I presume you took off like a rocket.

SCHOEMPERLEN: Yes, I did then. I finally felt comfortable with it and stopped trying to write a book that was more like my other books.

Which is not to say that I didn't labour over every sentence – I did, because that's the way I write. But once I knew this book should be written in a simpler, plainer voice than my fiction, then I was able to move on ahead more confidently.

SIMMINS: Do you have any more thoughts on the differences between writing fiction and non-fiction?

SHOEMPERLEN: Much of my fiction has an autobiographical element, but I could always say, 'Oh, I made it up, it's just fiction.' I could hide behind that. With this book, I was more anxious because I felt like I had nowhere to hide. But once it was done, once it was out there, I felt like it had blasted me wide open in such a fabulous way that I no longer wanted to hide.

SIMMINS: That's how Linden MacIntyre felt with his memoir, *Causeway*.

SCHOEMPERLEN: That's amazing that he would say the same sort of thing – the feeling of being blasted wide open. Now I feel like: why would I want to hide?

SIMMINS: This, too, is something to share with would-be memoir writers. You know, feeling scared and apprehensive at various points as you're writing, that's all normal. But once the piece of art is completed, the story told, you no longer feel any need to hide behind anything.

SCHOEMPERLEN: No, because whatever you're hiding, once you can put it out there, you are free on some deeper level. And for me, nothing bad happened after I'd put it out there – the world didn't end!

SIMMINS: In fact, good things happened.

SCHOEMPERLEN: Yes, many good things happened. I think we all have a lot of emotional energy invested in the things that we're hiding. Shame is a powerful force that is keeping many of us prisoners. But our prisons, unlike Shane's, are invisible. In writing this book I got angry about shame in a general way, angry about how we feel we have to hide things that we think we should be ashamed of. During the writing, I came to the conclusion that, I'll be damned, I am not going to feel ashamed of this, I'm just not. I had a favourite line that I sometimes said in interviews when I felt the interviewer was trying to get me to say I was ashamed of my relationship with Shane. I would say, 'I am not a skanky crack whore' and that, for sure, would finish that line of questioning.

SIMMINS: Good line!

SCHOEMPERLEN: I found that releasing these things into the world was very liberating. But certainly there have been awkward moments. Kingston can be a very small town. One day something happened that I now think of as "Awkward Moments at the Metro." Here in Kingston, we don't have a subway and the Metro is a downtown grocery store where I often shop. On this particular day, I was searching for a certain kind of bread that I especially like, when I realized there was somebody standing close beside me. I turned and it was a woman I'd known for twenty-five years or more, not a close friend, but an acquaintance. She said, 'Oh, I just finished reading your book!' She said it quite joyfully so I assumed she had liked it. I said, 'Oh, that's wonderful, thank you!' Then there was a long pause. Finally, she said, 'It was … interesting. I know a lot more about you now than I used to. Does that bother you?' And I'm thinking, Beam me up, Scotty, get me out of here. I grabbed any old loaf of bread and said, 'Nope, doesn't bother me at all,' and I took off.

SIMMINS: Beyond awkward.

SCHOEMPERLEN: Weird things have happened, yes, but this one makes me laugh when I think about it because – no ego on my part! – I assumed she loved my book because of the way she said it. But I also thought, I've known you long enough to know that you have some pretty deep dark secrets, too. Kingston is a small town. Maybe you should let them out.

SIMMINS: I'm delighted with this discussion because you've covered in a really beautiful, humorous way so many of the fears and anxieties that people have about memoir. First, there is the whole business of feeling exposed or even naked, which fortunately, and bit by bit, does fade. Then there are all the worries about the quality of the story you've produced. And all you can do is just get on with it.

SCHOEMPERLEN: Just get on with it, yes. That kind of thinking was part of how I wrote the book as well. I didn't write it in the order that it appears. This was another trick I played on myself that worked extremely well. I wrote the easy parts first.

SIMMINS: How did that work?

SCHOEMPERLEN: I wrote descriptions of the visiting room first. I wrote a long scene that doesn't appear in the finished book of me going to get my hair cut before a parole hearing. It took me quite a long time to work up to writing a scene in which Shane actually appeared. I wrote around it; I wrote around *him*. This proved to be a good way of easing into the more difficult scenes. The book is in five parts, plus the epilogue. I sometimes had five or six documents open on the computer at the same time. I would be working on a scene over here, and then I'd think, Oh, God, this is getting too hard, and then I'd go and work on a scene over there that was easier. This was an important part of how I managed to do it. I just kept warming up to the hard parts.

SIMMINS: This is pure gold, because it's pure problem-solving. This is strategy, the memoirist's good and necessary friend.

SCHOEMPERLEN: Yes, I just did it the way that I could handle it.

SIMMINS: This strategy should be so helpful to other writers. What I say to people over and over again, is, 'The rules are there are no rules.' Just do whatever works for you to get those precious words on the paper. As a journalist, I think I'd have a meltdown if I had to have five articles on the screen at once, all totally different but needing to be worked on. But I've never done that with personal writing. It almost sounds fun.

SCHOEMPERLEN: I certainly hadn't done this before, either. There were so many things about writing the memoir that were quite different than the habits I'd developed over years and years of writing fiction. This strategy was one of them. I would recommend it to anybody: start with the easy parts.

This was also part of what helped me in finding the voice. As I worked on those easy parts, I became more and more comfortable with the voice.

Another thing was that I did not write this book at my desk. I wrote it at the kitchen table, where there are two big windows looking onto the street. For all my other books I wrote in a room with the curtains closed so I wouldn't be distracted – I've always found a window to be almost as distracting as a TV set, even though there's nothing happening on my little street in the middle of the day. But this time I wrote at the kitchen table so I could look outside and say, 'This is now, that was then.' This was another thing that Shannon Moroney talked about in her Writing What Hurts workshop: try to find a way to keep yourself in the present moment so you don't get drawn too far back into the pain of the past.

SIMMINS: Or that you simply can't write.

SCHOEMPERLEN: Right, you don't want to get drawn so deep into the pain that you can't write. I could keep grounded in the present by looking out the window and thinking, Yes, here I am, I'm right here right now, and I'm okay.

SIMMINS: These are brilliant tips you're giving us. They should really help people to write about the hard stuff.

SCHOEMPERLEN: When I was trying to write something difficult, I would leap up from the table again and again, pushing my chair back and going to the fridge or the bathroom or getting myself another cup of coffee. It was like I was physically jumping away from the writing to catch my breath. Then I would come back and sit down and go at it again. What I didn't notice until well into the process was that I was doing this so often that I was wearing out the tile on the kitchen floor with my constant pushing back of the chair. I'm looking at that worn spot right now. At first I thought, Oh, my God, I'll have to replace those tiles. But now I look at them and think maybe I'll just leave them like that.

SIMMINS: Oh, no, you can't lose them. Those are bragging tiles. People think that writing is so stationary. And it is, a lot of the time. But it's also so physical! I'm laughing when you say this because I do the same thing. You stretch, you move, you get up, you turn around, whatever the heck it is, right? I also notice I do weird things with my hands. I'm looking for a word and I move my hands around almost like trying to scramble up my brain to find that word or idea. So yes, keep those tiles. If I were you, I would sign those bloody tiles.

SCHOEMPERLEN: That's a good idea! I'd also like to say one more thing. At the very beginning of our interview, before you started recording, you mentioned how well I'd done in the interviews about the memoir. So many people have said that to me. 'Oh, you were so calm and so poised.' The truth is, I was mostly terrified. I knew there were a lot of negative, even nasty, things that could be said. So before I headed to Toronto to start doing all the media when the book first came out, I downloaded that old Pat Benatar song "Hit Me With Your Best Shot" and I had her voice in my head every time I sat down to do an interview. It helped immensely every single time and that's another trick that nobody else is ever going to tell you!

SIMMINS: I'm laughing, but only because it's perfect. I love Benatar, and I know the song. So basically I should tell my poor students of memoir that when they're out there on their media tours, 'You need to choose your fighting song.'

SCHOEMPERLEN: Yes, choose your fighting song, whatever it happens to be, and just listen to it over and over again before you have to go up there in front of the mike or the cameras. You'll be fine.

SIMMINS: I'm going to do that myself.

SCHOEMPERLEN: I still use it if I'm getting a strange feeling from somebody about the book. When they're talking to me I can just flip that switch in my head and there Pat's voice in my head and I think, Okay, Pat's here. You go ahead and say whatever you want to say. I can handle it. And you know what's really strange? They've now got a TV commercial for Applebee's Loaded Fajitas that features this Pat Benatar song! Not sure how I feel about that!

Diane Shoemperlen
Craft

"I'll think about it tomorrow," said Scarlett O'Hara. "After all, tomorrow is another day!"

Diane Schoemperlen has lots of excellent advice for writers who are tackling memoir for the first time. Not thinking too far ahead is one strategy she recommended, along with finding the structure as she wrote.

For your memoir:

Decide on the central idea, or the approximate period of your life, around which you will build your memoir. Don't worry about the beginning, middle, or end of the memoir. Your job on this day is to write one small story that will go inside the bigger story of your memoir. It may be a half page long, or it may be five pages. The word count is unimportant. Choose an event or something "unforgettable" (overheard dialogue; something you saw that you weren't supposed to see; a family episode of great beauty or strangeness) and write a short story about it. Polish it and care for it, as though it were the only story going in the book. Then, the next day, write another one.

What to put in, what to leave out

This should be easy, right? Well, it's not always. In the case of Schoemperlen's memoir, she was struggling with how to present certain members of her lover's family – really struggling. Amusingly, it took a non-writer to point out the fairly obvious: just leave 'em out altogether. Schoemperlen, a fair-minded but serious professional, thought she had to put all the characters in the larger story in the book, because a true-to-life story had to have all the significant true-to-life characters in it. In fact, this is not the case.

When in doubt, the writer must always serve the story. Schoemperlen's narrative centred on the microcosm of her love affair (which of course felt huge, as it does to us all), and macrocosm of the prison system in Canada. Not everyone Schoemperlen met or interacted with – difficult or otherwise, related to the main characters or otherwise – deserved a seat in the theatre of her memoir. Of course it was hard to leave out people she'd come to like and respect and, in some cases, even admire, but she did what she had to do to free herself from indecision, and to safeguard the readability and pacing of the story, by not focusing on too many characters or allowing too much stage time to secondary characters. Your loyalty is always to the story.

For your memoir:

When you have a complete draft, it will be time to review and assess what you've assembled. As you reread, make a list of all the characters in the book. You may wish to put them in categories, such as family, friends, siblings, spouse(s), and so on, which will also show you which group has the greatest numbers (indicative of a theme, most likely).

Have a good hard look at your people. Is it, like the trilogy for *The Lord of the Rings*, a "cast of thousands"? Do you and the other main characters get lost in the crowd? You may even have to do some re-evaluations. Are there main or minor characters that should be demoted, combined – or removed altogether? Are there minor characters who support the narrative more than you realized? Above all, whose story is it? And by the way, if you hesitated for a fraction of a second too long to answer that … then you'd better learn to place yourself in a more central position in the memoir. You are not supposed to be a minor character – unless you are deliberately writing the memoir for someone else.

Making loving choices

I think I would have paid Diane Schoemperlen to suggest this one. I know I was happy to hear her talk about this aspect of writing true life stories. "Well, it might be nice to be in a book and *not* have cancer," said Diane's best friend. "Do you think …?"

Schoemperlen didn't hesitate. The cancer wasn't pertinent to the essential story, and was so huge and hideous, it could have taken over the memoir. Presto, cancer gone.

This was a good and loving decision that also had literary legs. You are allowed to make these decisions. We can't tell six stories at once. We can only tell the story we set out to tell – unless midway along, our head and heart really scream for another story we didn't know at first that we should be telling. If you absolutely must, you can change horses in mid-stream. But hey, you know, you can always write two separate stories …

For your memoir:

Write a sketch about a family member you love dearly. It may or may not be a part of your memoir, or only parts of it may be. In short form, write everything you know about that person. Describe their good points, and their not-so-good points. Detail how they look, and how they sound, and how they move. List essential-to-them points, as well. Do they snore? Do they have a pacemaker? Are they learning-disabled, gay, bi-sexual, or essentially fluid? A cheap tipper? Estranged from their only son? Prone to bouts of crying or heavy-handed sarcasm? Vote Conservative, but have supported you through every bad time you've ever had in your decidedly non-conservative life?

Now, take a hi-liter pen and highlight all the traits and realities you know for a fact this person wouldn't give a damn that other people knew. Secondly, and with a different-coloured pen, highlight the traits and realities you know they would cringe to see in print.

If they are a part of your memoir – then you can think about this bit of writing you've done. Can you gift them in any way – the way Schoemperlen did with her good friend? Omission is allowed. It's not dishonest or harmful. Of course you can't leave out anything that is of critical importance to your story. You … just … can't. But there are ways and ways to present your supporting cast.

Schoemperlen was similarly generous to her main cast, namely Shane. After all, as Schoemperlen noted, he didn't ask to be written about. Courtesy still counts – *if* you can make the points you need to make without being stingingly unkind.

Choices, so many choices. And thanks to Schoemperlen and our other guest interviews, you can see how much choice you have – to write a memoir that makes you stand tall – and belt out Pat Benatar.

The support onion.
Plainsong.
Writing what you can, when you can.
Start on the easy bits.

Think about all these ideas Schoemperlen offered to you.

Chapter Seven
Character and Setting in Literature and Memoir

You and everyone in your memoir are characters. As such, you will face adversity, near or total despair, and will then (we hope) regroup, take on new resolve, and either triumph or ... Every character has gifts, and flaws. We are complicated creatures. Our flaws cause us trouble; they also make us likeable, relatable, and real.

Remember: in a good memoir, it is not your job to hide your character or personality, but to tell the story, revealing yourself as required, as a multi-dimensional, imperfect, and interesting human being.

For your memoir:

List three gifts you have, and three flaws. Do any of these make you smile? Do any of these make you squirm? Blush, maybe? Have a good poke at the list. Are you working on some of the flaws, or have you accepted they're just a part of you and won't go away or be muzzled/held back? Perhaps you are smiling and resigned. Would you/do you forgive other people for these flaws? Would you/do you commend others for the gifts you have – while not commending yourself?

Your gifts and your flaws will be a part of your life story. How you choose to view them is also a part of the story. Own your flaws, indicate your gifts, and use humour to deflect vanity – unless you need to present yourself as vain, for whatever reasons may support your story. Memoir is not static. *You, the protagonist, must grow as the story is related.*

As important, your qualities will emerge from the story. Once again, it is show me, don't tell me. And omit any qualities that aren't relevant to the story. *You must always serve the story.*

Like a novel, memoir really is all about the story; every paragraph in it must support and develop your story. Also like a novel, each sentence should either *add to the setting, move the narrative along, or develop a character* (which may or may not be you).

Consider these famous characters (and animals) from literature:

Sherlock Holmes (and Dr. Watson, who relates the mysteries); Mma Precious Ramotswe; Scarlett O'Hara and Rhett Butler; Charles de Batz de Castelmore d'Artagnan; James Bond; Alice in Wonderland; Hermione Granger; Harry Potter; Voldemort; Yuri Zhivago; Jo March and her youngest sister, Beth March; Anna Karenina; Anne Shirley; Becky Sharp; Lisbeth Salander; Heathcliffe and Catherine Earnshaw; Stanley Kowalski and Blanche Dubois; Bigger Thomas; Philomena Moosetail; Satan; the Archangel Michael; Black Beauty and Ginger; Enzo (the golden retriever); Sweet William, a.k.a. Old Horse; Tao, the Siamese cat.

You're smiling, aren't you? You're seeing Scarlett O'Hara trying to hide her dancing feet at the ball, when she is still wearing widow's weeds. Or perhaps you're imagining James Bond (choose your favourite Bond actor; mine's Sean Connery) doing impossible stunts in his Aston Martin. Perhaps you envision the once-elegant feline, Tao, now gaunt and malnourished, along with his bedraggled canine friends, Luath the Labrador Retriever and Bodger the Bull Terrier, safely reunited with their human family again.

Or maybe you're not smiling. Maybe the hair on your arms is raised, as you think of Stanley Kowalski wailing "Stelllllaaaa," and almost beating his dirty, singlet-clad chest in anguish. Will he win his wife back – or will Blanche DuBois, Stella's sister, turn her against him? Will he, perhaps, take out a darker revenge on Blanche?

You might even be weeping, remembering the ghastly fate of Anna Karenina – and how, surely, she might have achieved a life of even meagre happiness.

What characteristics do you think of when you consider these characters, or other favourites? I think of cruelty, denial, lust, shallowness, courage, kindness, tenacity, adventurousness, cooperation, loyalty and love, among many others. Do you see yourself in any of these characters? How do you feel, when you think about these characters? Emotions are a journey, too, and good memoirs evoke them, by making us care about the central characters in them.

Consider any "characters" (authors) from favourite memoirs. When you have a list, look it over and ask yourself why these author-characters are memorable. Here's how mine would read: Nuala O'Faolain (*Are You Somebody?*), for her disarming honesty; Jenny Lawson (*Let's Pretend This Never Happened*), for her brilliant zaniness; Farley Mowat (*Bay of Spirits*), for making himself vulnerable; Pat Conroy (*The Death of Santini*), for his immense, forgiving heart; Sara Jewell (*Field Notes: A City Girl's Search for Heart and Home in Rural Nova Scotia*), for honouring roadkill on the country roads around her home with a lovely essay; Richard Ford (*Between Them: Remembering My Parents*), for making me remember parents can be a united, loving force; Wayson Choy (*Paper Shadows*), for his resolute bravery; Gloria Steinem (*My Life on the Road*), for her brilliant mind, capacious heart, and originality; and Terese Marie Mailhot (*Heart Berries*), for being broken, and then choosing to heal, with her writing.

Can you find yourself in the characteristics of your favourite author-characters? Again, what feelings do these people evoke, as they relate their life stories? Identify the times of greatest drama, and see how the authors respond to crisis and loss. Do you admire them, or does your heart sink, when you see them compound their mistakes or difficulties?

For your memoir:

Choose two characters from each of your two lists, and list their gifts and flaws. Think about why we love certain characters and memoirists, and why, sometimes, we hate them. Are the "bad" ones more memorable than the "good" ones? If so, why is that? Who are the good and bad characters in your memoir? Of course we're all a blend of good and bad, so are you presenting them, and yourself, honestly? If someone seems too good to be true, as though you suddenly got lost in a *Gidget* movie from the 1960s, or Forrest Gump took over the story, think about adding another, more thoughtful dimension to their passage through your memoir. This could be as simple as permitting them more than one mention, more than one memory-period, so they are presented as more fully rounded characters. Your mother wasn't always baking cookies; once she rounded on your father with a carving knife in hand. Nor was your father endlessly patient and accepting; his "needling" was in fact legendary. You get the idea.

Settings in Literature and Memoir

Think of André Alexis' *Fifteen Dogs*, or Tara Westover's *Educated*, or Mordecai Richler's *St. Urbain's Horseman*, or Christopher Skaife's *The Ravenmaster*, or Roald Dahl's *Charlie and the Chocolate Factory*, or Esi Edugyan's *Half-Blood Blues* and *Washington Black* (both Giller winners), or Audrey Thomas's *Intertidal Life*, or Michel Tremblay's *The Fat Woman Next Door is Pregnant* ... so many novels and memoirs with unforgettable settings. Think of J.K. Rowling's *Harry Potter* series. Wouldn't you live at Hogwarts in a heartbeat?

Think as well of Laura Beatrice Berton's *I Married the Klondike*, or Linda Greenlaw's *The Hungry Ocean*, or Annie Dillard's *Pilgrim at Tinker's Creek*, or Magie Dominic's *Street Angel*, or Gloria Steinem's *My Life on the Road* – all these memoirs are "of their time," providing evocative details of landscapes, oceanscapes, music, art, food, clothing, marriage, city and country lives. We linger in memoirs such as these, transported to settings we'll never see in reality. We walk slowly in these different worlds ... all our senses engaged.

This is your challenge, too. To make your reader turn the pages quickly at first, and then slow right down, not wanting to leave your world.

For your memoir:

Write a paragraph about a memorable place in your life. Would it appear in your memoir? Are there any connections between your flaws and gifts and this setting? For example, a love of winter landscapes and snowy mountaintops – and a fear of heights?

Setting also affects tone. Tone is something we crave, and seek out. Millions crave the particular tones of romance novels, or science fiction, or fantasy novels, or literary works, or even graphic novels.

And naturally tone changes over the course of a work. The story arc demands different tones for different parts of the book. We often employ longer descriptions and musings to start and finish, and short, driving sentences surrounding the action scenes and climax.

Finally, setting is interconnected to themes. There are no casual mentions of scenes and sights in our memoirs. They connect to our loves, losses, and longings, our joys and needs. We are all of us "of a place," and often, that place forms our character, affects our sensibilities. Consider how these place names and locations make you feel: the moors and dales of Northern England; "The Outback" of Australia; the steppes of Mongolia; the rain forests of South America; the South Pacific Islands; Tuktoyaktuk, Northwest Territories; Moscow; Nuuk, Greenland; Lima, Peru. How about the grasslands of Saskatchewan in summer, or the autumnal hillsides of the Cape Breton Highlands in Nova Scotia? What about Vancouver, British Columbia, in November – or much better yet, April? What do you see, hear, smell, feel, and touch? What stories have already started to play in your imagination or memory?

For your memoir:

Return to your writing on your memorable place. Identify the tone in the piece. How do you feel when you go to this place, either in reality or memory? Do you see this tone as being a constant in your memoir? What tone would you like to establish?

As you write, and rewrite, be aware that you are also crafting a particular reading experience in your memoir. To a large degree, the story will be the story you need to tell, but there are times, and there are ways, to offer your reader sensory and emotional experiences, as you tell that story.

Those "ways" all relate to the care you put into the crafting of your tale. If you've heard a phrase before, even often, find a new, fresher one. If your writing has entered the "purple" realm, pull way back and remove all adjectives and adverbs and shorten up those sentences. If you're so buttoned up the reader couldn't identify a single emotion in many pages, then you'll have to trust yourself more, trust the reader more, to accept the choices and circumstances that make up your life.

Finally, when you write, think of your reader as being close by – close enough that you can show them the scar on your arm, from when you broke it in two places trying to fly, and hear them whisper, "I'm so sorry … but you almost found the sky, didn't you?"

Conversation with Plum Johnson, author of *They Left Us Everything*

Born in Richmond, Virginia, Plum Johnson spent her early years in Hong Kong and Singapore before her family immigrated to Canada, settling in Oakville, Ontario.

After receiving her B.Sc. degree in education from Wheelock College in Boston, she returned to Toronto and enrolled in the M.F.A. Theatre program at York University.

In 1983, she founded KidsCanada Publishing Corp. to pioneer the first parenting publications in Canada and was awarded the *Toronto Sun*'s Women On The Move Award for outstanding achievement in business. Over the next ten years, her flagship news magazine, *KidsToronto*, won multiple international design awards and in 1992, Plum was awarded the Parenting Publications of America Association Award of Excellence for her monthly editorial column.

Plum Johnson's memoir, *They Left Us Everything*, won the 2015 RBC Taylor Prize for literary non-fiction and the 2016 Ontario Library Association Evergreen Award.

SIMMINS: For me, there were several reasons I thought your book would be appropriate for *Conversations and Craft*. One of these is the whole idea of the childhood home. The idea was just out there, like an apple on the tree waiting for somebody to pluck it and you did. There isn't a person on the planet that doesn't have very strong feelings one way or another, and usually both, about their childhood home.

JOHNSON: It's true and I think the other thing I'm learning, which I suspected anyway, is that there is an age range when one is in a home.

I think especially around eight, nine, ten years old, it's such an influential time in one's life. I don't know whether it's also true for men, but certainly for women. Whatever home you're in at that age seems to take on this incredible significance.

SIMMINS: Well, aged ten, eleven, you're becoming a little person. I think it was Lewis Carroll who said about age ten was a perfect age, certainly for girls, such as the delightful Alice.

JOHNSON: It's a very intense time before puberty. Though it's probably not before puberty these days, but it used to be.

SIMMINS: That's right. No, I think it's probably a very porous time in terms of intellect. You know, ideas are coming in and staying, affecting choices and decisions. I think for many of us, it's easy to close our eyes and be ten again. But it wasn't as though you woke up and said, 'Well, I'm going to write something that no one else has, all about childhood homes' – or maybe you did?

JOHNSON: No, no, I didn't, but I guess I had been affected by writing from my early schooling. I had a high school teacher who said, 'Don't write until you have something to say,' and she effectively shut me up for about fifty years! So I think I've been storing up [my ideas]. I now find I have a lot to say, but then, I'm a late bloomer. Now all of a sudden, the pressure's on, because the years are running out to take the time to write it. And of course I've been writing all my life, but I think I tried everything else first. I kind of circled the job, that career, and I just didn't have the confidence to think that anything I had to say was important enough.

SIMMINS: I'm cringing at the idea of that teacher.

JOHNSON: Yeah, she was wrong.

SIMMINS: No kidding, the harm done! But I am glad you felt strongly about your writing subject.

JOHNSON: She was right in that, I agree with her, that you shouldn't write until you have something to say but – but she was wrong in thinking that you couldn't have something to say when you're fifteen or twenty or whatever age you are.

SIMMINS: Agreed. We have enough trouble with our inner critics as it is. So could you tell me about your motivation for writing the book?

JOHNSON: It was a light bulb moment for that particular book because when I had moved out to Oakville and started clearing out Mum's house, every time I found an object that triggered a memory I would write the memory down, really for my grandchildren. That was my intent. So it wasn't until one day, when I was taking stuff to the thrift store, the local thrift store, and I noticed a couple of things. First of all, that the thrift store was filled to overflowing with objects identical to what I was bringing, all stuff from the '50s.

I had this sensation that we were throwing away the whole of the twentieth century. I also noticed that, especially on weekends, usually husbands driving up in their big SUVs and taking cardboard boxes to the curb and roaring off in a cloud of dust. We seemed to be doing all this in a big hurry, as though we wanted to get it over and done with. There were boxes I would see in the thrift store, boxes of, you know, personal postcards and things that shouldn't have been thrown away. I stood back and I thought, Wow, look at this picture. In my age group, we all seem to be doing this. We're doing it in a big hurry and why isn't anybody writing about this? Maybe there's a book here.

As I said, I had already been collecting the memories from a personal point of view, but then it occurred to me that a bigger thing was going on in the context of my generation. So then, I just felt compelled. I didn't even think of it as motivation, I just thought of it as something that I had to get out. My original book proposal was a *Goodnight Moon* for adults. I thought I was going to be writing this gentle tribute to the house and saying goodbye to the things. What I didn't anticipate was this mother-daughter theme that reared its ugly head. That terrified me when that came up in my writing.

I realized that that was a much bigger theme and I just didn't expect it. And then, of course, I was so insecure about my writing. I thought, Should I go there? and was I doing an injustice to Mum by confessing these things? I had tremendous guilt with how I had behaved towards her at the end of her life. And I worried I would be vilified by the reading public if I confessed those things.

SIMMINS: I thought you were so gentle and loving. You were frank, too, but because of that, I was able to put myself in your shoes. I didn't think you could've done any better. I had absolute sympathy with the fatigue.

JOHNSON: Well, this is what I didn't realize until I started getting reader reactions. I had steeled myself to having tomatoes thrown at me or whatever. Instead, the very first thing that happened to me was amazing. The book had just come out and I had just gone for an interview at TVO [Television Ontario]. I hadn't had the interview yet and I was nervous about it. I walked out of the elevators and a stranger, a woman, was standing waiting for the elevator. She did a double-take when I walked out and she said, 'Are you Plum Johnson?' And I was so taken aback I said, 'How did you know?' and she said, 'Because I recognized you from the cover of your book.' Then she said, 'Do you mind if I give you a hug? Because I had a mother just like yours.' And that was the first reader reaction that I got. I was so relieved and sort of stunned.

SIMMINS: What a blessing, to have that warm reaction to your work, before the interview.

JOHNSON: Exactly. I found that since then all these reactions have come tumbling out. It's almost like the book has been giving women permission to admit that they had these same feelings. I think a lot of us had been in a tunnel for a really long time. I remember thinking because I was forty-five when I went into the tunnel, the elder care tunnel, but I had sort of bought into the marketing men who said Freedom 55 was around the corner. And my children had just started to move back home and then Dad got Alzheimer's. So I was in this tunnel that I thought would never end, because you never know how long it is. For me it ended up being twenty years. I was sixty-five by the time I came through the other end. That whole twenty-year period when I had been looking forward to having freedom, I felt I'd been in some ways incarcerated. And I had been. Friends of mine and I had been confessing this to each other, but I didn't realize it was so prevalent.

SIMMINS: Oh, you spoke for many. Plum, I want to circle around here for a moment because we started on a very interesting vein, I thought, and that was you had made notes about what you were doing, primarily for the grandchildren when you started cleaning out the home. And then things started taking on a pretty good life in terms of the writing and then you were a little bit shocked and uneasy to realize that you had to write about your mother and the complexities there and that made you really worried. How did you push on?

JOHNSON: I just decided I would pour out everything and worry about the edit later.

SIMMINS: Perfect, yes.

JOHNSON: The writing, pouring it all out, took about nine months, but the editing took almost two years. I know a lot of writers do a plan first and I didn't do that. In the end about 30 percent of the stories got cut as I was shaping the book – with the help of a really wonderful independent editor, I might add, who deserves a lot of credit. And I was on a learning curve, too. I had tried to get into a memoir writing course at the library when I realized that I was on this trip to write a book.

SIMMINS: As I said to Diane Schoemperlen, I wish you'd come to one of my courses!

JOHNSON: Yeah, I wish so, too. I saw a sign one day at the local library, memoir course, six-week minimum, but it was full, so I couldn't get in, but they gave me the reading list. So I went out and bought all the books and read all the books and I was doing that at the same time as writing. You have to remember that I was in the house, the house didn't sell. So I didn't know how long I had, but I was just taking advantage of being in the house and being in what I considered this sacred setting of the house. Even as a child, it had always seemed a sacred setting to me, and I have always felt highly creative there. I have felt highly creative all my life, but in particular, it started there. I attribute those feelings to that setting, maybe most of all. I was back there with this unlimited horizon of lake and sky and so it fed my work ...

SIMMINS: That was the key point I was hoping you might say. You let the story work through you, and didn't question its route, or the overall journey. So you may have come late to writing books, but your creative soul knew that everything all around you was important. You'd write now, and deal with the intricacies of editing later. But you had a lot to deal with in terms of the emotional underpinnings of the project. It took courage to keep writing.

JOHNSON: You have to remember also that I was there alone so in terms of a writer's retreat, it couldn't have been better. I had no social life and I had every single evening blank, so I could just write.

SIMMINS: Nine months, though. That's an amazing bit of work.

JOHNSON: I actually had two years there, almost two years.

SIMMINS: Yes, but you said nine months to produce the manuscript first time around.

JOHNSON: Yes, I had something by the end of nine months. And I was also reading how-to memoir books during that time. It was a period of time teaching myself. I work best that way anyway. It took me a long time to realize I'm not really a good classroom learner. I'm not a good joiner. I'm much better at doing stuff on my own, learning from books.

SIMMINS: While you were writing and reading about memoir at the same time, was there a particular book that was very helpful?

JOHNSON: Actually, there was a whole list of books that I still have on my shelf. William Zinsser was my favourite and I took his advice very much to heart.

SIMMINS: You spoke for many family members in *They Left Us Everything* among these three live siblings, one late sibling, and your late parents. Some reviewers also consider your childhood home to be a character in the book. How did you manage the complexities of providing voice to all these characters, especially family?

JOHNSON: Because I had the dialogue, I love dialogue, and I remembered it, if that's what you're asking.

SIMMINS: Well, absolutely, yes.

JOHNSON: So I could recall. For some reason, I find it easy to recall dialogue. And also often when I write, I write what I call beads. Think of the string of beads on a necklace, which is sometimes used as a kind of chastisement to writers that, you know, you don't have a narrative arc, you're just writing beads on a necklace or whatever. So the beads are scenes and I love to write to like that. I actually think it's a very good way for a memoirist to write.

SIMMINS: I agree. Get the stories down.

JOHNSON: For me, anyway, I will often write, I will often make beads and just store them in a box; I mean visually, that's how I see it. And the beads can be very short, just snippets of dialogue even, but I often see words as colours and I see the beads as decorated. Some are tiny, some are big, some are, I don't know, imperfect, some are perfect, the different sizes, different colours and they're in a box – which is to say, they're in a file folder and they all have titles. So I can go into that box and pull out two different beads and see what I've got and then create a narrative arc. The string is the narrative arc and depending on where that goes, I might shift the beads around or whatever. That's just the way visually I see it. So dialogue often triggers a whole scene for me. I know it's not word for word, but I wasn't prepared to sacrifice any relationship for a book.

So I had promised my family that I would show the raw manuscript to them first, before it was published, and I promised I would take out anything they found hurtful. I asked them to help correct any inaccuracies that they found because I know memory can do weird things with timeframe. And I knew that our perspectives may all be different on the same event. The event had to be accurate, by which I mean, the event had to have actually happened. So they did that for me. I was lucky they didn't ask me to take out any parts.

Now they didn't see anything that they found hurtful, but there's a scene in there with one of my daughters where there's dialogue. That dialogue had to be absolutely correct; she fixed that herself. She said, 'I didn't say it like that, I said it like this,' so fine, I corrected that. And also whenever there was a peripheral character in the book like the doctor, for example, or where there was other dialogue, I sent those people only the pages where they were included and asked them if it was right, and if I had their permission to include it. I felt it was a really sensitive thing. I didn't want them to feel they were included in something they didn't approve of, or that I had been inaccurate in any way when I was using their real names. Almost like getting signed affidavits.

SIMMINS: Fascinating. I haven't spoken to another memoirist so far who has done things so expansively. I've never spoken to anyone who has shown their entire manuscript to their family.

JOHNSON: Oh, really?

SIMMINS: I've heard of the writer showing family bits and pieces of the manuscript that pertained to them, yes, but not showing them the whole manuscript. I'm actually flabbergasted that your family didn't tinker and didn't say, 'No, this happened earlier, not then,' etc. Was there a good deal of discussion or mostly, 'No, you have this right'?

JOHNSON: No, it was mostly I have this right.

SIMMINS: Isn't that wonderful? Because you mentioned one of your siblings was a bit of the family historian.

JOHNSON: Yes, and that was interesting because the other thing I did was to send each of them a separate manuscript. I was smart enough to do that, because I didn't want them to gang up on me in the margins. The rule was that they had to send it directly back to me.

SIMMINS: Brilliant.

JOHNSON: And so my brother Robin's copy – he's the sort of the family historian, so he's a real stickler for detail – his manuscript came back, and much to my astonishment, he'd written the word fiction on some of the margins. So I'd write back, 'What do you mean fiction?' And he'd say, 'You didn't find that in Mum's bottom drawer, you found that in Dad's filing cabinet.'

SIMMINS: Oh, for God's sake.

JOHNSON: And I'd write back and say, 'Oh, for God's sake, that doesn't matter,' and then he'd write back and say, 'Well, did you want my help, or didn't you?' And other times I'd write, 'Good catch, thanks,' because he did correct some things for me date-wise. Other times, I'd write, you know, 'Who are you anyway, what's the reason for this comment?' His daughter later asked if she could have that manuscript because she said she'd been so fascinated by our sibling relationship, which was all played out down the margins. Robin did ask me to remove one thing and that was the F-word. I used it once in a dialogue towards the end of the book. It was a dialogue of my brother Victor's and Victor had used the word and I liked the word, but Robin said, 'It lowers the tone of your book.' So I removed it. It didn't make any difference to me.

SIMMINS: You sound enormously accommodating. Do you have an example of one of the siblings disagreeing about something, and you stuck to your guns and said, 'No, that's how I remember it'?

JOHNSON: No, because that was the only thing he asked me to remove. That's the only thing I remember, anyway. It didn't make any difference. If that made him feel better, fine.

SIMMINS: And as you say, you didn't have an attachment to that word.

JOHNSON: And Victor was very alarmed that I was using everybody's real name.

SIMMINS: Did that surprise you?

JOHNSON: It surprised me because he's a very generous, gregarious people-person and I didn't expect him to feel so exposed by that.

SIMMINS: Yes, yes, I come from a whole writing family and we've had discussions like this. You do feel exposed, even if the person has said something very nice about you it's like, '*Eww, that's me, in a book.*'

JOHNSON: Yeah, so Victor said, 'You know, if you're going to use real names, I don't want any part of it.' And so I said, 'That's fine. I'll put a disclaimer in the front of the book and I'll say that all the names are real except for Victor's and I changed his to Paul.' And he huffed out of the room, but the compromise that we came up with was that I offered to remove all reference to my maiden name in the book. There are only a couple of occasions where I had used that and it was a bit tricky to remove them, but I did. So I said, 'If I take out all reference to my maiden name and since I write under my married name people will think your name is Victor Johnson, so is that okay with you?' And he said, 'Yeah.'

SIMMINS: Good for you. That took some careful thought.

JOHNSON: So that worked.

SIMMINS: Yes, it did and again, with some careful thought and respectful interactions. And that tells me a lot about your sibling relationships.

JOHNSON: But then when the book won the RBC Taylor Prize, he called me up and he said, 'Now that your book is doing so well, you can put my name back in.'

SIMMINS: No, he didn't!

JOHNSON: It was cute.

SIMMINS: I think it's splendid. This is obviously a huge testament to the friendship, the wonderful friendships siblings share that there wasn't a lot of argument and fussing. But at the same time, there's a candour which has to be there for the book to succeed. I am thinking about the lady who hugged you in the elevator. You wouldn't have had that hug had you not been as candid as you were in telling your story.

JOHNSON: I've always felt that there's no need to hold secrets in a family because I've always had a sense that we're all essentially the same. I believe that every family has the same skeletons, more or less, in a closet and that if you share those you can help each other. Probably if you took every family, maybe not every family, but most families, if you pull aside the curtain there's probably going to be an abortion somewhere, there's probably going to be a mistress somewhere, there's probably going to be alcohol, illness, there's probably a suicide, you know. If you go back far enough and wide enough I think all the drama and the romance and the problems, it's all essentially the same. So I never understood why people want to hide those things or why we should feel ashamed or embarrassed. I mean, I certainly have felt ashamed of things that I have done in my life or things that happened to me, but once I share them I'm comforted.

SIMMINS: Catharsis is something that comes up on a regular basis in discussions when I teach and so far in discussions with other memoirists I've been talking to. Did you find the process of writing your book cathartic?

JOHNSON: Yes, I did.

SIMMINS: Tell me about that.

JOHNSON: I felt that I made friends with Mum again.

SIMMINS: What an incalculable gift.

JOHNSON: Yes. I had the twenty years of elder care. We had a live-in couple for my parents so I wasn't there every day, but I found those years at the end gruelling, to such an extent that it had overlaid some lovely years that I'd had with Mum. I remember her as being very enthusiastic and loving and supportive, probably throughout my life, but what I remember is my early life and through my marriage and when my children were born. It got gnarly later, but the final years blocked all that love and support out of my memory. Once I had done all this thinking and writing of the memoir the latter years fell away. And the earlier years came to the fore and that gave her back to me.

SIMMINS: Again, what a gift for a memoir to have bestowed on you. The book is worth it if only for that. Now, could you tell me, was that part, this rediscovering the friendship and support and easier love that you shared as a young person with your mom, was part of that brought on by the household objects and letters and papers?

JOHNSON: It was the letters, not the objects. This is why I'm so alarmed when I see friends of mine now clearing out houses. I know we all do the best we can and I know a lot of them simply don't have the time or circumstances to make it work. Usually there's a great distance to travel when a parent dies and you have to rush out and do it in two weeks or whatever, but I'm quite alarmed that people are not realizing what they're throwing away.

I don't care about the furniture, the things, [it's] the personal diaries, those things are essential. I also think we may be the last generation to actually have these things, because with our digital technology now, e-mails aren't going to survive. Future generations aren't going to be able to even read the cursive writing and so all these letters and diaries from the past, our parents, are really precious. We don't know our parents before we were born, so the only way you can piece that together is to read what they wrote before then. And I was lucky that Mum was a pack rat and that people had returned all her letters because they found them so fascinating so we had all these bags in the trunk room that I was able to take the time to read. Although I didn't read it until the end. I didn't realize what was in them, the depth of what was in them. I had saved them as a reward for myself at the end.

SIMMINS: Yes, I can understand that.

JOHNSON: I think if I had read them first, it might have been a different kind of book, but I read them at the end. Actually the original manuscript didn't have any of the letters in it. I put the pieces in at the eleventh hour; some of them even went in after the galleys were done.

SIMMINS: How extraordinary! Under the wire, or what?

JOHNSON: I felt Mum deserved it and I felt I needed to have them in there. She was now gone from my life physically and I just saw her from a completely different point of view. It thrust me back into the early part of the century, the 1920s and 1930s. Reading what was going on in her life at the time rounded out her character for me. And so whereas before she died, if someone had said to me, 'If you had been a peer of hers, a contemporary of hers, would she have been a friend of yours?' I still had so much anger I would have said, 'No,' but after she died, when I started reading all these letters, and I thought, Would I have been a friend of hers? and I thought I would have given anything to be a friend of hers.

SIMMINS: What an incredible perspective to have gained.

JOHNSON: Yes. I wish I could have been a friend of hers at that time; she would have been a wonderful friend.

SIMMINS: What an extraordinary feeling that must have been. We've talked about the siblings having the opportunity to look at the manuscript before it was published and no great problems there. Was it much the same with your three children?

JOHNSON: Yes. They've been very supportive and generous all the way along; they've always been like that.

SIMMINS: After writing the memoir, are you more aware of your own legacy?

JOHNSON: (Laughing) Of course I hope I'm dead when my children write their book! Who knows what might come out on a psychiatrist couch later? But I'm not – how can I put this? I'm conscious of not throwing away juicy diaries or correspondence.

SIMMINS: Good for you. So you're not editing your life.

JOHNSON: Exactly. I don't want to self-edit. I think it's a mistake to self-edit because if you think about it, it's a controlling thing to try to do. We can't control how people think of us after we're dead and we're going to be dead so it shouldn't matter, but I think the more we leave behind of, of our foibles or the negative parts of us, the more our children, if they didn't realize it before, will realize that we were human. I think my children are pretty aware of all the mistakes I've made in my life and I think it's probably helpful to them to know, if they make the same mistakes. We never learn from our parents, anyway. We all need to make our mistakes. It's so sad we all make the same mistakes over and over again.

SIMMINS: Until some point it just gets too ouchy and you do stop making some mistakes.

JOHNSON: Yeah, but you don't learn from whomever went before you. You don't learn from your parents. I have a diary from an aunt and it's very dry. She talks about the weather and what flowers are blooming and all that stuff. Those kinds of diaries don't interest me much. It's the introspection and when somebody's really trying to figure out their life. That's what I find fascinating.

SIMMINS: Well, you're right that this is a bit of a dying art, too, both cursive writing, letters, journals, these forms of expression. It's not the same in electronic form, it simply isn't. When you're touching the paper that somebody else touched and you're looking at fountain pen script …

JOHNSON: The weight of the paper, you know, the use of that particular word or another …

SIMMINS: You would be particularly responsive to this as an artist.

JOHNSON: Yes, and I do think there's something to be said for the hand on the pen and the paper, what comes through your body, through your hand, I do. Even though I do a lot of writing straight onto the computer, I do find that I write differently when I'm writing ink on paper.

SIMMINS: Yes, and apparently our brains work differently as well. There has been quite a bit of research in to that. Is there anything you would say to someone preparing themselves to write a memoir? Are there any thoughts on that process that you would share?

JOHNSON: There are a couple things. The ten thousand hours to learn a new skill, what I learned is that ten thousand hours, whether it's on the brush or with the pen, I think it's important to have a learning curve in terms of your writing, to practise diligence and learning.

Also, one of the things that I couldn't figure out, I never understood what people meant by style. So I was always worried about that, like what's my style, what does that mean? I could read the explanations of it and the definitions of it but I couldn't grasp what that meant until I realized … it's just your voice.

SIMMINS: Yes, a steady, maintainable, likeable your-voice.

JOHNSON: Right, but it's not a question of writing in the style of some famous writer, it's that you've got to have confidence, you've got to be natural. It's your own speaking voice.

SIMMINS: Yes.

JOHNSON: And you have to have confidence that somebody will like it. Some people won't like it; you can't be all things to all people, but you just have to be yourself and find your own voice and put it out in the world and see what happens. And that's what style is, I think.

SIMMINS: I would agree, there's a certain naturalness and ease to a writer who has written a lot and is comfortable in their own writerly skin.

JOHNSON: And I think context also. Even though this was my first memoir, I've always read memoir and biography and autobiography. It's my favourite. For me it's the literary equivalent of reality TV. I think life is so full of drama that there's no need to read fiction. I always think most fiction is disguised memoir, anyway. So it's always my first choice. I do read some fiction but frankly, I get bored with it and I just love memoir, so yes, I think context is important.

The trap I started to get into was to get too close to the subject in memoir and I had to remind myself to stand back. I still find this a really important exercise for myself. Once I have what I'm thinking about in terms of *me*, to then stand back and research the context – the world context, the town, the time, and the era.

I'm working on something at the moment which is what was happening to me in the '70s and '80s, in a very personal way, a sort of slice of life. And then when I went to stand back to look at the context, I realized I actually had to research because I couldn't remember everything. Then when I started researching it, it flooded back more memories of the time and I could analyze why, if all these things were happening in Toronto at the time, why didn't I see that then? What was it about me that had isolated me from this event? All of that helps, I think. You really grow as a person or you become more enlightened about your own life. Even if you think you weren't influenced by the context of the time, you realize you were, and why. I find that all a fascinating dive back into history.

SIMMINS: It's not only your life, it's your life and *times*, as the phrase goes. Now you mentioned that you're working on something new.

JOHNSON: I hardly know where to start.

SIMMINS: Oh, isn't that splendid?

JOHNSON: Well, it's a muddle for me at the moment. I had all these beads started, some of them longer than others. I thought, Oh, my God, I've got eighteen manuscripts open on the desktop, and then I thought, Well, let's hope they're all chapters of the same book. I tried to cram them into one. It doesn't work. They're not all chapters of the same book, they're all different books. I'm weighing the options because if each book takes three to five years, which it probably will for me because I work slowly … I envy these people who can crank out a book every year. I turn seventy this year [2017]. So which of these books do I want to spend three to five years on?

SIMMINS: So the works you're focused on now, are they also memoirs?

JOHNSON: Yes.

SIMMINS: Okay, good. Nuala O'Faolain said she didn't understand why more people weren't serial memoirists. I completely agree. Once you're on a roll, you think, Well, this was an interesting period, too, and so was this.

JOHNSON: And not only that, but I realize you can write a memoir in any genre, in any style, right? You can have thrillers, you can have romance, you can do anything.

SIMMINS: Collections of poems.

JOHNSON: Graphic novels.

SIMMINS: Who knows, with your artist's background, you might consider doing a mixed-media memoir.

JOHNSON: Memoir is so popular now.

SIMMINS: There's never really been a time when it wasn't.

JOHNSON: I think reality TV has made a difference to it. Because I really do think it's a literary equivalent.

SIMMINS: That sounds a bit negative, doesn't it? I mean, reality TV is pretty vacuous, isn't it?

JOHNSON: No, I don't think so, it depends what the program is. There are lots of true crime shows on TV. I think there's a fascination with all this genealogical stuff now, too. You know, *Who Do You Think You Are?*, which is a reality TV program based on Ancestry.com.

SIMMINS: True. I like that one.

JOHNSON: And now there's a program about finding your birth family, called *Long Lost Family*, where people are searching for their biological parents when they were adopted. So there are all these programs popping up that are hugely popular. I think this whole trend towards watching [true life stories] has happened in the past twenty years. So I think that's giving a boost to the sales of memoir.

SIMMINS: Well, I hope one story of the eighteen you've started calls out to you more than the others.

JOHNSON: Thank you. I hope so, too.

Plum Johnson
Craft

From the personal to the universal

Plum Johnson was not far into the work on her memoir, *They Left Us Everything,* before she could see there would be a link from the personal to the universal. She was far from being the first in the exhausted "sandwich generation" to look after both failing parents and "boomerang children." A part of this care included dealing with her parents' lakeside estate property, all twenty-three gracious but crammed rooms of it, in Oakville, Ontario. Johnson had a whole generational context to acknowledge and investigate.

For your memoir:

Do some online research about your first decades of life. What happened in your village, town, or city? What happened in the country? What music was playing? What did you used to eat for lunch – who prepared that lunch? What did you wear to school? Were you home-schooled or did you leave school early? Had the expressions "litterbug" or "beatnik" or "hippie" or "cool" or "rad" or "what-ever" or "bae" or "selfie" or its cruder cousin "belfie" come into the language? Where were you when Nelson Mandela was released from prison, or Space Shuttle Challenger exploded, or 9/11 occurred, or the Boxing Day Tsunami slammed Indonesia, or Sid Vicious or Princess Diana or pop star Michael Jackson died? Make some fact lists.

Be open to the emotions that visiting the past brings up in you. In fact, be as open as you can be. Somewhere in that glorious mix of nostalgia and happiness and fear and surprise and persistent, foggy amnesia, the generational subject you need to write about may appear.

Setting and creativity

Like Linden MacIntyre, Plum Johnson hadn't been aware that subjects for memoir choose us, as much as we think we choose them. Both writers realized that, as they researched their decades, something else was going on in their psyches. As they unearthed facts, they also rediscovered memories about people and long-ago events. Some of these were closely attached to family members, others to the strangers. Either way, some memories were intense and dramatic. And sometimes, the memories were gut-wrenching to revisit. Johnson, like Schoemperlen, reviewed these memories one bite at a time. Both writers realized that slow and steady, or nibbling around the edges, however you might think of it, really can win the race.

For your memoir:

If you've settled on the period around which you'll be writing, you probably have a good idea of some of the difficult stories of those times. Make a list of these hard memories.

And that's it, for a little while. Just look at them, and remember you are not that person anymore. Nor can those words hurt you anymore. You may have to do as Schoemperlen did and write in front of a window, looking out, then in, and telling yourself, 'That was then, this is now.'

Skeletons in the closet

I was intrigued by Plum Johnson's calm and accepting attitude about "skeletons in the closet," which she believes every family has. Her essential attitude seemed to be, "Why hide these skeletons? If they're out in the open, we can talk about our troubles, and support each other. You have them, I have them, we all of us have them. Let's offer comfort, not judgement."

For your memoir:

Make a list of the skeletons in your family's closet(s). Choose the most "shocking" and secret of these – and write about it. Imagine the best and worst outcomes writing about this skeleton might cause. Write about both. Which feelings tug at you the hardest? Fear? (Good

– it's a worthwhile subject.) Excitement? (Also good – you may have something more than a simple story to relate; you may have a book!) Anger? (Great! Injustices were done, and the writing may create room for healing.) Push on!

Section II
Creating your Memoir

Chapter Eight
Style and Content

Style

Tone is influenced by the author's writing style. Is the writer aggressive and punchy? Gentle and inviting? Funny? Crabby? At one remove, or "TMI," too much information? Inclusive or chilly? Dreamy? Nostalgic? Quirky? Self-deprecating? Style – personality – develops over a lifetime. Now and again, a writer has "it" from the get-go, but that is relatively rare.

Style also includes rhythm. Perfected in the oral tradition of so many indigenous cultures, from Canada's First Nations, to the Highland Scottish Gaels, rhythm is something all cultures learn from youngest years. Our heartbeats are echoed by drumbeats, our imaginations caught by the rhyming of words, the repetition of words, the allure of alliteration, the humour of onomatopoeia, and much else. From fairy tales to folk songs, rhythm is something we know, and love. Rhythmic writing calls out to us and leads us along. We follow with eager footfalls and arms outstretched. Rhythm and the rules of storytelling – beginnings, middles, and ends; archetypes of heroes and villains, fools and mentors, magicians and jesters, lovers, rulers, and innocents, outlaws, explorers, and the everyman/woman; paradises lost, paradises regained, or at least glimpsed once again – are what the reader lives for, and demands.

For your memoir:

Can you identify your writing style? Is the style suited to the subject matter? Go to the library and take out a half-dozen books. Dip into each book several times over. Note each writer's style. What do you like? What rubs you the wrong way?

You are not, heaven forbid, looking for a voice you can copy, which, in any case, you couldn't sustain, anyway. You are doing this to help you hear your own voice more clearly. So while your tone may be affable and self-deprecating, similar to Alan Doyle's tone (*Where I Belong, A Newfoundlander in Canada: Always Going Somewhere, Always Coming Home*), your story delivery might have some sharper observations and darker overtones. That's fine, that's you.

More than anything, this exercise serves to underscore just how many different writing styles exist. Yours exists in your head and heart; you hear it in conversation with others, you hear it when you chatter to yourself. Now you need to relax and apply it on paper … one page after another.

Content

What goes in a memoir? Think of memoir as the anti-résumé. Memoirs are far more than a recitation of facts and figures. The following list was created by a memoir writing group I taught.

What is often included in a memoir:

- family: of origin; biological; adoptive; extended;
- friends and communities, of all sorts;
- pets, or animals we work and/or live with;
- achievements; our struggles; how do we overcome adversity and misfortune?
- life or birth roots; our survival skills;
- senses of humour; aspirations;
- optimism: bringing light into the lives we live, and other lives lived;
- sense of hope, for ourselves and others;
- dreams continuum;
- exuberance; our sense of adventure;
- vim and vigour;
- emotions – the good, the bad, the wretched – all of them;
- characters and convictions;
- mysteries, intrigues and, possibly, our violence;
- addictions and obsessions;
- religion and/or spiritual beliefs;

- needs and desires;
- deepest fears;
- COURAGE.

For your memoir:

Thinking about style and content, read the first paragraphs in six different memoirs you have in your library, or you randomly choose from a public library. Which ones pull you in, which ones leave you cold – which ones just bore you?

Below are the first opening sections from the memoirs of our seven memoir muses. I have added an eighth, from Newfoundland born and raised Magie Dominic, author of *Street Angel* – because I love it. All of these excellent examples show how to establish setting, tone, and voice.

MacIntyre, Linden. *Causeway: A Passage from Innocence.* Toronto, ON: Harper Collins Publishers Ltd, 2006.

It is late Saturday morning, and my mother is at the stove fishing the doughnuts out of a dangerous pot of boiling fat. My father is quietly watching her while sipping on instant coffee and tapping his spoon on the can of Carnation evaporated milk. The top of the can is punctured by two triangular holes, and one has a collar of yellowing acrylic scum. He puts the spoon on the table and reaches past her, plucks a new doughnut from a heaping plate, rolls it around in the sugar bowl, nibbles delicately. His thinning hair is dishevelled, his eyes watery.

Johnson, Plum. *They Left Us Everything: A Memoir.* Toronto, ON: Penguin, 2014.

The night before I turn sixty-three, I'm looking in the mirror, pulling my sagging jawline up to my ears, listening to voicemails on speakerphone. Three are from Mum:

Happy birthday, m'darlin'!
Promise you'll drive out first thing tomorrow!
Damn this machine! Call me!

Mum is ninety-three, and these are her messages just since dinner. Nineteen years, one month, and twenty-six days of elder care have brought me to my knees. But first thing next morning, I crawl to my car, hack at the ice on the windshield, and slump into the front seat with the heater cranked up.

Dominic, Magie. *Street Angel.* **Waterloo, ON: Wilfred Laurier University Press, 2014.**

It's 1956. 'Tennessee Waltz' on the radio in the kitchen. Ingrid Bergman and Marilyn Monroe. The Russians are sending dogs into space and the dogs have spacesuits and helmets. Ed Sullivan and the show of shows. *The Honeymooners* on Saturday night. Pat Boone and Nat King Cole. Food rationing has ended in England. *Lady and the Tramp* and *Peter Pan*. Elvis Presley appears on TV but we're not allowed to look at his legs. Polio shots in the school auditorium.

Schoemperlen, Diane. *This is Not My Life: A Memoir of Love, Prison, and Other Complications.* **Toronto, ON: HarperAvenue, 2016.**

It is safe to say that never once in my life had I dreamed of being in bed with a convicted killer, let alone one with his teeth in a margarine container in the kitchen, his mother in the next room, and the word HI! tattooed in tiny blue letters on his penis.

Hill, Lawrence. *Black Berry, Sweet Juice: On Being Black and White in Canada.* **Toronto, ON: Harper Perennial, 2001.**

My children once joined me in a meeting with members of a black women's book club, who had asked me to speak with them about my last novel. While I answered questions, the children did their best to put a dent in the prodigious quantity of food laid out for our enjoyment. I always have the hardest time getting Caroline, my middle child, to touch meat of any kind, but that night she dug into jerk chicken as if preparing for famine. This child of mine, who at home would eat plain pasta for days on end if she had her druthers, also tucked into fried plantain, peas and rice, and all sorts of dishes she had never seen before.

Metatawabin, Edmund. *Up Ghost River: A Chief's Journey Through the Turbulent Waters of Native History.* Toronto, ON: Alfred A. Knopf Canada, 2014.

The bush, 300 kilometres north of Fort Albany, Ontario, 1954.

I knew something was wrong before I got back to camp. I could hear my family's voices, but I felt it before that. It was like walking into cold mist – you were breathing it in before you'd seen it coming. The feeling hung there, chilling me inside, and I hurried to our mud house, hoping I could make it go away.

Morrissey, Donna. *Different Dirt: A Memoir.* Toronto, ON: Penguin Random House Canada, 2021.

I am small. I am standing on a bed in a dark room that is strange. My pajama bottoms are wet and stick to my legs and I shiver from the cold.

A door opens, a crack of yellow light falls over me and my mother is in the light.

She bends down and scoops me up and her face is warm against mine.

Mowat, Claire. *Travels with Farley.* (Originally published with Key Porter Books, 2005.) East Lawrencetown, NS: Pottersfield Press, 2015.

On a bright day in May 1969, the Dart Herald airplane departing from Charlottetown for the Magdalens was only half full. Most of the passengers were speaking quietly to one another in French. Across the aisle, a grey-haired woman was trying to amuse a fidgeting child with a brace on one of her skinny legs – in English. They must surely live in the Magdalen Islands, I thought to myself. Why else would they be on the flight? Perhaps they had gone to some mainland city to see a doctor. Why were any of these people heading out that morning to a speck of land in the middle of the Gulf of St. Lawrence? I knew why we were there – to make a film for the CBC. I passed the time guessing about the circumstances of the others.

Chapter Nine
The Outline Dilemma: Plotting versus "Pantsing"

In the writerly scheme of things, you are either a "plotter" (a writer who likes to plot, or use an outline) or a "pantser" (a writer who works "by the seat of their pants," or likes to create first, and then organizes). You may even be both, or go back and forth.

I am an evolving pantser (depends on the day, depends on the work). Overall, my creative brain is far bossier than my organized brain. But I have come to see how crucial that left-brain function is.

The biggest epiphany I've had in recent times is realizing that, for me, an outline gives me far *more freedom* than I ever could have imagined. You can change the outline whenever you want! You are not limited to your first idea of what the plot or structure should be. (I wonder, at times, did I think it was carved in stone? Is that where the anxiety came from?)

Either approach can work for a writer. There is no right or wrong. No matter how you sit down to write a memoir, your job is to create an entertaining, inspiring, reflective, thoughtful, inclusive, and well-crafted story. If you need to write an overall outline before you write one word, go for it. If it only works for you to do this chapter by chapter, on you go. Or if you want to write first, sort later, so be it.

What plotters tend to think about:

- their characters' lives – every detail about these
- their characters' characters
- their characters' goals and motivations, flaws and foibles, challenges and troubles
- major plot events; the story's climax, resolution, and ending
- subplots, and who gets the most dialogue and air time (well, paper time)

- exploring particular themes, ideas, plot twists, connections *before* they write

What pantsers tend to think about:

- taking a small plot idea – and running with it
- dreaming up the haziest outline of an appealing (or wicked, or humorous, or odd, etc.) character and running with it
- intriguing story openings
- imagining the coolest climax or ending ever, and writing a story around it
- how far their enthusiasm and imagination can take them, every time they sit down to write
- exploring particular themes/ideas/plot twists/connections *as* they write

Unlike many experienced plotters, pantsers may face plot tangles after writing the first draft. Logic and logistics might trip them up. They might even write themselves into a corner. What plotters often achieve through their outlining, pantsers must work on during rewrites.

Really, all you need to do is work with your natural inclinations, and remain open-minded about all the rest. I think of myself as a work in progress. But after three non-fiction books and one unpublished novel, I sure see the sense of outlines at this point.

Some ways to outline

- Create a bare-bones outline on paper (or computer).
- Create a detailed outline on paper (or computer).
- Or work backward from the climax or forward from the opening event, whichever makes sense for you.
- Write blurbs for each section, whether events or scenes or chapters.
- Draw a visual of your acts (three, four, or more) in graph form and add the high point/crisis moments. (Writer's Blocks, or Scrivener, or MasterWriter, three of many book writing softwares, may also be helpful.)
- Write out character sketches for major characters – include physical particulars, histories, relationships, goals and

motivations, dreams, fears, importance to other characters. (The software Story Bible works well for some writers.)
- Write out setting sketches – know the look and feel of each scene location. Consider the five senses.

A few more words about plotting:

Plotting takes the reader from here (the beginning and middle) to there (the end). Your feet need to be firmly planted on your story path – and you'll need a lot more than bread crumbs to lead your reader along. Think how firm Donna Morrissey was on this point; without plot, you simply go in circles – and really, no one likes getting dizzy.

What they do like to do is turn pages. And what makes a reader do that? Encountering, in memoir, the same elements that make them race through the pages of a work of fiction, such as a mystery.

1. Curiosity and connection
2. Danger and suspense
3. Timelines bearing down on our "hero/heroine"
4. Anger over injustice or roadblocks or setbacks; frustration and tension over simple bad luck
5. Resolution/redemption
6. An ending that makes thematic sense, and has emotional resonance.

Chapter Ten
Before You Start Writing; Finding Your Story

Before You Start Writing:

Do some reading. Read critically and attentively. How is the story affecting you, and how does the writer achieve those effects?

Now, reread some favourite childhood books. This may serve to take you back to the atmospheres of childhood, which still hold strong and even magical appeal for many of us. The best of children's books are exquisitely written, too (e.g. *The Narnia Chronicles,* by C.S. Lewis; *Charlotte's Web,* by E.B. White; *The Secret Garden,* by Frances Hodgson Burnett; *Le Chat Botté (Puss in Boots)*, by Charles Perrault; *Madeline,* by Ludwig Bemelmans; *The Little Mermaid,* by Hans Christian Andersen; *King of the Wind,* by Marguerite Henry).

While I've cited children's books from my own Eurocentric, West Coast of Canada childhood of the 1960s and '70s, the world of children's literature has never been more diverse and fascinating, offering books for children of every race, ethnicity, and religion, and every age, circumstance, and language.

Next, reread several favourite adult novels and non-fiction books. Read new ones. Read books from countries and cultures that are new to your experience. Ask teachers and librarians for recommendations of new titles.

Reading fiction and non-fiction will remind you what you love best about certain writing styles, and underscore the delicious imperative of *story*.

And, of course, read memoirs – buy as many as you can. You can also go to your local library or to thrift stores. But it's nice to put some money toward living writers, who, heaven knows, are rarely flush. Support local writers when you can, too.

In addition to reading, refresh your own memories. You can even revisit childhood haunts or neighbourhoods in order to live a while in your memories. As rewarding, visit with older relatives and neighbours to talk about "the good old days" – or whatever else it was they might have been. You may also wish to record these conversations. A small voice recorder is an invaluable tool.

Also, have a look at family photo albums and correspondence. Both of these will stir old memories, sometimes profoundly.

And finally, go to a museum. Immerse yourself in the worlds of yesteryear. Ask any curator about the value of historical journals and correspondence, and they will tell you how rarely they receive them – and how they wished they had more. Your life has many sorts of values, and historical value is among these. You may even consider willing your personal papers and memoirs to a favourite museum. Just imagine if, at the ends of their lives, sisters Catherine Parr Trail and Susanna Moody chucked out their journals and diaries – what would we know about the social history and pioneer lifestyle of Upper Canada in the mid-nineteenth century? And we would know nothing of the awesome, almost impenetrable North American woods, which European settlers saw only as a resource, not the majestic miracles they were. (Susanna Moodie, *Roughing it in the Bush*, 1852, and Catherine Parr Trail, *The Backwoods of Canada*, 1863.)

Which makes me think again of Edmund Metatawabin's point about the strictness of the oral storytelling tradition in indigenous and other traditional cultures, and how these stories *do not change* from generation to generation, and can be counted on to provide historical truths. (Atlantic Canada's Acadian peoples also have strong oral storytelling traditions.) For example, had the Canadian government, at any time, asked the Inuit where the HMS *Terror* had sunk, on its doomed attempt to complete the Northwest Passage, they might not have had to wait 168 years to "discover" her, on the bottom of an Arctic bay … exactly where the local peoples knew it rested.

Pre-Writing (using paper): Free-writing:

Sometimes people don't know how to start writing – as in, they don't know how to get their hands moving and their thoughts flowing. They may have ideas galore, but feel stuck.

Free-writing is a process that can free the hands and imaginations of people who want to start their memoirs. Sometimes called "stream of consciousness writing," it is a technique which requires a person to write continuously for a set period of time, paying absolutely no attention to spelling, grammar, or topic. This exercise usually produces a jumble of words and ideas – connected or separate – but its genius lies in bypassing self-criticism and inaction. Set out your paper and pen.

Set the timer for a short period to start (two minutes), then longer. If you really feel bottled up, you may need to do this for several days in a row or longer. You'll have a tidy collection of writing by then to mull over and perhaps pull bits out of, to expand and explore. Remember: with free writing the idea is to keep the pen moving and the ideas and images flowing down onto the paper. Do not stop and meditate on what you've written, or where you are headed next. Just write.

Journal writing:

Journals are the writer's friend. Their benefits are too numerous to list. Above all, journals can set the pattern for daily writing that every writer needs if they wish to improve their skills and complete longer writing projects, such as a memoir. You may find that several months of journal writing will help grease the wheels for beginning a memoir. It even helps to see your ideas and thoughts down on paper – stark and real. That paragraph right there could start your book …

Read the Obituaries:

Why? For ideas. For inspiration. For the pleasure of reading some very fine writing and fascinating tributes. These obituaries are bittersweet pleasures. Amidst all the sadness, so much love and respect shines through – and sometimes, frank and amusing facts. *The Globe and Mail* has a large obituary section, and on the weekend runs an excellent guest column called "Lives Lived." When a skilled writer sits down to write about life, love, and loss, it is always worth the read.

Write Your Own Obituary:

Not as zany an idea as you may first think! This is a useful exercise for deciding what you do and don't want to include in a memoir. If you write about yourself in the third person – "Abigail loved her job as a teacher, but secretly yearned to work as a welder" – you may find it much easier to be honest about the life you've lived, and how you feel about it. "She" is at one rather large remove from "I." Once you have the ideas written in this way, you can pick and choose what stays and what goes.

Cluster-writing:

This has become very popular in recent years, and is a helpful tool to collect up ideas. Using paper and pen, choose a word that might be central to your memoir. This could be "family," or it could be "ocean" or "animals." Write this one word in the centre of your page. Circle the word, then write words all around it – the words that come to you when you think about "family" or "ocean" or "animals." These words may seem random at first. Don't overthink the exercise; write quickly, circling each word, grouping words around your central word. Connect your new words to previous ones with lines; when you feel you have exhausted a particular avenue of associations, go back to your central word and begin again. This exercise is fun and pleasantly unpredictable, as you don't know what words may come to you. Try it. You'll have a great stockpile of subjects to think about.

Finding Your Story

There are many ways to find your story. But if your heart isn't guiding you as quickly as you thought it might, or you are indecisive for a variety of reasons, consider the following.

World or community events: Memoir is not a stand-alone idea, or construct. It often stands shoulder to shoulder with world or community events, which can include wars, catastrophes, celebrations, and changes. These can serve the memoir well, because they provide structure, drama, and, one hopes, rebirth. They can provide essential dimension of the memoir – e.g. a war bride's memoir; the pioneer's memoir, etc.

Our villages: Writing personal life stories always includes writing about other people, particularly family members. Our romantic loves, friends, neighbours, work mates, or adversaries often make appearances in our work as well; it all depends on the story. In the same way we hope to connect to the reader holding our book, we are connected in the pages of our stories to those who have affected our lives the most, in positive ways and otherwise. At times, memoir can seem like a whole busy village or town, or even city. As mentioned before, care must be taken not to include too large a cast. But if you do the job you must do, to make me care about your life, I must also care about the people in it. This means multi-dimensional, complex, flawed, and admirable people – just like the rest of us.

Setting: Readers often cherish memoirs that put setting first. This might mean places that are common in the popular imagination, such as Tuscany, Copenhagen, or Tahiti, or the more particular and individual desires a reader may have of visiting Canada's Far North, or Haida Gwaii, or travelling on a sailboat, or visiting the Ravenkeeper, at The Tower of London, in the United Kingdom. As with settings in novels, settings in memoir can add greatly to the reader's enjoyment – or any other emotion you may care to list, all of which keep the pages turning. Settings pull the reader in experientially, engaging all the senses. Don't forget to use the full spectrum: sight, sound, smell, touch, taste, and maybe even our sixth sense, of intuition, or ESP, extrasensory perception.

Our loves or passions: These, of course, spread far beyond the romantic realm. We'd most of us enjoy being madly proficient or brilliant at our sports and hobbies. Usually we are more modestly gifted. And so, while a lucky few of us can climb Everest, win medals at the Olympics, take a submersible to the *Titanic*'s deep, watery grave, win a ribbon at the Westminster Dog Show or a wreath of roses at the Kentucky Derby, most of us compile less flashy achievements. In either case, we should still aim to create memoirs of depth and beauty.

How do we do that? Emotional investment is key. This in turn invites your reader to be invested. No achievement, however grand or modest, is accomplished without some sort of struggle – and commonly, several or even many setbacks. You need to share these challenges with your reader. What's at stake for you, the protagonist? Your self-worth? Your self-respect, or sense of identity? Your deepest psychic peace and well-being? Your very life? It had better be something substantial and either life-altering or life-threatening. Slight, passing disappointments or relatively superficial happiness won't do.

Our struggles: Again, these, too, had better be substantial, worth my while as a reader to learn about. Connection here can come two ways. I may have had/do have the same struggles as you (or someone close to me may be struggling), and I am intensely curious how you've sorted yours out. Or I am simply curious, human being to human being, how you navigated major tragedy or troubles. In all cases, I, the reader, have a strong need to collect up information, which you, the writer, will provide, in readily consumable fashion (small bits, artfully inserted). After that, you will move quickly to action.

Learning/Discovery, from ignorant to wise: We are thoroughly curious about other people's successes and competencies, too. Michelle Obama fits this bill perfectly. She's the only First Lady who has not one but two degrees from Ivy-League colleges (Harvard Law School and Princeton University). Any of her three pre-White House careers are of interest to many: lawyer; Chicago city administrator; community outreach worker. *Becoming* and other memoirs of the hugely successful and popular are like food to the hungry: gobbled down with gusto.

Perfect moments in time: It's the rare person who doesn't have a perfect moment in time in their life. These include certain seasons, times of dizzying love, times of great creative productivity, times of radiant success, or of shimmering simplicity. The trick here is to still look outward, when memories keep our gaze turning inward. Using every literary device at your disposal (foreshadowing; imagery; simile and metaphor; the right point of view and structure; etc.) makes this perfect moment in time as exquisite a reading experience for others as it is in recollection for you. And it still has to be a story, not just a single event or day or experience. Why will the reader care? Did the moment very nearly not occur? Did the joyous time come after another time, of intense loss and grief? And my favourite – were epiphanies involved?

Other worlds: Memoir readers live for those books that take them to worlds to which they have no real-life entry. This could be to a Thoroughbred horse farm in Kentucky, or to the deck of a West Coast of Canada commercial fishing troller. It could be to the private palace home of a queen and her prince consort – or to the mean streets of a working girl in Southeast Los Angeles. Like the fatally curious cat, humans are voraciously curious about anything outside of their own experiences, though, unlike the unfortunate feline, readers can satisfy that curiosity without fear of death. That door that says "Private"? That's the one we want to step through – even run through. If you can find a door behind which is a world not too many people have written about, so much the better. Like a "breakthrough" or bestselling novel, you may have a wildly successful memoir on your hands. But, you say, it's only just my life! Indeed, and not mine. So I want to know more.

A visit back in time (for example, Expo 67, Montreal, Canada): Self-explanatory – though many older people have trouble thinking of their growing up years as "the good old days." It's just their childhood, or their young-adult years, or their striving and producing years. The patina of time, however, has worked some miracles on "those days." Look no further than your refrigerator. Does it look like the refrigerator of your youth – in appearance or in contents? What about your clothes? Wouldn't spandex have been great in the '40s, with all those sheath dresses the women wore?

Similarly, the places you visited as a young person are mostly much changed. The "Exposition" of my twenties – Expo 86, celebrated in Vancouver, British Columbia – is only a memory now, its oceanside lands then developed for offices, apartments, and townhouses. But stories? I and thousands of other people, both city residents and visitors, have Expo 86 stories, by the truckload. Are any worthy of inclusion in a memoir? With that high number, I'd guess yes – and as long as the stories intersect with more personal stories of change and turmoil, and as long as it all makes thematic and artistic sense.

Speaking for Many

In the truest sense, you can only speak for yourself in a memoir, unless you are purposely writing on behalf of someone else, and working with them to create a story. But you can speak as one of a group, especially if research and facts are involved. In his memoir *Up Ghost River*, author Edmund Metatawabin, of the Cree First Nation, does speak on behalf of himself and others who attended the St. Anne's Residential School in Fort Albany, Ontario – and they were grateful for it. Are you a member of a group about whose experiences you want to, need to, write? If so, this is a large and sacred responsibility. You must take great care to write only about that which you know to be true, with no guesswork or assumptions. Your memoir will be as much creative non-fiction ("True stories, well told.") as a memoir (a chapter of a life of an individual).

Chapter Eleven
Collecting up your Writing, and "The Truth"

Gathering

Write 50 words. That's a paragraph. It adds up.

Write 250 words. That's a page. It really adds up.

Write 300 pages. That's a manuscript. And typing "the end" or "-30-" feels amazing.

Write every day. That's a habit. And a good one.

Edit and rewrite. That's how you get better. You'll come to see this is the fun and satisfying part.

Share your writing for people to comment. That's called feedback. Choose your word-mates carefully. Preferably, share your work with writers who are more experienced than you are, but who know how to offer constructive criticism. There is always a way to build up a writer's enthusiasm and resolve, which you, too, will learn in the company of honest but kind writers.

Don't worry about rejection or publication or good and bad reviews. That's the life of a writer. Your skin may never get thicker, but you do learn how to press on, and that's something to be proud of.

When not writing, read. Read from writers better than you. Read, and spend some time thinking about what you've read. Keeping a book journal can be useful. Just a paragraph or two on the books you read, and what you liked best/least about them. Publish these reviews on sites such as Goodreads.

"The Truth"

There's a myth in the world known as "objective journalism." In fact, there is no such thing. All newspapers lean a bit more left, right, or centre, according to the publishers' and owners' biases and connections. This is further influenced by corporate connections and financial support. The reporters themselves bring suitcases of personal histories and opinions to each and every story they write, and can readily assemble facts to create the one that interests them the most.

Then there are other trite phrases, such as "Just the facts, ma'm," which is supposed to reassure a reader that a story in the newspaper presents only the facts, no fluff, and no opinion or prejudice, either. Newspaper or magazine articles, personal essays or memoirs, all contain facts (selectively chosen), and all present a story (as carefully chosen). Now, you can check on facts, though this has become laborious, in an age of real "fake news," and fake "fake news." Often we can only grasp onto basic facts, such as the date, time, and place an event occurred.

The writer will choose the story they do, according to their own wants, needs, and assorted, urgent imperatives. You can't even attempt to "check" on these. Or if you do, you could find everyone else connected to that story in complete disagreement. Or not.

A story in its simplest form consists of selected facts, presented as a single narrative. In every case, someone – a unique individual – made the selection. Someone else would have selected differently. And that's the deeply subjective process that underlies every story.

Being subjective does not mean being untruthful or unfair. It simply means acknowledging that you are the person who created the story, and doing your best to compensate for your own shortcomings and ignorance.

Adding to the oddity of it, everyone is "right." Your mental and emotional snapshot of an event or experience is as "true" as anything concrete and provable in this world, including mountains, bridges, and Japanese cherry trees – even if it's completely erroneous.

Your story may not even be your own. If you are a younger sibling, for example, you may have heard a certain story from an older sibling, many times over, and have incorporated their memory into your own set. I have even had the experience of asking an older sibling about a memory she'd told me about years before, only to have her say, "No, I don't remember that." A second-hand memory that was seared in my brain was apparently not even in my sister's recollection anymore.

This same sister said our mother had talked about having relatives from Britain who were among the first schoolteachers in Nova Scotia, but when she asked about this again, some years later, our mother denied it. And before you suggest otherwise, I know this sister to have a sharp and accurate memory. Of course she does: her memories often align with mine!

I once asked my father if he'd really said to my mother, "Your best is not good enough." I'd been angry about that for decades. My mother worked like a draft horse to look after her four kids when she and Dad were married, and like a team of draft horses after Dad left the family.

"No," said my startled father, "I never said that. But your mother said that to me."

Oh … and even as I tell this story, I am worried that it was indeed the other way around. Have I misremembered again? It's been twenty years since I lost my parents; I can't ask them about these things anymore. Perhaps the only "truth" is that I don't like thinking that either parent was capable of saying that to the other. That feels real.

In my family, I am known as having an acute memory. I have often teased my older brother about the apparent gaps in his memory related to childhood or teenage years. I don't do this as much anymore, as I've finally figured out there's a large pain link in there, which causes us to "forget" certain times in our lives. So I only tease about "gentle" lapses in memory. Memory, after all, has a way of revising reality so we really believe things that are not true. Memory even likes to protect us at times.

I protected myself, for example, about memories related to my maternal grandmother's funeral Why didn't we go to her funeral, I asked my brother, feeling confused about that lapse in memory, but certain that he and I had not attended the funeral.

"You didn't," he said promptly, "but I did."

I didn't believe him. "Why would you go, and I wouldn't?" I asked him.

"Because Mum asked us if we wanted to go – she gave us the option. You said no, I said yes."

I still didn't know how to believe him. I asked him a bunch of questions to which I knew the answers, from around that exact time and he answered every one correctly. So he had gone to the funeral at the Presbyterian Church in Kerrisdale, Vancouver, 1974 – he really had gone.

But why, I wailed, would I not go to the funeral? To myself I thought, How could I be so heartless not to support my mother, and show respect for my grandmother? At fifteen years old, I was more than old enough to manage a funeral.

"I don't know," my brother shrugged. "You just didn't."

Not only had I forgotten why I didn't attend the funeral, I had also forgotten that my brother had gone to it. Do not ask me if my older sister attended: I have no idea.

In this book, I have suggested to you that you should be both honest and truthful in your memoir. It is a suggestion seemingly as straightforward as "Turn right at the next corner," said to the driver of a car by his navigator. And of course it is not.

Whenever possible, support your story by checking family documents such as letters, journals, personal papers, and so on; you can also check newspapers of the times. After that, and only if you wish to (because it could completely rock your memory/un-memory), check with older siblings and older family members about the comings and goings of others in the family. Mostly, focus on your own understanding of an event or transition – as it affected you.

Had I written about the "funeral of my grandmother," I would have skipped the actual funeral, thinking that for some reason, I just didn't remember it very well. Most likely I would have written about how the death of my grandmother affected my mother, who was heartbroken, and her apparently less emotional granddaughter. (I apologize, Grandma Josie, and I do have nice memories about you, especially the stories you told about the St. Bernard dogs you had growing up. Now that I think of it, didn't your mother, the fine watercolour painter, Josephine "Joe" Dickson, have a whole kennel of these dogs? There, see, my memory's not bad at all.).

I might also have written about my lack of deep connection with my grandmother, but also about my deep respect for her as a veteran of World War One, and a front-line nurse, in France, seeing some of the worst injuries and deaths imaginable, of men and animals. I knew this because Mum had told us about her nursing career so often – and speculated that that was why her hands shook so much.

There are times when a writer can speak with great authority. How did the loss of your first-born child change your world? You know, as no one else could possibly know. When did you feel that complete loss of innocence that a child should have had for so much longer than you did? Tell me about that. What changes did you make to your life after your divorce, and why did you move from the city to the country? There shouldn't be too many wobblies in these accounts.

And if there are, you will deal with them, as an artist is allowed to, with imagination, research, and careful, intuitive thought.

Memoir is a blend of truth and art. I cannot remember the dress I was wearing when I went to my first day of school. But I can remember dresses of the time, and my favourites among these. I can remember wanting patent leather shoes more than the moon and stars, of being envious to the point of feeling sick that so many of my classmates had them, in black! in white! in pink! – but I wore black and white oxfords, because I needed "arch support," due to my (dear God) flat feet.

I also remember tearing two sets of cotton tights in one week – and my mum looking stricken. Just where was the money going to come from for more stockings?

Trust these memories that speak to you. I believe with all my heart in the memories I just shared with you. I can write whole stories around those memories, not just present the bare bones. I believe in my truths, however abbreviated or incomplete they may be. I also believe that I want to share those truths, as I have lived them, and now safeguard in memory.

Section III
The Audacity of Memoir

Chapter Twelve
Maps of the Heart and Mind

The best memoirs are maps of the heart and mind. My hope for *Conversations and Craft* is that you explore the map of your own life, as you reflect on conversations with bestselling Canadian memoirists and decide how their offerings and mine will help you craft a memoir.

I wrote *Conversations and Craft* because when I looked for a particular type of book I wanted to read on memoir, I couldn't find it. Here are some more questions I had, along with some answers I found, during the course of teaching, and writing my book.

Q How do you access the details of your earliest memories, make them immediate and dramatic?

A I believe we access our oldest memories through side doors. You can't remember who came to your fifth birthday party? You can't see their faces at all, or remember any names? Well, then, can you remember the food your mother served? The clothes you wore? The games you played? Oh! You didn't have a party at your house? You went to the city zoo – and one of your friends tried to climb in the polar bear enclosure – and your mum was scared witless? Sound the bell, there's a story right there. As for making the memories immediate and dramatic, try this exercise.

For your memoir:

Write about the first time you saw either your mother or father or parental guardian was truly frightened. Write about this episode in the past tense. Jump in with all your memory-senses: sight, sound, taste, touch, and smell.

Secondly, write about the same episode in the present tense. Read both versions aloud.

Often, the present tense will really pull your reader into the story. It can be powerful and immediate. But not always. Sometimes the past tense works a charm. It all depends on the details you include, and your ease in one tense or another. Occasionally, both versions are equally dramatic and evocative. Usually, one has stardust on it.

Q How do you drive the story forward?

A You have to want something badly. I mean crawl-over-a-field-of-broken-glass badly. Or, and again with all your heart, you may want to understand something that has occurred, or to heal from an event, or to share coping mechanisms and spiritual perspectives, after coming through a difficult or perhaps life-changing period.

You include the whole kit-bag of emotions, including your vulnerabilities, your weaknesses and vanities, your misguided moves toward happiness and fulfillment, and your elemental, worthy humanity. In your story, I see myself, or my sister, or my mother, brother, grandmother, or dearest friend. I connect with your story, heart to heart, life to life, no matter that you live on a sailboat in New Zealand, and I live in a Victorian cottage, in a small coastal village in Nova Scotia.

Q How do you make a stranger care about your life?

A As above, except you might reach him or her on an even more personal level by writing about a subject of shared interest. Sometimes when I ask people in a workshop, "What are you good at?" I get the most astonishing answers. People are good at: beekeeping; candle-making; making wedding cakes; hammering shoes on horses; helping autistic children ride horses; tuning pianos; playing the kazoo; building sandcastles; solving mathematical equations; reading aloud; choosing the right people to do the right jobs; coaching children; doing crossword puzzles; swimming large bodies of water; communicating with animals; beachcombing; quilting; designing museums.

For your memoir:

What are you good at? What specialized worlds could you lead people into, and tell them stories about? Can you see yourself writing a book of essays, sharing the details of your special world? Could you write a single narrative about that world? In the same way Linden MacIntyre chose a causeway to literally link up public events with more personal stories in his life, you could use your area of expertise to be the front story of your memoir. Instantly, you have visuals, specialized language, even smells (sweet beeswax, or the tang of iodine on the beach) to bring into your memoir. And in terms of our passions of every sort, these are always complex and layered subjects, well worth investigating and ruminating on.

Q Can anyone write a memoir?

A Yes. The only proviso I have is that you need to enjoy time with yourself, time with your memories, and time with words and stories. I think the biggest trick is also the smallest, in some ways. If you can decide on the *scope* of your project, you might save yourself from having some discouraged days. For some, it could be a Year of Saturdays, when you write a memory each Saturday morning, about your childhood on up to the present. That's fifty-two or possibly fifty-three Saturdays in a year memories, as long or as short as they need to be. Still too much? The Holidays of my Youth, perhaps, where you would write about how you celebrated each one of the holidays of your faith and culture, within a calendar year.

For the more ambitious memoir writers, they already know what they'll be writing about, and at length. The trick then is to choose the structure and style that suits you best. I do believe anyone motivated and supported enough can write a memoir.

My hope for each and every one of you memoirists is that your dynamic life stories demand to be read, refuse to be forgotten.

Remember, you hold the magic of connection and universality in your hands.

Chapter Thirteen
The Minefields of Memoir

As we've touched on in the interviews, there are some potential minefields to writing a memoir. Families can be volatile entities, even violent. Even "good ones" can be "shirty," or prone to offense or holding grudges. Memoirs can push a lot of family buttons, anger even the mildest of people, if they feel exposed or ridiculed (even if that was the last thing you intended). Even if it's "her" memoir, or "his," you, the sibling, aunt, uncle, mother, father, cousin, friend, might feel as though you've been dragged into the circle of scrutiny – or criticism.

And then there's the old saw, "You can please some of the people some of the time, but not all of the people all of the time," and for sure, you're likely to encounter these hot and cold reactions to your memoir.

It is what it is. Don't say I didn't warn you.

And do say I gave you some strategies and more positive ideas to think about, before you started your memoir. (As for the after of memoir, a friend of mine taught me to respond to every incomprehensible or dispiriting remark a person might make by saying, "No kidding?" You're not being rude, and generally, it closes down the conversation nicely. This works well for any written work!)

Within the memoirs themselves, what are the most common minefields, and how do we want to write about them?

Here's a brief description I wrote about minefields, for a workshop I put on.

"Minefields are: secrets; shared, hidden histories; shocking events, followed by complicated decisions or estrangements; affairs, addictions, and compulsions; multiple failures, escalating betrayals; incest, violence, and murders. Minefields are also the negative patterns that go on in families, generation after generation, and in individual lives, for some or all of that life. Minefields are whatever weighs on your heart, but needs to be worked out – on paper."

You know, the good stuff: sweaty, lustful, objectionable, rule-breaking, jaw-dropping, shocking, embarrassing, shivery, delicious stuff. We all want to read about that. Of course we stray into prurient territory at times, but that's forgivable, too.

Reading about the more peculiar or non-mainstream side of life can have all sorts of good effects, too. Maybe you learn about something you knew nothing about – and want to aid or somehow assist troubled or abused individuals in that group. That could mean something as small as changing your own attitudes and actions, as you move through the world, or something as big as studying to be in the helping professions. Think of that! Perhaps a memoir you write could change someone's life, in a broadening, excellent way. Worth a few blushes, that.

There is life after the minefields of memoir. They blow up around you and you cover your ears and pray there's no loss of life or limbs. You didn't ask, necessarily, to have certain less than optimal life experiences, about which you then wrote. You wrote about them bravely and well, or even tentatively and adequately, but either way, you did try your best to come to terms with the cards you were dealt. Maybe, as many of the interviews here have shown, you, too, came away from writing a difficult memoir with a great and expanding sense of healing and well-being. I hope so.

I really hope so.

Appendix

Seven Tips for Writing a Memoir

1. Narrow your focus

Remember, this isn't your whole life you are writing about. Choose that one magic summer of childhood or early adulthood, or one of the toughest times in your life, or the day, like memoirist Karen Blixen, you bought a coffee farm in Africa.

2. Then widen your focus

You aren't the only "character" in your memoir. Your friends, family, animals, and even strangers will appear on the pages. The landscape, or setting, may also be significant enough to be a character. The wider world will, and should, insert itself. Politics and history, even, as they pertain to change or challenge in our lives. Of course readers want to know about you. However, the backstory and vivid details also make for a powerful memoir.

3. Tell the truth

The most resonant memoirs require the writer to be honest and genuine. For women, who are socialized to put the feelings of others before their own, this can be difficult. A memoir doesn't give you *carte blanche* to criticize and betray, but if it's all sunshine and roses the reader will be bored quickly. Telling the truth can be hard, but the effort is worth it. The good news is – you will find the level of honesty you are comfortable with fairly quickly, and can push up and down from that position, *according to what is needed in the story.*

The only "master/mistress" you serve in memoir is *The Story*. If a revelation about someone or yourself doesn't push the storyline ahead, or reveal something about their/your character and its development, then guess what? You don't need it! I've also found you can dispatch a nasty bug as easily with a newspaper as a hammer. You can say a lot with a little.

Ultimately, and with luck, you will find and articulate wisdom.

4. Put your readers in your shoes

Remember the old adage "Show, don't tell." That's the difference between "When Bob came home drunk for the third time that week, Jeanette was very upset," and "When Jeanette heard Bob's car door slam shut, she gasped, and her hand went to her throat, where the bruises from last night still showed purple and red." Bring your reader in as close as you can to your perspective.

5. Use elements of fiction to bring your story to life

Your memoir is your journey, but it is the reader's journey, too. They will want to cheer you on. But they need to like you first, and then truly care about you. You don't have to confess to every flaw you have, but you do need to be vulnerable, and you do need to have some hard times, so you aren't unapproachable on an emotional level.

As a "character" (and you are one), you need to be multi-dimensional and complex. Your other main or supporting characters also need to be fully realized. Build tension with conflict and drama – I know you've had some of that in your life! Create atmosphere by using all five senses to describe the worlds you inhabit. Welcome your readers into different and evocative settings; soon, they'll know these as well as you do. And feel free to add lots of action and dialogue. I'll just repeat that last one: lots of action and dialogue – so important! Last, the six elements of fiction – setting, characters, plot/action, conflict, themes, and narrative arc – always pull a story along at a good clip.

6. Create an emotional journey

Memoirs are all about connection. I may not have bought a farm in Africa, but I have been blessed with several wonderful homes, and love them dearly for what they gave/give me. Similarly, I've never loved a baron (Karen Blixen's husband was Baron Bror von Blixen-Finecke), but my life has been graced with both love and heartbreak, the latter serving to open my heart to others in distress. When I sit down to write a story, I want to "leave 'em crying in the aisles."

And not just crying, but howling with laughter or shocked by my reckless derring-do, or praying I won't hurt myself too badly – *again*. Keep your readers close! Write a page-turner packed with emotions. (And again, *show*, don't tell those feelings!)

7. The Narrative Arc

As a reader, you are familiar with the narrative arc. Remember the "mountain" your English teacher used to draw on the chalk board? Once we reached the precipice, we were to fill in the climatic point of the book or story. Your memoir is the same. You need to create enough tension to shape your overall story, *as well as each individual chapter*, with that narrative arc.

Writing Prompts and Lists

Sometimes it's hard to access the stories inside us without a prompt. Lists can also help to stir up ideas. Dip into these prompts and lists whenever you're in need of a fresh breeze to set sail with your writing. You never know which idea may work its way to the centre of your memoir, or which themes may serve to support it.

Prompts:

The homes of your life: Write about all the homes or places you have lived. Think about what made them special/not special and reflect upon those periods of your life.

Summer: Write about the happiest/saddest/simplest/most complicated summers of your life.

Seasons: Write about your favourite season(s), and the events and memories attached to those seasons. Write about your least favourite season. Do you attach past events to the seasons? (I once had a boyfriend break up with me under a magnificent arc of Japanese cherry blossoms; never felt quite the same about them.)

Precious objects: Your house is on fire and you have only a few minutes to gather up precious items in it. What do you take with you?

Friendships: So many different kinds! Write about a lifelong friend, or a brand-new friend, or the circle of friends you couldn't imagine living without. (Write about the loss of a friend, too – either through death or circumstance or choosing.)

Your pet – or Furry Family, as I call them. Write about the animals you have shared your life with/do share your life with. If you're not an "animal person," write about your feelings of disconnection to them, and your inability to understand why so many people seem to find them essential to their well-being.

Emotions: What's the angriest you've ever been? The most heartbroken? The most crazy-in-love?

Also, think about the subtler emotions: feeling protective, fragile, uneasy, confused or bewildered, creeped out, shocked. Write about all these, as connected to the stories of your life.

Highs and Lows: Most people can readily cite the highs and lows of their lives. Write about these. If it helps you get started, list the five worst and five best times of your life, and start writing about them. Show the reader how you were affected by these times. Did you lose weight? Abuse drugs or alcohol? Lose sight of the important things and people in your life? Lose your job? Take the reader into the heart of these bright and dark years with dialogue and vivid settings.

Coincidence: What's the strangest/most amusing/most inexplicable coincidence you've ever experienced? Some people even say that there is no such thing as coincidence. Do you believe that? If you believe that "everything happens for a reason," then why do good people suffer, and bad people get away with … murder? Surely the world is more random than we'd like to believe?

Otherworldly: Do you believe in ESP, or extrasensory perception? Do you believe in an afterlife? Who can you imagine being before this life, in another, previous life? Who do you believe you were, in another, previous life? Can you write about that?

World Religions/Spirituality: Are you Muslim, Hindu, Sikh, Jewish, Christian, or Wiccan? Write about your spiritual or religious beliefs and how these may have changed or strengthened over a lifetime. Secondly, write about a time when your faith was sorely tested … and …

Cultural influences: Perhaps you have a varied cultural background. Do you lean more to one than the other? Are there certain types of music you are drawn to because they were always played at home, or in conjunction with religious ceremonies? Did you have a Mi'kmaw grandfather who used to sing in Mi'kmaw or play the drum? An African Nova Scotian mother who took you to church every Sunday? Are the traditions of the heritage you grew up with of great importance to you, or are you determined to spurn these in favour of a different kind of life? Does the traditional dress/uniform of the culture strike a chord with you (the Scot's swinging kilt, the feather headdress or jingle dress of First Nations, the fur and animal-skin clothes, mitts, and boots of the Inuit? Do you wear a hijab, or a niqab, or a burka?)

Food: Do you live to eat, or eat to live? If the former, write about a time you prepared a meal with great care and love, for someone you hadn't seen in a long time. If the latter, write about a food that even you, a disinterested eater, still thinks is wonderful.

Your last meal: What would you choose for your last meal on earth?

Storms: What's the wildest storm you've ever endured? Describe it in detail, and your accompanying emotions.

Our heroes or mentors: Write about someone who changed your life, or the life of someone you love, but who lives far away.

Music: What role does music play in your life?

"Our song": Write about a love song that you and your sweetheart think of as yours.

Your profession: If you could choose all over again – would you have the same profession?

The Settings of Our Lives

Many memoirs are set in childhood, and many pertain to our families. But not all, or not entirely. We all have deeply magical and mystical places or settings, in our lives. The family summer cottage. Our first apartment with our first sweetheart. A beach we love to walk along. A river we swim in. A tree house, built by our father. A warm and cosy home library, where we read the weekends away. The barn where we rode a horse for the first time. A forest path where we take our dog for long walks, in every season of the year. The float home we live on, now. These settings represent our past, the present, and, we hope, the future. And so on.

For fifteen minutes, choose one of the memorable settings in your life, past or present, and write about it in the present tense, as though you are there, right now. Go!

Lists

- Daily rituals you love.
- Yearly holidays you love – or detest.
- The most difficult times of your life.
- The most joyous days of your life.
- The grossest things you've ever had to do.

- The best teachers, ministers, rabbis, mentors you've ever known.
- Moments you would give anything to relive.
- Moments of choice – where you'd choose differently now.
- Ways you find peace amidst storms.
- Ways you've broken the laws of your land and not been caught.
- Snippets of poetry or song lyrics always close to mind.
- Objects you like to collect.
- All the activities you love to do alone.
- All the ways you show love for your sweetheart.
- All the ways you make him/her/they grind their teeth.
- Ten talents you wished you had; now, list in order of desire.
- Ten world cultures you'd love to know more about.
- The times when you feel beautiful.
- The times you feel most capable and alive.
- The times you knew you had no business doing what you did.
- The times you were given a second chance.
- The times you've asked a Higher Power for a favour.
- Exactly what you'd do if you had a year to live.
- Exactly what you'd do if you had a week to live.
- Exactly what you'd do if you had a day to live.
- All the problems you've had with a given name.
- All the problems you've had with a patronym.
- All the problems you've had with a married name.
- Ten first names you'd rather have than your own; pair these with professions which interest you.
- Ten middle names you'd rather have than your own.
- Ten things you'd enact instantly, if you ruled the world.
- Freedoms you take for granted.
- The greatest loves of your life.
- The people you'd like to marry – if it weren't forever.
- The people you need to forgive.
- The things that scare you most.
- The ways you've been really lucky.
- Your most treasured possessions.
- Your favourite foods from childhood.
- Your favourite foods now.

- The strangest foods you've ever eaten.
- Your plans for having a great and meaningful old age.
- The people you'd like near you when you die.
- Your hopes and beliefs of the life thereafter/reincarnation/heaven/that other, hotter place.

Ghosts of Our Past

1. Make a list of five people who are "ghosts" in your past, who live inside you. They may or may not be alive, but they are not currently present in your life, and *they are beloved.* Second, attach a theme-word to every name. (e.g. mother: artist, or, cousin: musician.) And third, write *one sentence,* which begins, "I remember …" that you could make into a story.
2. Make a list of five other "ghosts" in your past, who *make you uneasy to think about.* Second, attach a theme-word to every name. (e.g. mother: anger, or cousin: liar.) And third, write *one sentence*, which begins, "I remember …" that you could make into a story.
3. In a separate list, write down the ten themes that emerged from the first two exercises. Can you see the themes you would like to write more about in this list?

The Voices of Our Ancestors – Finding Joy, Humour, and Authenticity in our Writing

As the years pass, it can be difficult to summon up the face of a loved one who has died. Often, it's easier to remember stories they told, or expressions they used often. Some of these are humorous, some still make our hearts bump. Many sayings or jokes or exhortations do bring back their smiles or frowns to our mind's eye. Others, best of all, bring back the cadence of their voices, and the warm emotions they were conveying to us. Sometimes it feels as though we *are* these family words, that our spines grow taller when we hear them again, or we find comfort where none existed, minutes before. We can even feel guided and protected by the words of our ancestors.

What did your family say to you?

1. Write three of your mother's or main caregiver's favourite expressions.
2. What did your father say when he was really angry, and really cheerful? One of each.
3. What is the happiest sound of your childhood?
4. What is the scariest sound?
5. What is the music of your childhood, both in the home, and in the larger world? How did it make you feel?
6. What are some of your favourite foods from childhood?

Acknowledgements

When you can count up the decades, you know you have been teaching memoir writing for a long time (1995 -). For me, it has been a privilege and a pleasure to learn about so many different people's lives, by being permitted entry into their life stories as a teacher, an editor, and, often, as a friend.

My teaching adventures began in a small, stuffy room at the New Westminster Library, in New Westminster, British Columbia. There I taught a charming seniors' group called The Writers' Discovery group. These people were warm, welcoming, polite, and eager to learn and to write. Nor did I ever have to explain the concept of beginning, middle, and end to these older, traditionally and/or rurally educated people. We met once a month and they gave me $50 to be their instructor, though a formidable former teacher (by name of Marguerite, as I recall) was their group leader. I made up assignments, spent countless hours reviewing their writings. I corrected, suggested, expanded, encouraged, congratulated, and learned. I showed up, for at least a year. I enjoyed.

Thank you, Writers' Discovery Group.

In 2008, I taught my first memoir writing workshop at the offices of the Writers' Federation of Nova Scotia (WFNS). It was eight sessions long, and we met at the weekends. They were an extraordinarily worldly and diverse group, some professional writers, most amateurs, ranging in age from around thirty to eighty. They were kind enough to say they learned much from me. I was honest enough to say I learned more. Again, I spent countless hours preparing lessons, reviewing writing, responding to question after question, for modest pay. I loved every moment. I cherish memories of that time. In particular, I wish to thank the then-executive director of the Writers Federation of Nova

Scotia, the late Jane Buss, for trusting me to lead a workshop for Federation members.

"Can I really give a workshop here at the Fed office?" I asked Jane, the ink of my newly received Certificate in Adult Education from Dalhousie University still wet, and me feeling rusty after years away from teaching.

"Of course!" the tall, beaming Jane said, arms thrown out in that lovely big-energy way that she had, ready to hug me. "They're lucky to have you!"

Perhaps, dear Jane, but those members were, we all were, so lucky to have you.

Thank you, to all of you who came to my first workshop in Halifax.

Now I teach all over Nova Scotia, and across Canada. I've taught in museums, heritage homes, National Historic Sites, at university alumni buildings, junior and high schools, private clubs, and libraries. I teach seniors, middle-agers, and young people.

Bottomless thanks to each and every one of the workshop participants who have come out to these workshops. Such civility in these gatherings! And so much laughter. I have seen patience, too, and delight and surprise. *You mean my life matters?*

More than I, or we, your fellow learners, could ever say.

I'll conclude with deep and loving thanks to my Simmins and Cameron families for their love and encouragement, and my beloved husband, Silver Donald Cameron, for his.

Bibliography
Selected Memoirs and More

Ackerley, J.R. *My Dog Tulip*. New York, NY: New York Review of Books Classics, 1956.

Ackerley, J.R. *My Father and Myself*. New York: NY: New York Review of Books, 1968.

Aguirre, Carmen. *Something Fierce: Memoirs of a Revolutionary Daughter*. Toronto, ON: Vintage Canada, 2014.

Alexander, Elizabeth. *The Light of the World*. New York, NY: Grand Central Publishing, 2016.

Alexander, William. *52 Loaves: A Half-Baked Adventure*. Chapel Hill, NC: Algonquin Books of Chapel Hill, 2010.

Andrews, Julie. *Home: A Memoir of my Early Years*. New York, NY: Hyperion, 2008.

Arden, Jann. *Feeding My Mother: Comfort and Laughter in the Kitchen as a Daughter Lives with her Mom's Memory Loss*. Toronto, ON: Penguin Books, 2017.

Armstrong, Luanne. *Blue Valley: A Memoir*. Nelson, BC: Maa Press, 2007.

Armstrong, Luanne, and Zoë Landale, eds. *Slice Me Some Truth: An Anthology of Canadian Creative Non-Fiction*. Hamilton, ON: Wolsak and Wynn, 2011.

Armstrong, Sally. *The Nine Lives of Charlotte Taylor*. Toronto, ON: Vintage Canada Ltd., 2008.

Bacall, Lauren. *By Myself*. New York, NY: Ballantine Books, 1985.

Barrington, Judith. *Writing the Memoir: From Truth to Art*. Portland, OR: Eighth Mountain Press, Open Library, 1997.

Bayley, John. *Elegy for Iris*. New York, NY: First Picador USA Paperback Edition, 2000.

Bégin, Monique. Ladies, Upstairs! My Life in Politics and After. Montreal, Quebec: McGill-Queen's University Press, 2019.

Berton, Laura Beatrice. *I Married the Klondike.* Toronto, ON: McClelland & Stewart, 1967.

Blackburn, Julia. *The Three of Us.* New York, NY: Pantheon, 2008.

Blackburn, Thomas. *A Clip of Steel.* London, UK: Macgibbon & Kee, 1969.

Borel, Kathyrn, Jr. *Corked: A Memoir.* Mississauga, ON: John Wiley & Sons Ltd., 2009.

Boswell, Patricia. *Montgomery Clift, a Biography.* Pompton Plains, NJ: Limelight Editions, 2004.

Brown, Ian. *The Boy in the Moon: A Father's Search for his Disabled Son.* Manhattan, NY: St. Martin's Press, 2011.

Bryson, Bill. *The Road to Little Dribbling – Adventures of an American in Britain.* New York, NY: Doubleday, 2015.

Burroughs, Augusten. *Dry.* New York, NY: Picador, 2013.

Burroughs, Augusten. *Running with Scissors.* New York, NY: Picador/Macmillan, 2002.

Burroughs, William. *The Naked Lunch.* (novel) London, UK: Corgi Books, Transworld Publishers, 1959.

Butala, Sharon. *Where I Live Now: A Journey Through Love and Loss to Healing and Hope.* Toronto, ON: Simon & Schuster, 2017.

Campbell, Maria. *Half-Breed.* Halifax, NS: Goodread Biographies, 1983.

Carr, Emily. *Growing Pains: The Autobiography of Emily Carr.* Vancouver, BC: Clarke, Irwin & Company Ltd., 1946.

Chong, Denise. *The Concubine's Children.* Toronto, ON: Penguin Books, 1995.

Chow, Olivia. *My Journey.* Toronto, ON: Harper Collins Publishers, 2014.

Clinton, Bill. *My Life.* New York, NY: Alfred A. Knopf, 2004.

Connolly, Billy. *Tall Tales and Wee Stories.* London, UK: Hatchette/Hodder & Stoughton, 2019.

Connolly, Karen. *Burmese Lessons, a True Love Story.* New York, NY: Nan A. Talese, 2009.

Conway, Jill Ker. *True North.* Toronto, ON: Alfred A. Knopf Canada, 1994.

Corey, Deborah Joy. *Settling Twice.* Yarmouth, Maine: Islandport Press, 2017.

Crosley, Sloane. *I Was Told There'd Be Cake: Essays.* New York, NY: Riverhead Books, 2008.

Cusk, Rachel. *Aftermath: On Marriage and Separation.* London, UK: Faber & Faber, 2012.

Dakin, Pauline: *Run, Hide, Repeat: A Memoir of a Fugitive Childhood.* Toronto, ON: Viking, 2017.

Darlington, Terry. *Narrow Dog to Carcassonne.* London, UK: A Bantam Book, 2006.

Davies, Libby. *Outside In: A Political Memoir.* Toronto, ON: Between the Lines, 2019.

Dawn, Amber. *How Poetry Saved My Life.* Vancouver, BC: Arsenal Pulp Press, 2013.

Defoe, Daniel. *Journal of the Plague Year* (fictional memoir). London, UK: Penguin Classics, 2003. (First published in 1722.)

Defoe, Daniel. *Moll Flanders* (fictional memoir). London, UK: Penguin Classics, 1989. (First published in 1722.)

DeQuincey, Thomas. *Confessions of an English Opium-Eater.* Hertfordshire, UK: Wordsworth Editions, 1999. (First published in 1821.)

Dillard, Annie. *Three by Annie Dillard.* New York, NY: Harper Collins Publishers, 2001.

Diski, Jenny. *On Trying to Keep Still.* London, UK: Little, Brown, 2006.

Dominic, Magie. *Street Angel.* Waterloo, ON: Wilfred Laurier University Press, 2014.

Doyle, Alan. *Where I Belong: Small Town to Great Big Sea.* Toronto, ON: Doubleday Canada, 2014.

Edwards, Helen and Smith, Jenny Lee (with Jacqui Buttriss). *My Secret Sister.* London, UK: Pan Books, 2015.

Edugyan, Esi. *Half Blood Blues.* London, UK: Serpent's Tail, 2011.

Edugyan, Esi. *Washington Black.* New York, NY: Penguin, Random House, 2019.

Ephron, Delia. *Sister, Mother, Husband, Dog.* New York, NY: Blue Rider Press, 2013.

Epstein, Howard. *Rise Again: Nova Scotia's NDP on the Rocks.* Halifax, NS: Empty Mirrors Press, 2015.

Ferguson, Will. *Hokkaido Highway Blues: Hitchhiking Japan.* New York: NY: Soho Press, Inc., 1998.

Fetherling, George, editor. *The Vintage Book of Canadian Memoirs.* Toronto, ON: Vintage Canada Edition, 2001.

Flinn, Kathleen. *The Sharper Your Knife, The Less You Cry: Love, Laughter, and Tears, at the World's Most Famous Cooking School.* New York, NY: Viking, published by the Penguin Group, 2007.

Freedman, Karyn L. *One Hour in Paris: A True Story of Rape and Recovery.* Calgary, AB: Freehand Books, 2014.

Frey, James. James Frey, *A Million Little Pieces,* 2005. London, UK: John Murray Publishers, 2005.

Gallear, Richard. *The Forgotten Child.* London, UK: HarperElement, 2019.

Gates, Henry Louis, Jr., editor. *The Classic Slave Narratives.* New York, NY: Signet Classic, 1987.

Gerard, André. Fathers: A Literary Anthology. Patremoir Press: Vancouver, BC, 2011.

Gildiner, Catherine. *Too Close to the Falls: A Memoir.* Toronto, ON: ECW Press, 1999.

Gillis, Tessie. *Stories from the Woman From Away.* (novel) Wreck Cove, Cape Breton, NS: Breton Books, 1998.

Gilman, Susan Jane. *Hyprocrite in a Pouffy White Dress.* New York, NY: Warner Books, 2005.

Gillmor, Don. *To the River: Losing my Brother.* Toronto, ON: Random House Canada, 2019.

Goldbloom, Richard B. *A Lucky Life.* Halifax, NS: Formac Publishing Co. Ltd, 2013.

Grealy, Lucy. *Autobiography of a Face.* New York, NY: Harper Perennial, 1994.

Greenlaw, Linda. *All Fishermen are Liars.* New York, NY: Hyperion, 2004.

Greenlaw, Linda. *The Lobster Chronicles: Life on a Very Small Island.* New York, NY: Hyperion, 2002.

Greenlaw, Linda. *Seaworthy: A Swordfish Captain Returns to the Sea.* New York, NY: Viking, 2010.

Greenlaw, Linda. *The Hungry Ocean.* New York, NY: Hyperion, 1999.

Halliday, E. M. *John Berryman and the Thirties.* Boston, MA: University of Massachusetts Press, 1988.

Hamilton, Hugo. *The Speckled People.* New York, NY: Harper Perennial, 2003.

Hancock, Herbie (with Lisa Dickey). *Possibilities.* New York, NY: Viking Books, 2014.

Handke, Peter. A *Sorrow Beyond Dreams.* New York, NY: NYRB Classics, 2002.

Harris, CoCo, ed. *Impact: An Anthology of Short Memoirs.* Greenville, SC: Telling Our Stories Press, 2012.

Harrison, Kathryn. *The Kiss.* Toronto, ON: Harper Collins, 1998.

Hawkes, John. *Sweet William: A Memoir of Old Horse.* New York, NY: Penguin Books, 1993.

Hely, Steve. *How I Became a Famous Novelist.* New York, NY: Black Cat, imprint of Grove/Atlantic, Inc., 2009.

Hesse, Benjamin. *Memoirs of a Gaijin: E-mails from Japan.* Bloomington, IN: iUniverse Inc. Publishing, 2007.

Hillen, Ernest. *The Way of a Boy: A Memoir of Java.* Toronto, ON: Penguin Books, 1994.

Hillen, Ernest. *Small Mercies: A Boy After War.* Toronto, ON: Penguin Canada, 2008.

Hodgman, George. *Bettyville: A Memoir.* New York, NY: Penguin Books, 2015.

Homes, A.M. *The Mistress's Daughter.* New York, NY: Viking, 2007.

Hotchner, A.E. *Papa Hemingway: A Personal Memoir.* New York, NY: Random House, 1966.

Hughes, Molly. *A London Child of the 1870s.* London, UK: Persephone Books, reprinted 2008.

Hui, Ann. *Chop Suey Nation: The Surprising History and Vibrant Present of Small-Town Chinese Restaurants from Victoria, BC, to Fogo Island, NL.* Pender Harbour, BC: Douglas & MacIntyre, 2019.

Huston, Anjelica. *A Story Lately Told: Coming of Age in Ireland, London, and New York.* New York, NY: Scribner, a division of Simon & Schuster, Inc., 2013.

Iglauer, Edith. *Fishing with John.* Madeira Park, BC: Harbour Publishing Co., Ltd., 1988.

James, P.D. *Time to be in Earnest: A Fragment of an Autobiography.* Toronto, ON: Vintage Canada, a division of Random House of Canada Ltd., 1999.

Joe, Rita. *Song of Rita Joe: Autobiography of a Mi'kmaq Poet.* Charlottetown, PEI: Ragweed Press, 1996.

John, Elton. *Me.* London, UK: Pan Macmillan, 2019.

Johnson, Plum. *They Left Us Everything: A Memoir.* Toronto, ON: Penguin Canada, 2014.

"Jones, Margaret B." *Love and Consequences* (memoir hoax). Riverhead Books: New York, NY: 2009.

Jong, Erica. *Fear of Fifty: A Mid-Life Memoir.* New York, NY: Harper Collins Publishers, 1994.

Karr, Mary. *The Art of Memoir.* New York, NY: Harper, 2015.

Kawatski, Deanna. *Wilderness Mother: A Chronicle of a Modern Pioneer.* Vancouver, BC: Whitecap Books, 1994.

Kawatski, Deanna Barnhardt. *Burning Man, Slaying Dragon: My True and Transformative Travel Tale.* Celista, BC: Gracesprings Collective, 2013.

Kay, Adam. *Twas The Nightshift Before Christmas.* London, UK: Pan Macmillan, 2019.

Kay, Adam. *This is Going to Hurt.* London, UK: Picador, 2017.

Kay, Jackie. *Red Dust Road: An Autobiographical Journey.* London, UK: Picador Books, 2011.

Keith, Newton Agnes. *Land Below the Wind.* Kota Kinabalu, Borneo: Natural History Publications, 2006 (first published January 1, 1939).

Kelly, Deirdre. *Paris Times Eight.* Vancouver, BC: Greystone Books, D & M Publishers, Inc., 2009.

Kelly, Deirdre. *Paris Times Eight.* Vancouver, BC: Greystone Books, D & Publishers, Inc., 2009.

Kimmel, Haven. *A Girl Named Zippy: Growing Up Small in Mooreland, Indiana.* New York, NY: Broadway Books, 2001.

Kimmel, Haven. *She Got Up Off The Couch: And Other Heroic Acts from Mooreland, Indiana.* New York, NY: Free Press, a division of Simon & Schuster Inc., 2006.

Kincaid, Jamaica. *Among Flowers: A Walk in the Himalaya.* Washington, DC: National Geographic, 2007.

Kincaid, Jamaica. *My Brother.* New York, NY: Macmillan, 1997.

Kincaid, Jamaica. *My Garden (Book).* New York, NY: Macmillan, 2001.

Kincaid, Jamaica. *Talk Stories.* New York: NY: Macmillan, 2001.

Knausgaard, Karl Ove. *My Struggle: Book I (six volumes in total).* Oslo, Norway: Vintage Digital, 2012.

Kostash, Myrna. *All of Baba's Children.* Edmonton, AB: NeWest Press, 1977.

Kostash, Myrna. *Bloodlines: A Journey into Eastern Europe.* Vancouver, BC: Douglas & MacIntyre, 1993.

Lancaster, Jen. *Bright Lights, Big Ass.* New York, NY: New American Library, a division of Penguin Group, 2007.

Landale, Zoë. *Harvest of Salmon.* Saanichton, BC: Hancock House Publishers Ltd., 1977.

Landry, Janice. *The Sixty Second Story: When Lives are on the Line.* (non-fiction) Lawrencetown, NS: Pottersfield Press, 2013.

Lasdun, James. *Give Me Everything You Have: On Being Stalked.* New York, NY: Farrar, Straus and Giroux, 2013.

Lau, Evelyn. *Runaway: Diary of a Street Kid.* Toronto, ON: Harper Perennial, 1989.

Lau, Evelyn. *Inside Out.* Toronto, ON: Doubleday Canada, 2001.

Laumann, Silken. *Unsinkable: My Untold Story.* Toronto, ON: Harper Collins Publishers Ltd., 2014.

Lawrence, Grant. *Adventures in Solitude: What Not To Wear to a Nude Potluck, and Other Stories from Desolation Sound.* Madeira Park, BC: Harbour Publishing Co., Ltd., 2010.

Lawson, Jenny, The Bloggess. *Let's Pretend this Never Happened: (A Mostly True Memoir).* New York, NY: G.P. Putnam's Sons, 2012.

Loudon, Mary. *Relative Stranger: Piecing Together a Life Plagued by Madness.* Edinburgh, Scotland, UK: Canongate US, 2007.

Louttit, Ernie. *The Unexpected Cop: Indian Ernie on a Life of Leadership.* Regina, SK: University of Regina Press, 2019.

MacIntyre, Linden. *Causeway: A Passage from Innocence.* Toronto, ON: Harper Collins Publishers, Ltd., 2006.

MacIntyre, Linden. *The Bishop's Man.* (novel, Giller-Prize winner). Toronto, ON: Random House Canada, 2009.

MacKinnon, J.B. Smith & Smith, Alison. *The 100-Mile Diet: A Year of Local Eating.* Toronto, ON: Vintage Canada Edition, 2007.

MacMillan, Dr. C. Lamont. *Memoirs of a Canadian Doctor.* Markham, ON: PaperJacks Ltd., 1977.

Matheson, Grant. *The Golden Boy: A Doctor's Journey with Addiction.* Charlottetown, PEI: The Acorn Press, 2017.

Maynard, Rona. *My Mother's Daughter.* Toronto, ON: Douglas Gibson Books, 2007.

McCourt, Frank. *Angela's Ashes.* New York, NY: Charles Scribner's Sons, 1996.

McFarlane, Judy. *Writing with Grace: A Journey Beyond Down Syndrome.* Vancouver, BC: Douglas & McIntyre, 2014.

McGahearn, John. *All Will Be Well: Memoir.* Toronto, ON: Knopf Canada, 2007.

McGahearn, John. *Amongst Women* (novel). Republic of Ireland: Faber and Faber, 2009.

McLachlin, Beverley. *Truth Be Told: My Journey Through Life and Law.* Toronto, ON: Simon & Schuster, 2019.

Metatawabin, Edmund. *Up Ghost River: A Chief's Journey Through the Turbulent Waters of Native History.* Toronto, ON: Alfred A. Knopf Canada, 2014.

Mitchell, Joni. *Morning Glory on the Vine: Early Songs and Drawing.* Boston, MA: Houghton Mifflin Harcourt, 2019.

Moody, Anne. *Coming of Age in Mississippi: The Classic Autobiography of Growing Up Poor and Black in the Rural South.* New York, NY: Bantam Dell, 1968.

Moroney, Shannon. *Through the Glass.* Toronto, ON: Doubleday Canada, 2011.

Moss, Barbara Robinette. *Change Me Into Zeus's Daughter: A Memoir.* New York, NY: Scribner, 1999.

Morrissey, Donna. *Downhill Chance.* (novel) Boston, MA: Mariner Books, 2002.

Morrissey, Donna. *Kit's Law.* (novel) Toronto, ON: Penguin Books, 1999.

Morrissey, Donna. *Sylvanus Now.* (novel) Toronto, ON: Penguin Canada, 2005.

Morrissey, Donna. *What They Wanted.* (novel) Toronto, ON: 2009

Morrissey, Donna. *The Deception of Livvy Higgs.* (novel) Toronto, ON: Viking Canada, publisher 2012.

Morrissey, Donna. *The Fortunate Brother.* (novel) Toronto, ON: Penguin Random House, 2016.

Mowat, Claire. *Travels with Farley.* Lawrencetown, NS: Pottersfield Press, 2015.

Mowat, Farley. *Bay of Spirits, A Love Story.* Toronto, ON: McClelland & Stewart Ltd., 2006.

Mowat, Farley. *A Whale for the Killing.* Toronto, ON: McClelland & Stewart, 1972.

Mowat, Farley. *High Altitudes.* Toronto, ON: Key Porter Books Ltd., 2002.

Mowat, Farley. *Never Cry Wolf.* New York, NY: Dell Publishing Co., Inc., 1963.

Mowat, Farley. *Otherwise.* Toronto, ON: McClelland & Stewart Ltd., 2008.

Mowat, Farley. *The Serpent's Coil.* Toronto, ON: A Seal Book/ McClelland & Stewart Ltd., 1961.

Mowat, Farley. *Aftermath: Travels in a Post-War World.* Toronto, ON: Seal Books/McClelland- Bantam, Inc. 1996.

Mutch, Maria. *Know the Night: A Memoir of Survival in the Small Hours.* Toronto, ON: Alfred A. Knopf Canada, 2014.

Nelson, Maggie. *The Argonauts.* Minneapolis, Minnesota: Greywolf Press, 2015.

Newman, Kristin. *What I Was Doing While You Were Breeding: A Memoir.* New York, NY: Three Rivers Press, 2014.

Norman, Renee. *House of Mirrors.* New York, NY: Peter Lang Publishing, 1992.

Obama, Michelle. *Becoming.* New York, NY: Crown Publishing, 2018.

O'Faolain, Nuala. *Are You Somebody? The Accidental Memoir of a Dublin Woman.* New York, NY: Holt Paperbacks, 1999.

O'Faolain, Nuala. *Almost There: The Onward Journey of a Dublin Woman, A Memoir.* New York, NY: Riverhead Books, 2003.

Osborne, Stephen. *Fire and Ice.* Vancouver, BC: Arsenal Pulp Press, 1998.

Ostlere, Cathy. *Lost: A Memoir.* Toronto, ON: Key Porter Books Ltd., 2008.

Ovid. *Amores.* (a collection of 49 elegies, first published in 16 BCE, or earlier) London, UK: John Murray Publishers, 1968.

Patterson, Kevin. *The Water In Between: A Journey at Sea.* New York, NY: Doubleday, 1999.

Pick, Alison, *Between Gods.* Toronto, ON: Doubleday Canada, 2014.

Plath, Sylvia. *The Bell Jar.* Boston, Massachusetts: Harper Perennial Modern Classics, 2006 (first published January 1963).

Pottier, Anna. *Good as Gone: My Life with Irving Layton.* Toronto, ON: Dundurn Group, 2015.

Powell, Julie. *Julie & Julia: My Year of Cooking Dangerously.* New York, NY: Back Bay Books, Little, Brown and Company, 2005.

Quinton, Dave. *The Grand Tour: My Months of Hitchhiking, Biking, and Serving Her Royal Majesty.* Portugal Cove-St. Philip's, NL: Boulder Publications, 2017.

Rainier, Tristine. *Your Life As Story.* Toronto, ON: Penguin Random House, 1998.

Rebanks, James. *The Shepherd's Life: A Tale of the Lake District.* London, UK: Penguin Books, 2015.

Resnick, Rachel. *Love Junkie: A Memoir.* New York, NY: Bloomsbury, USA, 2008.

Richardson, E.M. *We Keep a Light.* Toronto, ON: McGraw-Hill Ryerson Ltd., 1945.

Roberts, Siobhan, for John Horton Conway (biography). *Genius at Play: The Curious Mind of John Horton Conway.* Toronto, ON: Bloomsbury Press, 2015.

Rosenblat, Herman. *The Angel at the Fence* (memoir hoax). Berkley, CA: Berkley Books, 2008.

Rossant, Colette. *Return to Paris: A Memoir.* New York, NY: Atria Books, 2003.

Rousseau, Jean Jacques. *The Confessions of Jean Jacques Rousseau.* First published in 1782. London, UK: Penguin Random House, 1963.

Ryan, Michael. *Secret Life.* New York, NY: Pantheon, 1995.

Saint Augustine. *Confessions of a Sinner.* Written in Latin between AD 397 and 400. London, U.K. Penguin Books, Great Ideas: 2004.

Sage, Lorna. *Bad Blood.* Toronto, ON: Harper Collins, 2000.

Schoemperlen, Diane. *This is Not My Life: A Memoir of Love, Prison, and Other Complications.* Toronto, ON: Harper Collins Canada, 2016.

Sexton, Linda Gray. *Searching for Mercy Street: My Journey Back to My Mother, Anne Sexton.* Berkeley, CA: Counterpoint, 2011.

Sheridan, Peter. *44: Dublin Made Me: A Memoir.* New York, NY: Viking Books, 1999.

Silcott, Jane. *Everything Rustles.* Vancouver, BC: Anvil Press, 2013.

Simmins, Marjorie. *Coastal Lives.* East Lawrencetown, NS: Pottersfield Press, 2014.

Simmins, Marjorie. *Year of the Horse.* East Lawrencetown, NS: Pottersfield Press, 2016.

Singer, Natalie. *Scraping by in the Big Eighties.* Lincoln, NE: University of Nebraska Press, 2004.

Smith, Patti. *Just Kids.* New York, NY: Harper Collins Publishers, 2010.

Smith Magazine, Fershleiser, Rachel & Smith, Larry, eds. *Not Quite What I was Planning: Six-Word Memoirs.* New York, NY: Harper Perennial, 2008.

Snodgrass, W. D. *Heart's Needle.* New York, NY: Knopf, 1959

Spero, Wendy. *Microthrills: True Stories from a Life of Small Highs.* New York, NY: Plume, by Penguin Group, 2006.

Strayed, Cheryl. *Wild: From Lost to Found on the Pacific Crest Trail.* Vintage Books, a division of Random House, Inc.: New York, NY, 2013.

Styron, William. *Darkness Visible: A Memoir of Madness.* New York, NY: Random House, 1990.

St. Germain, Justin. *Son of a Gun.* New York, NY: Random House, 2013.

Stuart, Julia. *The Matchmaker of Périgord.* New York, NY: Harper Collins Publishers, 2008.

Sutin, Jack and Rochelle; edited by Lawrence Sutin. *Jack & Rochelle: A Holocaust Story of Love and Resistance.* St. Paul, MN: Graywolf Press, 1995.

Thanh, Yasuko. *Mistakes to Run With.* Toronto, ON: Penguin Random House, 2019.

Thoreau, Henry. *Walden.* Boston, MA: Ticknor and Fields, 1854.

Traill, Catherine Parr. *The Backwoods of Canada.* Toronto, ON: McClelland & Stewart, 1966.

Trudeau, Margaret. *Changing my Mind.* Toronto, ON: Harper Collins Publishers, 2010.

Uppal, Priscilla. *Drunk Mum: A Memoir.* Toronto, ON: Doubleday Canada, 2013.

Vaughan, Betty Boudreau. *I'll Buy You an Ox.* Halifax, NS: Nimbus Publishing, 1997.

Wagamese, Richard. *One Native Life.* Vancouver, BC: Douglas & MacIntyre, 2005.

Walls, Jeanette. *The Glass Castle.* New York, NY: Scribner, 2005.

Walls, Jeanette. *Half Broke Horses: A True Life Novel.* New York, NY: Scribner, 2009.

Wearing, Alison. *Confessions of a Fairy's Daughter: Growing Up with a Gay Dad.* Toronto, ON: A. Knopf Canada, 2013.

Westover, Tara. *Educated.* Toronto, ON: Random House, 2018.

Wilson, Mara. *Where Am I Now? True Stories of Girlhood and Accidental Fame.* New York, NY: Penguin Books, 2016

Wolff, Tobias. *This Boy's Life: A Memoir.* New York, NY: Grove Press, 1989.

Wong, Joanna Claire. *Wong Family Feast: Our Recipes and Stories.* Vancouver, BC: self-published, 2007.

Worth, Jennifer. *Call the Midwife: A Memoir of Birth, Joy, and Hard Times.* New York, NY: Penguin Books, 2002.

Worth, Jennifer. *Call the Midwife: Shadows of the Workhouse.* New York, NY: Harper Collins Publishers, 2005.

Worth, Jennifer. *Call the Midwife: Farewell to the East End.* New York, NY: Harper Collins Publishers, 2009.

Zeppa, Jamie. *Beyond the Sky and the Earth.* London, UK: Pan Books/MacMillan Publishers Ltd., 2000.

Non-fiction:

Benjamin, Chris. *Indian School Road: Legacies of the Shubenacadie Residential School.* Halifax, NS: Nimbus Publishing, 2014.

DeMont, John. *A Good Day's Work: In Pursuit of a Disappearing Canada.* Toronto, ON: Doubleday Canada, 2013.

DeMont, John. *The Long Way Home: A Personal History of Nova Scotia.* Toronto, ON: McClelland & Stewart, 2017.

Horwood, Harold. *The Foxes of Beachy Cove.* Don Mills, ON: PaperJacks, a division of General Publishing Co., Ltd., 1967.

LeBlanc, Barbara. *Postcards from Acadie.* Kentville, NS: Gaspereau Press, 2003.

Macdonald, Helen. *H is for Hawk.* Toronto, ON: Hamish Hamilton, an imprint of Penguin Canada Books, Inc., 2014.

Ouston, Rick. *Finding Family.* Vancouver, BC: New Star Books, 1994.

Paul, Daniel N. *We Were Not the Savages.* Halifax, NS: Fernwood Publishing, 2000.

Pollan, Michael. *In Defense of Food.* New York, NY: The Penguin Press, 2008.

Thurston, Harry. *The Atlantic Coast: A Natural History.* Vancouver, BC: Greystone Books, D & M Publishers, 2011.

Books about creative non-fiction writing:

(With thanks to Alison DeLory, writer, editor, teacher, and Associate Director, Communications, at the University of King's College, Halifax, Nova Scotia, for these next three sections.)

Berton, Pierre. *The Joy of Writing. A Guide for Writers, Disguised as a Memoir.* Toronto, ON: Anchor Canada, 2003.

Clark, Roy Peter. *Writing Tools: 50 Essential Strategies for Every Writer.* LLC Gildan Media, 2011.

Goldberg, Natalie. *Writing Down the Bones: Freeing the Writer Within.* Boston, MA: Shambhala Publications, 2005.

Goldberg, Natalie. *The True Secret of Writing: Connecting Life with Language.* New York, NY: Atria Books, 2013.

Gutkind, Lee. *You Can't Make This Stuff Up*. New York, NY: De Capo Press, 2012.

Kidder, Tracy and Todd, Richard. *Good Prose: The Art of Nonfiction*. New York, NY: Random House, 2013.

King, Stephen. *On Writing: A Memoir of the Craft*. New York, NY: Pocket Books, 2000.

Kramer, Mark and Call, Wendy. (Eds) *Telling true stories*. New York, NY: Penguin Group, 2007.

Lamott, Anne. *Bird by Bird: Some Instructions on Writing and Life*. New York, NY: Anchor Press, 1994.

Zinsser, William. *Inventing the Truth: The Art and Craft of Memoir*. New York, NY: Houghton Mifflin Company, 1998.

Zinsser, William. *On Writing Well: The Classic Guide to Creative Nonfiction*. New York, NY: Harper Collins, 2006.

Grammar, mechanics and syntax:

Grammar Girl online grammar resource: www.quickanddirtytips.com.

Messenger, William E., De Bruyn, Jan, Brown, Judy, and Montagnes, Ramona. *The Canadian Writer's Handbook* (4th ed.). Don Mills, ON: Oxford University Press, 2005.

O'Conner, Patricia T. *Woe is I: The Grammarphobe's Guide to Better English in Plain English*. New York, NY: Riverhead Books, 1996.

Purdue Online Writing Lab. Punctuation & Grammar: http://owl.english.purdue.edu/owl/section/1/6/ http://owl.english.purdue.edu/owl/section/1/5/

Ruvinsky, Maxine. *Practical grammar: a Canadian writer's resource*. Don Mills, ON: Oxford University Press, 2006.

Strunk, William Jr., and White, E.B. *The Elements of Style*. New York, NY: Macmillan, 1972.

Creative nonfiction online:

thewalrus.ca

www.theglobeandmail.com/life/facts-and-arguments/

vanityfair.com

creativenonfiction.org

newyorker.com

rollingstone.com

brainpickings.org (many excellent essays here about writing)

Reference Books:

Atlas, Nava. *The Literary Ladies Guide to the Writing Life.* South Portland, ME: Sellers Publishing, Inc., 2011.

Atwood, Margaret. *Good Bones and Simple Murders.* New York, NY: Nan A. Talese, imprint of Doubleday, 1983.

Atwood, Margaret. *Negotiating with the Dead: A Writer on Writing.* Toronto, ON: O.W. Anchor Canada edition, division of Random House of Canada, Ltd., 2003.

Baldwin, Christina. *Storycatcher: Making Sense of Our Lives Through the Power and Practice of Story.* Novato, CA: New World Library, 2005.

Birkerts, Sven. *The Art of Time in Memoir: Then, Again.* Minneapolis, Minnesota: Graywolf Press, 2007.

Bollman, Stephan. *Women Who Write.* New York, NY: Merrell Publishers Ltd., 2006.

Cameron, Julia. *The Artist's Way: A Spiritual Path to Higher Creativity.* New York, NY: Putnam, a member of Penguin Putnam Inc., 1992.

Clarke, Andrea, editor. *Love Letters: 2000 Years of Romance.* London, UK: The British Library (no date issued).

Conroy, Frank. *The Eleventh Draft: The Craft and the Writing Life from the Iowa Writers' Workshop.* New York, NY: Harper Collins Publishers, 1999.

Conroy, Pat. *My Reading Life.* New York, NY: Nan A. Talese, imprint of Doubleday, 2010.

Elbow, Peter. *Writing Without Teachers.* Oxford, UK: Oxford University Press, 1998.

Goldberg, Natalie. *Old Friend From Far Away: The Practice of Writing Memoir.* New York, NY: Freepress, a division of Simon & Schuster, 2007.

Goldberg, Natalie. *Writing Down the Bones.* Boston, MA: Shambala, 1986.

Graham, Barbara Florio. *Five Fast Steps to Better Writing.* Ottawa, ON: Opus Mundi Canada, 1985.

Heffron, Jack. *The Writer's Idea Book.* Cincinnati, OH: Writers Digest Books, 2000.

Hemingway, Ernest. *Ernest Hemingway on Writing*, edited by Larry W. Phillips. New York, NY: Touchstone, 1984.

Herbert, Robert, L, editor. *Ten Unabridged Essays.* Eaglewood Cliffs, NJ: Prentice-Hall Inc., 1964.

Loehr, Jim. *The Power of Story.* New York, NY: Freepress, a division of Simon & Schuster Inc., 2007.

Lopate, Phillip (a Teachers and Writers Collaborative Book). *The Art of the Personal Essay: An Anthology from the Classical Era to the Present.* New York, NY: Anchor Books, division of Random House Inc., 1995.

McKee, Robert. *Story: Substance, Structure, Style, and the Principles of Screenwriting.* Los Angeles, CA: Harper Collins, 2010.

Murdoch, Maureen. *Unreliable Truth: On Memoir and Memory.* New York, NY: Seal Press, an imprint of Avalon Publishing Group Inc., 2003.

Oxford English Dictionary. Oxford, UK: Oxford University Press, 2011.

Queneau, Raymond. *Exercises in Style.* New York, NY: New Direction Paperbook 513, 1981.

Rak, Julie. *Boom! Manufacturing Memoir for the Popular Market.* Waterloo, ON: Wilfred Laurier Press, 2013.

Styne, Marlys Marshall. *Senior Writing: A Brief Guide for Seniors Who Want to Write.* (self-published) West Conshohocken, PA: Infinity Publishing.com, 2007.

Thomas, Abigail. *Thinking about Memoir.* New York, NY: Sterling Publishing Co., Inc., 2008.

Truss, Lynne. *Eats, Shoots & Leaves.* New York, NY: Gotham Books, 2003.

Vance, Terry. *Letters Home: How Writing Can Change Your Life.* New York, NY: Pantheon Books, 1998.

Waller, Adrian. *Writing! An Informal, Anecdotal Guide to the Secrets of Crafting and Selling Non- Fiction.* Toronto, ON: McClelland & Stewart, 1987.

Yagoda, Ben. *Memoir: A History.* New York, NY: Riverhead Books, a member of Penguin Group (USA) Inc., 2009.

Magazines and URLs:

Bateson, Mary Catherine. http://storyteller.net/quotes-about-storytelling/

https://emergentcognition.com/2015/06/01/mary-catherine-bateson-our-species-thinks-in-metaphors-and-learns-through-stories/(Original source: Peripheral Vision: Learning Along the Way.)

Bhalla, Jag, "It Is in Our Nature to Need Stories." *Scientific American*. Guest blog: May 8, 2013. https://blogs.scientificamerican.com/guest-blog/it-is-in-our-nature-to-need-stories/

Hsu, Jeremy, "The Secrets of Storytelling: Why We Love a Good Yarn." *Scientific American*. Volume 19, Issue 4 (August/September), 2008. August 10, 2015.

Article on recovery memoirs versus memoirs that focus on good stories and good writing: www.kirkusreviews.com/features/memoir-discovery-not-recovery/

Monroe, Debra. "The Memoir of Discovery (Not Recovery)." *Kirkus*. October 1, 2015.

Recommended list of First Nations novelists and memoirists:

http://49thshelf.com/Blog/2016/02/04/Indigenous-Readers-Recommend

https://owlcation.com/humanities/Muses-Nine-Goddesses-of-Greek-Mythology

www.nytimes.com/books/97/08/03/lifetimes/white-essays.html

About the Author

Marjorie Simmins is an award-winning journalist. She has won Gold at the National Magazine Awards, for Best One-of-a-Kind Journalism, and Gold at the Atlantic Journalism Awards, for Best Magazine Article. She is the author of two non-fiction books, *Coastal Lives* and *Year of the Horse*.

Simmins has a Bachelor of Arts in English Literature from the University of British Columbia, a Certificate in Adult Education from Dalhousie University, and a Research Master of Arts in Literacy Education from Mount Saint Vincent University.

Raised in Vancouver, Simmins now lives in Nova Scotia and British Columbia, with her husband, author and filmmaker Silver Donald Cameron, and their two Shetland sheepdogs, MacTavish and Franki. When not writing, she teaches memoir writing across Canada. Her latest passion is learning how to drive miniature horses in a two-seater cart. She is currently working on a fourth non-fiction title, *Somebeachsomewhere: A Harness Racing Legend from a One-Horse Stable*, due out in the spring of 2021.

See more of her work on her website, *Memoirs and More* (www.marjoriesimmins.ca).

Books by Marjorie Simmins

Coastal Lives: a memoir

This is an unabashed love story – a tale of two coasts, east and west, two writers, Marjorie Simmins and Silver Donald Cameron, and many definitions of home, evolving and complex. She was a single and sad freelance fisheries reporter and writer living in Vancouver, on the West Coast of Canada. He was a widowed and heartbroken journalist and author, living in a small village on Isle Madame, Cape Breton. They met in Vancouver on a brilliant spring morning at a coffee shop. He was on a book tour and she was the reporter sent to interview him. "Hi, I'm Don," he said; "Hi, I'm Marjorie," she replied – and their lives changed forever.

It took 800 e-mails, countless phone calls and three PFO letters, but in the end, she, age 37, agreed to start seeing him, age 59. But there was no way she was going to leave her beloved West Coast, and her family, friends, horses, and dogs. That just wasn't going to happen.

This is a tale of love and resistance written with humour and candour. There are times of overwhelming happiness and flattening grief. Simmins writes of these times and the gentler ones as well, all against the backdrop of an East Coast Canadian world so new to her, she said she'd found a trip to Turkey less foreign. After all, she had thought the two coastal worlds would be similar. To her surprise, the two coasts had little in common. Food, fish, music, language, history and cultures were all different. Even the ocean smelled different, the saltier Atlantic so much more pungent. To her greater surprise, she came to fiercely love those differences, in ways both expected and surprising. She also fiercely loves the man who told her she was brave enough to "jump off a cliff – and tell a damn fine story at the other end."

Year of the Horse: A Journey of Healing and Adventure

After a severe horseback riding accident in 2011, journalist and author Marjorie Simmins finds herself unable to walk. During the slow months of recovery, she replays a lifetime of memories related to her beloved horse companions and the adventures they shared. Finally back on her feet, she makes a bold and surprising decision: she will ride again, in a discipline that is new for her, and she will even compete in a horse show – her first in 42 years. Simmins decides that 2014, the Chinese Year of the Horse, is her time for a comeback. Exhilarated but nervous, the former hunter-jumper of modest ability commits to full-time training as a Western rider.

Dynamic and lyrical, *Year of the Horse* shares the heart-lurching highs and lows of a 55-year-old horsewoman determined to put the pain behind her and to create the sunniest of futures with new, extraordinary horses in it. Simmins' initially modest goals take fire and she finds the support of a whole new horse community across Nova Scotia. These individuals welcome her, with a warmth that reminds her of the vibrant horse community of Southlands in Vancouver, where she rode in the 1970s, '80s, and '90s.

Year of the Horse is written for every horsewoman or -man who's had a serious setback and never lost the love of the sport, or the animal. It's for every person who at some point has had a serious physical or emotional injury and said, "I can't heal, I can't go forward" and then did.